Praise For

Ten Talks Parents Must Have With Their Children About Sex and Character

"Finally, a book that helps parents and their children have those vital talks about sex, health, relationships, and most importantly, strength of character."

—Rita Creighton, Washington State PTA President

"Easy-to-use strategies that get young people talking."

—Frieda Takamura, Washington Education Association

"What do sex education and character education have in common? Everything! And parents now have the perfect book to help them talk with their kids about sex, love, and character—everything from setting personal boundaries to keeping commitments."

—Judith Bradford, Ph.D., Virginia Commonwealth University

"Finally, the facts, skills, and guidance parents need in order to begin what are likely to be the most important conversations they will ever have with their children. *Ten Talks'* creative approach is practical for parents and engaging for children of all ages."

—Vicki Harrison, MSW,
National Education Association Health Information Network

"*Ten Talks'* approach is respectful, creative, and family-friendly. *Ten Talks* is a 21st-century approach to providing much needed sexuality and character education. *Ten Talks* gets parents and children talking about important issues such as sexuality, responsibility, and family beliefs."

—Dennis Worsham, "Washington, Can We Talk?"

Ten
Talks

Parents Must Have
With Their Children

About Sex
and Character

Ten Talks

Parents Must Have
With Their Children

About Sex and Character

**Pepper Schwartz, Ph.D.,
and Dominic Cappello**

New York

ISBN 0-7868-8548-3

First Edition
10   9   8   7   6   5   4   3   2   1

To Cooper and Ryder—I am privileged to be your mother. Thanks so much for your early comments on *Ten Talks*— and for all the talks we have had and will have for the rest of our lives.   P.S.

To Paula—whose compassionate and creative approach to raising two boys continues to inspire me. Your unconditional support and encouragement helped make this book possible.   D.C.

Acknowledgments

The Ten Talks Team

The development of *Ten Talks* was a team effort. This book is the result of thousands of conversations with parents, educators, children, and representatives from religious organizations and public health departments across the country. Packaging their insights into book form involved the invaluable contributions of some very committed colleagues and thoughtful editorial consultants: Susan Durón, Ph.D., an education specialist and evaluator in Denver, Colorado; Bonnie Faddis, Ph.D., a researcher and education specialist in Portland, Oregon; Susan Holmberg, Ph.D., a researcher and media analyst in Seattle, Washington; Susan Burgess, M.S., M.A., an organizational development consultant and therapist in Seattle, Washington; Xenia Becher, M.S.W., C.S.W., in Syracuse, New York; Susan Coots, a sexuality educator and program development consultant in Syracuse, New York; April Roseman, M.A., M.P.H., a therapist in private practice in Seattle; and Skylar Fein at Training for Change in Philadelphia. Special thanks to Paula Brooks for her editorial review of the entire manuscript in addition to coordinating the sample talks with parents and children.

We are indebted to our national reviewers and advisors: Laura Davis, Debra Hafner, Tracy Flynn, Christine Luong, Elaini Gardiner, Lauri Halderman, Laurie Trotta, Kate Folb, Michael Day, Lisa Frank, Nancy Tartt, Betsy Nagle-McNaughton, Susan Martin, Lisa Perry, Ted Eytan, M.D., Norma Straw, Mary Jo McHaney, Rita Creighton, Diana Rivera, Suzanne Hidde, Dennis Worsham, Julia Mitchell, Leah Hall, John Henry Kuhlmann, Brooke McDonald, and Richard Pargament. We also want to thank our family reviewers: Paula, Joe, Lee, and Robert Brooks; Aubyn, Sara, and Taylor Gwinn; Chelsea, Timothy, and Gabriel Becher; Debra and Max Kabin; Shireen, Gauri, and Sumi Holman; Cindy, Rachel, and Leah Rosin; Megen, Matt, and Kevin Opsahl; Patricia, Alexander, and Anne Goodling; Norman, Caitlin, and Justin Vinner; and the other families, who wish to remain anonymous.

Special thanks to Jerald Newberry, Paul Sathrum, Vicki Harrison, Ari Lopez, and Robert Kaiser at the National Education Association Health Information Network for their strong support of the "Can We Talk?" parent-child communication program and their commitment to health promotion for parents, youth, and educators. Thanks to Jerry Painter and Frieda Takamura at the Washington Education Association, Debra Delgado at the Annie E. Casey Foundation, and Lynne Whitt and Kristina Rudiger at the National Center for Health Education. We offer our gratitude to Fred Morris for supporting *Ten Talks* through its many incarnations and to our thoughtful editor at Hyperion, Mary Ellen O'Neill.

Of course, this book would not have been possible without the thousands of parents across the country who attended our presentations and workshops and helped us refine the *Ten Talks* approach.

Acknowledgments

Those moms and dads proved that parents are the experts, and with the right resources they can nurture family-talks about sexuality and controversial social issues. A big thank-you to the families in Dayton, Georgia; New York City, Syracuse, and Jamestown, New York; Seattle, Yakima, Olympia, Vancouver, and Everett, Washington; Portland, Bend, and Salem, Oregon; Memphis, Tennessee; Kansas City, Missouri; Austin, Dallas, and San Antonio, Texas; Great Falls, Montana; Pine Ridge Indian Reservation, South Dakota; Flint, Michigan; Idaho Falls and Boise, Idaho; Orlando and Miami, Florida; Oklahoma City, Oklahoma; Asheville, Greenville, Lafayette, and Charlotte, North Carolina; Virginia Beach and Fairfax, Virginia; Columbia, South Carolina; and Albuquerque and Las Cruces, New Mexico.

We are especially grateful to Ray Damazo and Gail Sage Damazo for the gift they gave us when they invited us to stay at their fantastic home, Burley On The Hill, in Rutland, England. Ray and Gail gave us their country place as a retreat where we could write and collaborate without interruption. They are people of rare generosity.

Contents

WELCOME TO TEN TALKS   1

How to Use This Book

1   HOW WE TREAT PEOPLE   14

Talking about Sex and Character

2   LIFE CHANGES   50

Talking about Puberty

3   PERSONAL SPACE   95

Talking about Boundaries

4   FRIENDS FOR LIFE   135

Talking about Healthy Relationships

Contents

5   THOSE FIRST FEELINGS   176

    Talking about Attraction and Love

6   KEEPING COMMITMENTS   218

    Talking about Trust and Honesty

7   WHAT'S ON?   256

    Talking about TV, Movies, and Music

8   CYBERSPACE AND SEXUALITY   294

    Talking about What's Online

9   HOW ARE YOU FEELING?   322

    Talking about Alcohol and Other Drugs

10   WHAT WE BELIEVE   347

    Talking about Your Family's Values

Ten
Talks

Parents Must Have
With Their Children

About Sex
and Character

Welcome to Ten Talks

How to Use This Book

When I was in sixth grade I had a health class about how bodies work. But I didn't know what to do the first time a boy showed any interest in me. My mom never talked about anything like that.
—Nancy, mother of one, Memphis, Tennessee

My parents always told me that the schools should not talk about sex and since it was optional, they didn't sign me up for that class. But they never talked about it to me at all. I learned stuff from the guys at school. —Jeff, father of two, Orlando, Florida

In school we were taught how the sperm meet the egg. Nothing about sexual feelings or relationships. I can remember a school slide presentation showing a husband serving his pregnant wife breakfast in bed. I think the comment was something like, "When a woman is pregnant she can become moody—it is then important for her to have an understanding and caring husband."
—Pia, mother of one, Stockholm, Sweden

A lot of adults grew up without ever having talked to their parents about sexual conduct. Even if their parents made sure they took the school health class—or gave them a book about puberty—they never talked about values or how to put those values into practice. How could that have happened? Pretty easily. Parents aren't sex education experts just because they are parents. And even

1

if they were, it's different talking about sexuality with your own child (believe me, we know!). Since most parents didn't have open and frank talks on sexual topics with their own folks, they didn't learn how to introduce intimate and potentially embarrassing topics to their kids.

That's why many parents, though not all, are relieved when they hear sexuality education is being taught in the schools. They figure their child will get the essential information without parents having to agonize about the conversation themselves.

But parents soon find out that their children are not getting the information that they really need. The education they get is most often about fallopian tubes and sperm and egg chases—not about how they feel about their body, or how to interpret the sex scenes in just about every movie on TV. There are a lot of complex questions out there that kids are not equipped to answer, and they need their parents to put sexuality in context. Children need their moms or dads to listen to their concerns and to help them think through the sexual issues that arise in everyday life.

And these days, sexual issues are everywhere. Parents shake their heads at the sexy ads and billboards, the sexual jokes in sitcoms, the sexual scenes on daytime TV, and the explicit and often vulgar talk in afternoon talk shows. Parents can't even count on the news to be safe to watch; everyday reports include horror stories about incest, rape, and sexual scandal.

The low point for many families came when the sexual transgressions of no less than the President of the United States became a fixture of the nightly news. During impeachment proceedings, young children innocently asked their parents about oral sex and the stains on Monica's dress. Parents who had exalted the office of the presidency now found themselves flustered trying to explain terms and acts that they had hoped would never come up in conversations.

This was the moment when millions of parents realized that they did not have the tools to conduct a conversation about sexuality with their children. Many parents just ducked the issue because they felt so embarrassed and ill equipped to discuss it. But most knew that they really did have to give their children an explanation and a personal opinion. They did want to weigh in on moral and sexual questions, but they wanted to be able to do it right.

They wanted to do it right because so much is at stake these days. Teenage pregnancy is not only possible but also common; in the U.S., more than one million girls get pregnant every year. Among teens, it's estimated that over 70 percent of all pregnancies are unplanned. Rape and sexual molestation are more common than we want to believe and sexual diseases are on the rise, even among teenagers. The stakes are high and parents are desperate to find an easy and effective way to approach what often seems like a weighty topic.

Why Ten Talks?

This book was written as a collaborative effort between a university sociology professor specializing in sexuality research and a parent education specialist. Both of us have spoken to young people and their parents all over the country and have realized how few families are talking about sexuality and character at home. Parents in workshops around the country speak candidly about having gotten little guidance about sexual conduct from their own parents (aside from the classic "If you have sex, I'll kill you") and admit to struggling to break the cycle of silence with their children. Parents want to keep their children safe and help them to develop healthy relationships. *Ten Talks* is designed to do just that. Our mutual concern and our different professional perspectives have been brought together in this book. The result is a process that parents can use to help their kids understand the complexities of sexual relationships and their families' own values.

How to Use This Book

Each chapter focuses on a different aspect of sex and character and is divided into four sections. In the first section, "Preparing for the Talk," you'll find ways to clarify your values and family rules about each aspect of sexuality we are discussing. The second section, "The Talk," is centered around stories for you and your child to read and includes illustrations to help set the scene in your child's mind. These stories illustrate challenging situations that your child might find herself in. Each story is followed by questions for you to ask your child. Your child's answers will give you insights into how she thinks and acts in particular situations. The questions encourage your child to share her views, and may help you articulate your personal values and the importance of following family rules and guidelines. The third section, "After the Talk," gives you an opportunity to reflect on your child's responses and to identify any potential problems.

The fourth section contains sample talks, excerpts of actual conversations between parents and their children. Some talks are very animated and show what can happen when a child is fully engaged. Others illustrate what happens when a child starts squirming from the moment the parent starts the conversation. Some talks will engage a child more than others. Even conversations with resistant children show that they learn something about the topic and the parents learn more about the child. Each of the ten talks may range from five minutes to an unhurried hour. Even a five-minute talk should be considered worth doing.

Every Talk Is a Success

It's not always clear during discussions whether your child is getting the message. It's particularly hard when you feel you are barely being tolerated, or when your child feels that he is doing you a big favor to sit through one or two talks. But remember that often, when you don't think you've made an impact, you'll find at some future date that you really did make an impression. And even if your child didn't get everything out of the talk you would have wanted, remember that he's getting this: the knowledge that you care. He knows you want him to know how you feel and that what you think is important. He will see that safety and ethical conduct are critical issues when it comes to sex. And he will know that you are approachable when there is a problem that confuses or scares him. Think of it this way: you are building pathways of communication between you and your child. There is no wasted effort. Yes, there may be very long pauses in your conversations and we hope you allow your child to fill in the silence. And remember, even though a given talk might be a struggle, the next time around your child may surprise you with his interested and mature questions and wise answers. It's happened time and again.

One, Two, or Ten Talks

You know your child. You know which chapters of this book will be most important for her level of development. Of course, not every chapter pertains to your child's life and your family's situation, so choose the chapters that make the most sense to you. Also, each chapter contains more than one story—you do not need to read each one with your child for the talk to be effective. Feel free to innovate. For example, you may wish to change the sequence of the talks depending on you or your child's interest. There are two chapters, however, that we feel you should not skip: Chapter 1, How We Treat People: Talking about Sex and Character, and Chapter 6, Keeping Commitments: Talking about Trust and Honesty. Each chapter will help you establish the larger framework of values that your family works within.

What Can You Expect from *Ten Talks*?

The *Ten Talks* process, first published in *Ten Talks Parents Must Have With Their Children About Violence*, has shown that following the guidelines in this book can bring huge rewards for both parent and child. Stick with the ten conversations and you may

- increase the amount of time you spend in meaningful discussions with your child.
- increase your understanding of your child's views about sex and character.
- feel more confident that your child can keep herself safe.
- be able to describe your family rules about developing relationships, sexual activity, using sexual language, or viewing sexual imagery.

Do these objectives seem daunting? Don't worry, there won't be a test! *Ten Talks* just wants you to have meaningful conversations with your child; we're not concerned with having your child come up with the "right" answer. Please don't be intimidated. You may be thinking, "Can I really do this?" The answer is, yes, you can. Thousands of parents in cities across the country have proved it. You are an expert when it comes to your child, and we are merely giving you better resources and tools to do your jobs even more effectively.

The Role of School

When you start to talk with your child about sexuality, be prepared to hear, "I don't want to talk about THIS with you." Or, "I've already had health education in school—you don't need to talk to me about this." You can reassure your child that these talks are not meant to embarrass (though they sometimes may) and that the talks will be more about potentially awkward or stressful situations than about body parts. You can reassure her that you are not going to pry; that you are going to share opinions about what to do under certain circumstances. Reassure her that you'll back off if there's a topic she really doesn't want to talk about. You can be pretty sure they didn't get this kind of education in health class. Don't lose heart. Remember, even if your child's teachers are providing lessons on sex and character, these lessons are *not* a substitute for communicating your values and house rules on the subject. This means, for better or worse, that the ultimate responsibility for sex and character education rests with the parents—in other words, you.

Talking with the Non-Communicative Child

When you sit down to have your first talk, your child may make a face that suggests gagging on a foul-tasting substance, or roll his

eyes and make a quick exit. Don't worry, you're not alone in trying to engage a "less than enthusiastic" child. Here are five common ways your child may try to derail the discussion.

Child's rejection #1: I've already learned this in school.
Child's rejection #2: I'll talk about this, but I don't want to
talk about it with you.
Child's rejection #3: I'm too old for this.
Child's rejection #4: I'm not gonna do it.
Child's rejection #5: It's none of your business.

Here are some ways other parents have steered their conversations back on track.

"I've taken a look at what you were taught in school and it
really didn't cover a lot of the topics that I think are important."
"Okay, let's talk about the chapters that aren't so personal, and
then we'll see how we feel about the other ones. If you still
don't want to discuss it with me, I'll let you pick someone
else from our family or friends to discuss it with."
"I'm not too old for this discussion—so you can't be! There is
always something interesting to think about when it comes to
important questions about relationships and choices about
sexual behavior."
"I don't always want to do some of the things I do for you, but
I do it because it means a lot to you. This means a lot to me."
"You know you are my business. My job is making sure you
have considered how you would behave before you are presented with an important choice. All I am doing is helping

you prepare for that moment. I wouldn't be doing my job as a parent if I didn't help you think about this topic."

If all else fails, each talk contains a section called The Bare Minimum for a quick review of terms and family rules. You may also find that talking with your child one-on-one, rather than with other people present, will give you the best results. And remember that some places are better than others to initiate a talk. Some parents have had their best luck in, of all places, the car. One mom in Seattle said that talking while driving was perfect for her son: he didn't have to maintain eye contact with her, and he "couldn't escape!"

Family Rules: Your Duty as a Parent

It seems fair to say that our culture is obsessed with sex. You can't keep your child from being exposed to the topic—and to the temptations. We can't pretend that all young people have their first sexual experiences on the first night of their honeymoon. (Did you?)

Data clearly indicates that all kinds of pairings take place within the context of various types of short- and long-term relationships. And even if you could be sure that your child was in the minority, that he was someone who'd wait until he was married to be sexual, you'd still know that in the meantime, his friends and his favorite TV shows would be filling his head with all kinds of other ideas. We live in a society where potentially dangerous opportunities present themselves early and often to the children we cherish. This alone should persuade parents to overcome their own or their children's reluctance to talk about sexuality.

At the very least, you need to come up with some family rules about sexual safety and sexual ethics, communicate them to your child, and review them to make sure your child understands them. Enforcing these rules is not something we suggest will be easy, but it's vital to establish them early on.

I thought I knew how my child would react to these stories when we first started Ten Talks. I was surprised how often my child did not feel entitled to make the decision he knew was best. I was relieved to have the opportunity to tell him how I thought he should act, and why I thought he should act that way. He was surprised by how many of these things had never occurred to him and how much he enjoyed thinking through them out loud.

—Margaret, mother of one, St. Paul, Minnesota

Yes, There Is Help

If you get stressed at the thought of having these talks with your child, consider calling in the reserves! Ask for some help from another adult—a grandparent, aunt, uncle, step-parent, trusted friend, or someone from your church or temple. For example, if a boy simply doesn't want to talk to a woman about body image or puberty, a single mom might want to have an adult male friend or relative talk with him about these issues. (This is something we wholeheartedly recommend, as many young males report being starved for healthy adult male role models they can trust and depend on.) Just make sure that if you ask another adult to talk with your child, his or her values are compatible with your own. You are not handing off responsibility for the whole set of conversations. There will be several of these talks you can do with little or no anxiety.

When Is a Child Old Enough for Ten Talks?

Ten Talks is designed for children from fourth to twelfth grade. However, most sexuality educators believe that even very young children can talk about sexual topics as long as you use simple words and don't introduce issues that are totally irrelevant to them. You need to tailor the talks to your child's age and maturity level; obviously, the talk you would have with a fourth-grader would not be the same as the one you'd have with a high school senior.

Many of the discussion topics in *Ten Talks* will be familiar to them through TV or life at school. The main ingredient of the *Ten Talks* process, storytelling, is an activity that young children are familiar with. We have found that parents talking with their fourth-, fifth-, and sixth-graders were the most successful. Younger kids are usually old enough to understand the importance of at least one or two of the topics. For example, in the chapter on boundaries, young children understand what is at stake in the story on bedroom privacy or having a bra strap snapped in the school yard. The nice part about talking to the younger children is that they are most willing to seek guidance from a parent. Some middle and many high school students may see this book as something for "kids," but the family rules outlined in each chapter are relevant to any child living under your roof. If your child watches TV, uses the Internet, or goes to school, then the ten topics in this book need to be discussed. You know best how you can frame the talks in a way that your child will understand.

You will find that your child's reaction to the talks will change as she moves from elementary school to middle school to high school. Just as a good schoolteacher does, you can revisit the topics in this book yearly to reinforce the lessons learned, review the family rules, and make adjustments if needed.

About Quotes and Pronouns

Many of the quotes from parents and youths come from feedback we received during presentations and workshops on parent-child communication that we conducted across the country. Quite a few also have been added from parents who tested the *Ten Talks* book for us. Their names have been changed to protect their privacy. Also, in the interest of succinctness, *Ten Talks* alternates pronouns throughout the text. Thus, as you probably have already noticed, in one paragraph we may refer to your child as "she" and in the next as "he."

Special Note

Ten Talks has been developed to help parents and children talk about sexuality and building character. *Ten Talks* is not intended to replace professional evaluation and treatment by a licensed mental health professional, if needed. If any concerns about sexual abuse or mistreatment arise, please contact a licensed child psychologist, psychiatrist, physician, or social worker.

Is it "sex" or "sexuality"?

Professional organizations and sexuality educators use the term "sexuality" to convey the broad range of topics that fall within the human sexual experience. Professionals prefer to use the word "sex" just to designate males and females—and occasionally to refer to intercourse (just because that's the way the public uses the word).

While we are both professionals in the sexual education field, and like the term "sexuality," we also felt that we needed to include the use of the word "sex" as it is used by parents and children in everyday life. Most kids—and their parents—use it to cover every kind of sexual interaction they can think of. Kids use the word "sex" to mean anything from kissing to intercourse. (Some young ones even use it as a verb, "Are you gonna sex?") So, our compromise, to make parents feel comfortable and let educators know that we know that they know that "sexuality" is the most inclusive word available, is to use both words in this book interchangeably.

Speaking of Character . . .

Families come in all shapes and sizes. Some have a mom and a dad, others have one mom, or one dad, or two moms or two dads or extended families filled with grandparents, uncles, aunts, and cousins, or blended families with lots of interaction between diverse households. Some families are headed by guardians or foster parents. We hope you customize the strategies in *Ten Talks* to share with your child your own unique family values.

1

How We Treat People

Talking about Sex and Character

I learned about body parts in school. The teacher never talked about relationships or morals or character. It was strictly how to make a baby. Of course, I told my mom I already learned everything in school. —Suzanne, mother of one, Seattle, Washington

I know that they don't know what they are saying when they hurl such words as "sluts" and "gay" at one another on the playground, but hearing third-graders acting out that way is upsetting.
—Christine, mother of two, New York City

I had not talked with my sons about sex, assuming that school would take care of it. One day I heard that a neighbor's thirteen-year-old daughter was pregnant. I immediately drove to the drug-store and bought two boxes of condoms—one each for my twelve- and ten-year-old sons. I sat them down, gave them each a box, and explained in detail how that pregnancy could have been prevented. I also explained that boys who become fathers have to pay for that child for eighteen years. The thirteen-year-old kept saying, "Calm down, mom." The ten-year-old looked at me like I was from outer space. —Pam, mother of two, Gaithersburg, Maryland

What do we mean when we say "sex and character"? We chose these words carefully, because we didn't want to write another book about body parts. While we thought understanding how the body works is very important, we also felt that what parents really need is a book that helps them talk to their children about ethical sexual conduct. Children need information about how their bodies work, but they also need to understand how they feel about their bodies themselves as they mature sexually and emotionally, and how to set guidelines about sexual relationships. Parents need a way to tell their children about the rules and values that they believe in, and they need a way to show their child how these values are expressed in everyday decision making. Children and parents need a comfortable way of learning about each other's feelings and beliefs about sexual situations. There is a lot of wisdom and intimate conversation that never gets shared because parents don't know how to bring up the topic in a way that feels acceptable. The purpose of this chapter is to help you think about what you mean by "sex," what you mean by "character," and how the two interact. In this talk, you'll be helping your child develop the kind of character traits that will allow her to have an emotionally and sexually healthy relationship someday.

Talking about sex and character together is a bit complex, so let's talk about each independently before we put them together. Let's start with what might seem an obvious question.

Talking about Sex

What do you mean when you say "sex"? Would your child agree with you? From an early age, children know that there is something called "sex," but their idea of what it means may vary from kissing or hugging to some hazy idea about bodies rubbing together. However, as they get older, they get more information—

especially from TV. By the time most children have started school they have viewed thousands of different kinds of sexual relationships on TV. Sexual words may be an ordinary part of their vocabulary—and most of these words aren't used in a very nice way. Kids on the playground call each other sexually charged names, often used as insults: "virgin," "slut," "gay," and "fag" are common school yard insults. Children today encounter sexually explicit images on the Internet. Kids are bombarded with sexual imagery in advertising wherever there's a TV, radio, magazine, or billboard. Kids today have seen so much sexual imagery that most middle-schoolers consider themselves teenage sex experts. They may be so sure that they know "all about sex" that they don't even ask questions. But when you talk to them, you'll find out that they haven't really thought through their own values or how they'd handle specific situations. You may also find that they have different definitions about what constitutes a sexual act than most adults would have.

How does a parent set rules about sexual activity when the parent and child define "sex" differently? Is kissing sex? Is oral sex really sex? Sexual conduct guidelines become more and more important as children get older and begin to interact with grownups with their own beliefs and desires. Once those interactions begin, important decisions about sexual behavior begin. And of course parents want their voice—their family values—to have an impact on those decisions.

The talk in this chapter will give you a chance to discuss how your child views sex. The talk is about sex and character because you and your child will want to discuss all of the personal qualities that each person needs to have in order for sexual relationships to be happy, healthy, and safe.

My fifth-grader says sex is "skin-to-skin" contact. My eighth-grader says it's kissing. I used to think of it as meaning sexual intercourse. In our family, with five different people, we have five different definitions of what sex is.

—Mara, mother of three, Jamestown, New York

Talking about Character

What do we mean when we say someone has character? Here are some character traits most people would agree should be nurtured.

- Honesty
- Respect for oneself and others
- Honor
- Tolerance
- Caring for others
- Sticking up for what you believe in
- Keeping promises
- Courage under pressure

Perhaps you can think of other traits equally as important. A person who had all these traits would be set for life and love—but even a few of these traits would help make our relationships more meaningful and satisfying. If you could stick to your convictions, you would never do something you'd be sorry about later. If you had courage under pressure, you could pick when to follow and when to lead—and be willing to take whatever consequences were caused by your behavior. If you were a caring, trustworthy person, you would be the kind of person others would want to love and depend on. Aren't these the kind of characteristics we want our children to have? In the course of this talk (and the entire book) you will have many opportunities to discuss your child's character traits and the traits she should look for in others.

Sex Can Be a Wonderful Part of Life

Even though this talk is about sex and character, your conversation with your child should not be about frightening, shaming, or intimidating her to the point that she doesn't want to ever have a relationship. Many parents believe that sexuality is healthy and wonderful. A relationship that is sexual can be one of the most pleasurable experiences in life. We also know that life is complicated and that decisions about being sexual come with big responsibilities. This talk is about empowering your child by giving her skills, primarily communication and critical-thinking skills. These skills can help her navigate through her daily life and as she matures make informed decisions about whom to be involved with. At the end of this talk, your child should understand that there are ethical ways to behave. She'll also understand that sex can have many meanings—and that there are many choices she can make based on her own and her family's values. Most important, she'll understand that sex and character are things families can and should discuss.

Preparing for the Talk

This talk opens the door for ongoing conversations that will deepen your child's understanding of sex and character.

In this talk you will let your child know that

- it's okay to talk about these kinds of topics.
- he can depend on you for support when facing problems about sex or character.
- you have expectations about her behavior as it relates to sexuality and relationships.
- there are family rules about sexual activity and how people are to be treated.

What You Can Expect from This Talk

After the talk your child will

- be able to identify healthy sexual relationships and the character traits needed to maintain them.
- understand that there are many types of relationships, both non-sexual and sexual.
- understand your family rules about sex and character.

How Do You Define Sex?

There is plenty of disagreement among adults about what "sex" is. In 1998 President Bill Clinton defended himself against charges of infidelity by saying that he had not had sex outside of his marriage. Later, when it became clear that oral sex had occurred, President Clinton defended his version of the truth by claiming that only intercourse qualified as "sex."

In general, the public rejected that definition, but it's true that many people disagree about what sex is. National surveys show that a sizable minority of people believe that sex is intercourse, plain and simple. In one women's survey, women who had had oral sex said that they were virgins and had therefore not had sex.

How should we define sex? Sociologists study sexuality as a part of human interaction. Psychologists are more interested in sexuality at the individual level; for them, even fantasies could be considered sexual experiences. Legal definitions of sex vary from state to state.

Religious groups often have different ideas about what constitutes sex. One denomination might label kissing as sexual conduct and condemn it outside of marriage, while another might call it harmless. Some religions would call an act sexual only if it aided procreation. Others would see any feelings or thoughts that are about the body or even about love as sexual.

We don't mean to avoid giving you a definition, but this is where your own family values come into play. There are a million ways to describe sex. What will matter most, as you explore *Ten Talks* with your child, is how you define sexuality and your values in relation to sexual behavior.

It's a matter of semantics. Whether you call it sex or sexuality, your child needs to know your attitudes about appropriate sexual behavior.
—Lisa, mother of one, Seattle, Washington

All of the hype around sexual conduct at the White House made me realize that I had a definition of what was appropriate that was different for males than for females. I've had to readjust my thinking.
—Dana, mother of two, Portland, Oregon

I want my child to wait until she is in a committed loving relationship before she has sex. But I expect that she will experiment during dating.
—Sandra, mother of two, Orlando, Florida

First, you need to find out what your child thinks sex is and what she thinks sex is for. Does she think of sex as recreation or procreation? Is sex another form of play, or is it a bond at the highest spiritual level? If you talk to your child about these themes you might be surprised by what she thinks.

This chapter's talk will also give you a chance to tell your child what you think sex is.

Your child learns about sex and relationships from you in all kinds of ways. You are the primary role model. How you comment on TV shows or advertising affects your child's perceptions. How you and your family and friends relate to one another helps your child define healthy relationships. When you communicate your feelings and thoughts, you help define sex.

Which of the following are instances of sexual situations? Two people kiss. A young person in the shower fantasizes about sex. A boy goes into an Internet chat room. A teenage girl has some beers with older students at an unchaperoned party. A teenager watches an afternoon talk show on "Men who Cheat."

What do the behaviors listed above have to do with sex? Most parents would say kissing and fantasy relate to sex. But when a child views sexually explicit sites on the Internet, a young girl gets drunk around older boys, or anyone watches afternoon TV, there are explicit sexual themes and at least the potential for sexual behavior. As you read this chapter, there will be opportunities to discuss your definition of sex, along with your personal values, with your child.

Your Home, Your Rules

Carrie and her mom have been fighting about Carrie's boyfriend. Her mom thinks he is too old to go out with Carrie (he is eighteen and she is fifteen). Carrie says that he is very nice to her. Her mom says that she knows that all he wants from Carrie is sex. Carrie has been promising her mother for weeks that she won't have sex. During a fight with her mom, Carrie breaks down, cries, and admits to having had intercourse with her boyfriend. Her mom is furious. Carrie's little sister hears the entire fight.

Many parents would call this situation every parent's nightmare. How would you respond to this situation?

First we need some background information. What are the family rules about being sexual? How much time has the mother given her daughter to discuss sexuality, relationships, pregnancy and parenting, sexually transmitted diseases, and the law? How can a parent know if her child has the skills and character traits to postpone sexual activity?

In a situation like the one above, what is the younger daughter learning from this experience? What are the consequences for breaking the family rules? What can the mother do? Should she call the boy's parents? Report the boy to the police? This all gets pretty complicated. Once a young person has already had a sexual relationship, the parent's dialogue has to be about future conduct and practical safety guidelines.

Your Parents' Family Rules and Yours

When you were growing up, did your family have spoken or unspoken rules about sexual activity? Or was it linked to the phrase, "If you have sex, I'll kill you"? Some families have a lot of house rules about sex. Other families have almost none. *Ten Talks* refers to family rules throughout. Family rules are also known as "guidelines" or "expectations for your behavior."

If you were to ask your child, "What are the family rules about sexual activity, including viewing sexually themed videos, TV, web sites, or sexually explicit magazines in our home?" what would she say? A goal of *Ten Talks* is to help you identify and set the rules that you feel comfortable with and to make sure that your child knows what they are.

My husband and I conflict over rules. He would let our son get away with behavior that I'm uncomfortable with. It's an ongoing discussion.
—Tracy, mother of two, Gaithersburg, Maryland

My parents had one simple rule: No hands go under clothing.
—Brad, father of one, Yakima, Washington

Because my parents never talked with us girls about rules, every encounter with a boy was like exploring new territory.
—Donna, mother of two, Orlando, Florida

Our church has a program where teens sign a contract about sexual restraint.
—Marie, mother of two, Bend, Oregon

Influence of the Media

The media often broadcasts images of sexual situations as entertainment. These images are not designed to offer insights into the complex issues surrounding sexual behavior and relationships. That's your job.

The media plays a big role in shaping our ideas about sex. Because the media rarely examines its own treatment of sex, it leaves the separation of reality and fantasy to parents. While the impact of TV programming on young people is debated in many circles, two characteristics of the U.S. media are clear: first, sexual activity outside of marriage or a committed relationship is portrayed as a common occurrence, and, second, negative consequences of sexual activity are rarely shown. How often do people in soap operas talk about unplanned pregnancy, chlamydia, or HIV? In Chapter 7: What's On?: Talking about TV, Movies, and Music, this is explored in greater detail.

Pressure from Peers

We've traveled around the country talking with parents about how to communicate with their children about sexuality, relationships, and character. Parents often find it helpful to think back to their own childhood and what motivated them to become sexual or to wait. Parents say that pressure from their schoolmates and neighborhood friends was the single largest factor influencing their decisions about when to become sexual.

Think back to your childhood and how important it was to be accepted by your peers. Did this kind of pressure increase as you moved from elementary to middle to high school? (It did for most people.)

I remember when I was a freshman in high school, and my friend Gary told me that he "did it" with Karen. Suddenly, I felt that if I didn't "do it," there was something wrong with me.

—Rich, father of three, Boise, Idaho

I never felt peer pressure to get sexually involved when I was a kid. I just wanted to have lots of sex when I was in college.

—Jeffrey, New York City

For me, the pressure from my girlfriends wasn't to have sex. It was to have a boyfriend, to be in a relationship. And this was at age eleven!

—Gretchen, mother of one, Denver, Colorado

Giving Your Child the Big Picture

Divorce rate: estimated at 41% to 50%

Percentage of all males who get married: 92%

Percentage of all females who get married: 85%

Average age of marriage for males: 27

Average age of marriage for females: 26

Percentage of all marriages that are remarriages: 33%

Households that are headed by single moms: 28%

Percentage of U.S. households with a married couple with their children, with Dad as the only breadwinner: 10%

(Source: Frank D. Cox, Human Intimacy, *Wadsworth Press, 1999)*

Percentage of teenage girls who have had sexual intercourse by age 18: 56%

Percentage of teenage boys who have had sexual intercourse by age 18: 73%

(Source: Kaiser Family Foundation, 1999)

What do these numbers tell you about sexual relationships and character?

Once upon a time, it looked like every family had a working dad, a mom who stayed home to raise the kids, and kids in the home who were biologically related to both parents. As our statistics show, however, this type of model represents only 10 percent of U.S. families. The majority of Americans are in blended families. Sometimes moms work outside the home. Sometimes households are headed by only one parent. Sometimes there are two dads or two moms or parents who have been married numerous times with kids from each union spending time with different parents throughout the week. Sound confusing? It is. And yet your child is exposed, through TV and peers, to a variety of models that need explaining.

The good news is that you have considerable control over the development of your child's attitudes about sex and character. You are the most important influence on your child. You are your child's role model for developing healthy relationships and communicating feelings.

Points of View

In the twenty-first century, more and more people are living together without feeling social pressure to share sacred or legal vows first. "Serial monogamy" is also the norm, with more and more people having a series of committed relationships over a long lifetime. The model of youthful virginity followed by marriage and lifelong fidelity has not been achievable for the majority of Americans for many decades. Your child will have friends with parents who are divorced or remarried, or who never married. Which model of relationship do you wish to pass down to your child?

My parents were married for fifty-five years. My wife and I have been married for nineteen years. I want my kids to see that lifetime relationships are possible.

—Drew, father of two, Bend, Oregon

I remember when I was a kid my mom talked about how shameful it would be to have a child out of wedlock. My son thinks that's funny, since so many of his friends' parents aren't married—to him it's no big deal.

—Nina, mother of three, Denver, Colorado

My fourth-grade son wanted to know why his Aunt Ann has been married three times, and me only once. I told him that sometimes people change and fall out of love.

—Ted, father of two, Memphis, Tennessee

When I was a kid, we always asked why Uncle Art never got married and never had kids. And we never got a straight answer! Now I realize that Uncle Art was gay.

—Rachel, mother of one, Everett, Washington

Different Families: Different Values

Your child is presented with many values about sexual activity. You have your own values and rules. But your child's friends, teachers, or coaches may have different ones. The following scenarios illustrate how your child may receive different messages all the time.

Your child is playing at a neighbor's home with a group of boys. One boy pulls up a site on the Internet that shows sexually explicit materials.

The friend's dad sees this and thinks this is acceptable and just "boys being boys." Another parent might see young people viewing certain types of erotica as inappropriate or disrespectful of women. How would you react? What if it was girls looking at the porn site?

■

In gym class, some sixth-graders are playing baseball. Your son is in left field when he picks up a ball and throws it to second base. One of the guys yells, "You throw like a fag," and laughs.

The coach sees this happen and thinks that it's no big deal. He feels it's up to the students to work out their own problems. Another coach would follow strict zero-tolerance guidelines to prevent verbal harassment of any kind and discipline the student who used sexual slang. How would you want to see this situation addressed?

■

Your daughter is going out with a guy a few years older than she is. They are kissing in the car and he wants to have intercourse. Your daughter does not. He says he loves her. She is very flattered and feels great. He is pressuring her to relax and have fun. She feels in love with him and doesn't want to disappoint him. She also knows that her parents would not approve of her having intercourse.

How would you want a daughter of yours to respond? If you were the boy's parent, how would you want him to behave?

The neighbor's dad, the coaches, and the boyfriend all have their own values about sexuality and character. In real life, your child may face situations similar to these all the time. Other people are communicating their values to your child in subtle or not-so-subtle ways. Your values need to be communicated in a way that's equally loud and clear.

Last-Minute Checkups before the Talk

This is a good time to think about your childhood experiences of talking with your parents about sex. When you were a child:

- Did a parent ever talk to you about sex?
- Did you ever tell your parents about the sexual behavior of your peers? What did they say?
- Did your family ever discuss pregnancy or sexually transmitted diseases?
- Did your parents ever discuss sexual orientation?
- Did a parent ever talk to you about inappropriate touching and what you could do in response to it?

How do you think your childhood experiences have affected the way you're raising your child?

- What have you told your child about sex?
- Have you told her to expect some pressure to be sexual from

schoolmates? Is she supposed to avoid kids who are having sex?
- Has your family discussed inappropriate touching and how people can respond to it?

Do you have any stories that you could share with your child? For example:

- A story about a neighbor or schoolmate who wanted to be sexual
- An experience confronting a sexually aggressive person

Keep these stories in mind as you talk with your child. She needs to hear that you have faced these situations and made your own decisions.

What Are Your Family Rules?

Do you have family rules about when people are old enough to have "boyfriends" or "girlfriends," to kiss, or to have sex? If not, this is a good time to think about them. The talk outlined in this chapter highlights the following situations:

- Two students are learning about sex during a classroom lecture.
- Two students are learning about character during a classroom lecture.
- At a girl's slumber party, sex is discussed.
- At a boy's sleepover, sex is discussed.

Discussing these situations will give you a chance to discuss your family rules. What would you want your child to do in each situation? What are your expectations? Before the talk, think about what rules you want to communicate to your child. At the end of the talk, you will have the chance to review the rules together.

The Talk

Introduce the Talk

All right—you are almost ready to have the talk about defining sex and character with your child. To fully understand the *Ten Talks* process, make sure to read the entire chapter before starting the talk. You may find the sample talks at the end of this chapter particularly helpful.

Find a time for an uninterrupted ten minutes or so. With this book in hand, tell your child:

> "I'm reading this chapter about sex and character. I need to talk to you for five or ten minutes."

Some younger children may be happy to talk with you, while others may be completely uninterested. Many children assume that they actually know more about real life than you do. A common response is, "I already know all this," or "I learned that in school."

If your child doesn't want to talk, be patient. Many parents report that their children don't get enthusiastic until the third or fourth talk. And remember, you can use the following statement as many times as necessary: "It's part of my job as a parent to have this talk, to listen to you and answer your questions. It's part of your job as my child to listen and ask me questions."

Remember how you liked to be spoken to when you were young—kids still don't want to be talked down to or be treated like babies. At the first sign of a patronizing speech, they shut down.

Next, you could say, "I've got some questions to discuss. First, what have you learned about sex in school?" Next, ask if she's had any lessons on character in school. Courses on character may or may not have anything to do with sex education. Sessions on character may be general talks about how to treat one another on the playground. For older students there may have been some lessons about sexual ethics—about how you are supposed to deal with sexuality in relationships.

Your child may offer some examples. If your child goes to a school with programs on sex education and character, you can expect some feedback. If so, proceed with the next section.

If your child doesn't offer some examples, you could say something like, "There are many ways to talk about sex and character. I'd like to start by talking about the kind of person you want to be when you are making decisions about your sexuality. Talking about sex and character means talking about how you treat people and expect to be treated by them in situations that might have sexual overtones. Treating people with respect starts way before people start having any sexual relationships."

Courses on "sex" can come under a lot of different headings. In some schools, HIV education is mandated. In early grades, courses may focus on germs and hand-washing. Other courses may be about "good touching" and "bad touching." So when parents ask about what their child has learned about sex in school, the question can be hard to answer.
—Susan Coots, sexuality educator and parent educator,
Syracuse, New York

Review These Words

Please review the terms in this section. Discussing all of them with your child is optional. You know what's appropriate for your child's age and maturity level. Keep in mind that more than likely, even the youngest children have heard these words on TV.

sex: sometimes used to define biological sex, meaning male or female; sometimes used to mean sexual intercourse; sometimes used to mean some kind of bodily contact. Consequently, when people say "sex" it might be difficult to know what they have in mind. It depends on the context.

sexuality: a broad term referring to the sum total of our sexual desire, behavior, and self-identity.

character: behavior demonstrates character, the core of a person's ethics and values.

platonic relationship: a non-sexual relationship. The word "platonic" comes from the ancient Greek philosopher Plato, who talked about the pure and deep love of friends. His name has been used to talk about close relationships that do not include eroticism or sexual contact.

monogamous: having only one sexual partner, traditionally, one's spouse.

serial monogamy: people who are monogamous for a while, then break up and become monogamous with someone else. The opposite of this would be lifetime monogamy, whereby a commitment is made and kept forever.

Why Is Talking about Sex and Character Important?

Ask your child whether she thinks talking about sex and character is important. Here are some reasons you might want to offer: Talking about sex and character helps us

- identify standards of behavior.
- understand the skills needed to form a healthy relationship.
- learn how to treat others.
- clarify our family rules on sexual activity, using sexual language, and viewing sexually explicit materials.

The Stories

In the next part of the talk, you'll be reading short stories to your child and discussing them together. You don't have to read all of the stories. Pick the ones that you think are appropriate. The stories are very simple. Feel free to embellish them, adding details that you think might make them more believable. For example, some parents change the gender of the characters to make a story mirror their own families.

Some children will express their concerns in a straightforward way. Others may say, "Well, I know this kid at school who has some problems," while they may really be talking about themselves. Remember that you may have to read between the lines to get to your child's true feelings and concerns.

The Story about the Classroom

This story gives you an opportunity to talk about what your child has learned about sexuality in school.

"A boy and girl are sitting in the front row listening to their teacher. The teacher is talking about human reproduction in class. She has already taught how flowers, frogs, and cats reproduce. Now she points to a picture of the male and female reproductive system on the board."

Ask these questions of your child:

- What is the teacher thinking?
- What is the girl thinking?
- What is the boy thinking?

Now that your child has completed this scenario, ask the following questions:

- What kinds of sexual information do teachers talk about in school?
- What would the girl's and boy's parents say about this situation?
- Have you seen or been in a situation like this? If so, how did you feel? What did you do?

Clarify Your Family's Values

Discuss this question with your child as a way of sharing your values about sex education.

Ask your child: "What do your teachers tell you about sex?"

> *Child:* You mean how babies are born?
> *Parent:* Yes, very good. What do you know about it?

The Story about the Classroom and Character Lessons

This story gives you a chance to talk about what your child has learned about character in school.

"A boy and girl are sitting in the front row listening to their teacher. The teacher is talking about character. He is asking the class to name character traits that they admire."

Ask these questions of your child:

- What is the teacher thinking?
- What is the girl thinking?
- What is the boy thinking?

Now that your child has completed this scenario, ask the following questions:

- What kinds of information about character and how to treat people do teachers talk about in school?
- What would the girl's and boy's parents say about this situation?
- Have you seen or been in a situation like this? If so, how did you feel? What did you do?

Clarify Your Family's Values

Discuss this question with your child as a way of sharing your values about character education.

Ask your child: "What do your teachers tell you about character?"

Child response #1: Nothing.
Parent: Nothing. Then I guess it is up to me to give you all the information you need. It's good that we have this book to help us.

Child response #2: We have a character class.
Parent: Tell me what you have learned about character. I want to make sure you have all the information you need about sex and character.

Stories for Older Children

The following stories deal with more mature behaviors. While some younger children may not be able to relate to them, you may find that to your child, these stories make perfect sense.

The Story about the Slumber Party

This story gives you an opportunity to discuss how your child hears about sex from peers.

"A girl is having a slumber party with friends. They are up late and one of the girls is talking all about sex."

Ask these questions of your child:

- What is the girl saying about sex?
- What is the girl thinking?
- What are the other girls thinking?
- What are the other girls saying?

Now that your child has completed this scenario, ask the following questions:

- How do you know if what others say about sex is true?
- Have you seen or been in a situation like this? If so, how did you feel? What did you do?

The Story about the Sleepover

This story gives you an opportunity to discuss how your child hears about sex from peers.

"A boy is having some friends stay overnight. They are up late and one of the boys is talking all about sex."

Ask these questions of your child:

- What is the boy saying about sex?
- What is he thinking?
- What are the other boys thinking?
- What are the other boys saying?

Now that your child has completed this scenario, ask the following questions:

- How do you know if what others say about sex is true?
- Have you seen or been in a situation like this? If so, how did you feel? What did you do?

The Bare Minimum: A Quick Quiz for Kids

Ask your child the following questions to assess her knowledge of sex and character.

1. What is sex?
   Sample answers:
- Sex is how babies are born.
- Sex is what people do when they are attracted to one another.
- Sex is a special way to show love for someone.
- Sex is fun.
2. What is character?
   Sample answers:
- It is what makes a personality.
- It is the way a person acts.
- It is about traits a person has, like being nice or mean, honest or dishonest.

3. Why is it important to talk about sex and character?
- Sex and character are the kinds of things people need to know about to have a healthy sexual relationship or a good attitude about sexuality.
4. Can you give me one example of how a person learns about sex and character?
  Sample answers:
- School
- Friends
- A parent
5. Why does a person need a strong character in order to have a healthy relationship?
  Sample answers:
- You need to know yourself and be able to stick to your own values before you can have a healthy relationship with someone else.
- You need to be trustworthy and honest in order to maintain a healthy, long-term relationship.

Talk about Your Family Rules

Family rules must be *your* rules. Be prepared for your child to ask about the reasons behind them. You may find it helpful to talk with relatives or friends about developing your family rules. Sample answers from parents across the country follow.

Ask your child the following questions:

1. What is our family rule about asking questions about sexuality?
  Sample answers:
- All questions are allowed. But talks about sexuality need to happen at the appropriate place and time.

- There is no such thing as a stupid question.
- Sometimes talking about sexuality can lead to disagreements. Talking about different points of view is okay in this family.
2. What is one family rule about using sexual terms and language as jokes or insults?
   Sample answers:
- When you are called names or hear jokes of a sexual nature, I want to hear about it.
- We do not use sexual words or jokes in this house or as a way to insult others.

Rewarding Your Child

For some parents, having a talk with a child is a huge accomplishment and they feel like rewarding their son or daughter. Others don't feel they have to reward their child for having a talk—to them it's just part of the job of being a parent and a kid. How you choose to acknowledge your child's openness and candor is up to you, but many parents have found that a special acknowledgment—whether in the form of a thank-you, a hug, or a special video rental—can work wonders.

After the Talk

A Moment to Reflect

Take a moment to reflect on the talk you just had with your child. How do you feel about it?

- What surprised you about your child's definitions of sex and character?

- How do you feel about your ability to talk with your child about sex and character?
- How much of the time were you listening to your child?
- How do you think your child felt about the talk?
- What will you do differently in the next talk?

After the talk with their child, many parents report a variety of feelings: accomplishment at sustaining a five-minute talk of substance, frustration at not being able to get more information from their child, or even a sense of fear that their child may be involved in situations he can't handle.

Warning Signs

The talks also may reveal potential problems that your child is facing. Was your child reluctant to talk about any situations? Did he avoid eye contact or get angry? Did his responses to your questions seem like normal behavior or did you get the feeling that something may be wrong?

There may be cause for concern if you hear from the school, from other parents, or from child-care providers that your child

- is touching other children inappropriately.
- has been touched in inappropriate ways.
- is using sexual language in jokes or insults.

In any of these situations, you need to find out what is happening by talking with your child. If, after your discussion, you feel your child needs more help than you alone can offer, visit the school counselor or social worker to find out about other resources available in your community.

Finding Help

If needed, support and help for your child are available. Most schoolteachers, principals, and religious leaders can refer parents to professionals with expertise in working with young people. Often a short-term intervention can do a world of good. If you have a good relationship with your child's grandparents or other extended family members, tell them what's going on with your child and seek out the support you and your child need.

Success Stories

You have made it through talk number one. It's a good beginning. Many parents say that getting their kids to have the first talk was like pulling teeth. And some of the things they found out were hard to hear. In the course of the talks, some children have told stories of being called sexual names or insults at school, or of having fights with siblings. Other children have shared great news—about how they learned about character at school, for example. A mom in San Antonio was happy to find that her fourth-grade daughter was very open to talking about sex and character issues, and they stayed up chatting for three hours having one of the best talks of their life.

But no matter what you've heard from your child, you've started an important process that will have a powerful ripple effect. You're now raising a child whose family discusses sex and character and whose parents don't shy away from discussing vital issues. You've become the kind of family that addresses these topics openly and honestly. You're the thoughtful parent who's taken the time to listen attentively and get a clearer picture of your child's real world.

Remember, this is only your first talk. Future talks could become easier. You're planting a seed that may not bear fruit until you've got a few more talks behind you.

Sample Talks

Between Parents and Children

Before you begin your first talk, you might want to read this sample conversation. The following are excerpts of actual talks between parents and children.

Discussing the Story about the Classroom

Participants: a father and his ten-year-old daughter.

Dad: A boy and girl are sitting in the front row listening to their teacher. The teacher is talking about human reproduction in class. She has already taught how flowers, frogs, and cats reproduce. Now she points to a picture of the male and female reproductive system on the board. What is the teacher thinking?

Daughter: That the kids might say, "Oooh!"

Dad: What is the girl thinking?

Daughter: I don't know. Maybe, "This could be important."

Dad: What is the boy thinking?

Daughter: "Oh no, not THAT!"

Dad: What kinds of sexual information do teachers talk about in school?

Daughter: Nothing.

Dad: Nothing?

Daughter: They do that in fifth grade, don't they?

Dad: What would the girl's and boy's parents say about this?

Daughter: Maybe the parents think, "You should listen and learn and you'll know what happens."

Dad: Have you seen or been in a situation like this?

Daughter: No.

Dad: Do your teachers tell you anything about sex?

Daughter: No.

Lessons Learned from This Sample Talk

At first glance it seems to be a fairly short and uneventful talk. But there is some important information being shared. Already, there is a perception that boys and girls view information about sex differently. The parent understands that this fourth-grader won't get information about puberty and sex until the next grade. If a girl were to start her period in fourth grade and the parent was depending on the teacher to explain the menstrual cycle, there would be a problem.

Discussing the Story about the Classroom

Participants: a mother and her twelve-year-old son.

Mom: This is a story about a classroom. A boy and girl are sitting in the front row listening to their teacher. The teacher is talking about human reproduction in class. She has already taught how flowers, frogs, and cats reproduce. Now she points to a picture of the male and female reproductive system on the board. What is the teacher thinking while she's doing this?

Son: The teacher's thinking, "Everybody should know this be-cause this is a fact in life."

Mom: What do you think the girl is thinking?

Son: She's thinking, "I might learn something. When I'm older this might be helpful."

Mom: What kinds of sexual information do teachers talk about in school?

Son: Um, about how people reproduce.

Mom: Do they only talk about the body or about the emotions and feelings too?

Son: How sometimes it's hard on people at a young age and that it's better to wait.

Mom: Okay. What would the girl's and boy's parents say about this situation of the teacher giving information about sex in class?

Son: I think they wouldn't care because it's part of health and how to take care of yourself and part of life.

Mom: When you were in a class like that, how did you feel?

Son: A little bit embarrassed.

Mom: Okay, I have simple questions and you can give simple an-swers. What is sex?

Son: That's how a man and a woman reproduce.

Mom: Okay, is that all there is about sex?

Son: I guess.

Lessons Learned from This Sample Talk

The son talked very softly and reluctantly, but Mom was able to coax a little information out and encouraged him whenever he did say something. The son said that sex was "how a man and woman reproduce." This is a good starting point to expand the definition of sexuality and introduce the topics of sexual ethics, orientation, and character. The son admitted he was embarrassed, and this gave his mom a way to address that feeling as normal and help her son feel more comfortable discussing issues.

Discussing the Story about the Classroom and Character Lessons

Participants: a mother and her twelve-year-old son.

Mom: A boy and girl are sitting in the front row listening to their teacher. The teacher is talking about character. He is asking the class to name character traits that they admire. What do you think the teacher is thinking?

Son: It's good to have good character traits. Like being smart and friendly. That it's not good to have bad character traits, like being mean and selfish and stuff like that.

Mom: What do you think the girl and boy are thinking?

Son: That it's better to have good character traits than bad because they want to be a good person.

Mom: The teacher is asking them to name some traits that they admire. What kinds of traits do you think they are thinking about?

Son: Caring, trustworthiness, being smart, friendly, getting away from other people who do wrong.

Mom: Okay. Do you think it is the same for the boy and girl?

Son: Yes.

Lessons Learned from This Sample Talk

This talk was very brief and revealed some important information. The child offered up his definitions of "bad" character traits and "good" traits. In this situation the child and parent shared similar definitions—which is not always the case with this activity. It might be interesting for the parent to explore in future talks how one's character can be tested by peers, and how one can steer clear of people with traits one doesn't respect (or as the child said, "do wrong").

Discussing the Story about the Sleepover

Participants: a mother and her twelve-year-old son.

Mom: A boy is having some friends stay overnight. They are up late and one of the boys is talking about sex. What is the boy saying about sex? We're trying to get the boy's perspective of this. What is he talking about?

Son: He wants to have sex with girls and all that other inappropriate stuff.

Mom: Okay, what kind of inappropriate stuff? Like his feelings?

Son: I don't know.

Mom: What are the other boys thinking?

Son: They aren't thinking.

Mom: Okay, son.

Lessons Learned from This Sample Talk

If you are thinking this is the shortest talk in history, you may be right. This does not mean it wasn't a success. The parent learned some things about her son's willingness to discuss sexuality with her. The mom did not push her son to explain his glib responses. But she can refer back to this talk when asking her son (in a future talk) to explain what "inappropriate stuff" means. The parent can probe to see if her son really has no idea what boys think about when they talk about sex, or if he is just too embarrassed to discuss it.

2
Life Changes
Talking about Puberty

My mom handed me a book about puberty. She said if I had any questions I could ask her. I had tons of questions and I never asked her anything. —Burt, father of three, Dalton, Georgia

When I was thirteen I would look in the mirror in despair. I thought I would never get breasts. I never did get the ones I wanted and it kept me from feeling sexy until way into my thirties.
—Lynne, mother of two, Kansas City, Missouri

I was raised by my mom with no brothers. I was convinced that my penis was smaller than other guys' were. No one told me that a flaccid penis looked a lot different from an erect one and I just thought I was much smaller than most guys were. I was afraid to go to the urinal, so when I had to pee, I went into the toilet with closed doors. —Phil, father of one, New York City

A child's body changes every year. Most children and teenagers are preoccupied with those changes, and with their looks, physique, chest, and genitals. And yet, most parents are not talking with their children, finding out what they know, what they need to know, and how they feel.

The most dramatic physical and emotional changes happen during puberty. It's a time of transition your child has already entered or will enter soon. Do you remember your life right before you entered puberty? Do you remember how your friends and school-mates joked about sex or certain parts of the body? Do you remember how nervous your teacher was in health class? Do you remember parents fumbling with the right words and asking, "You've learned about this stuff in school, right?" You may be surprised, and perhaps dismayed, to learn that in the past thirty years very little has changed when it comes to the way most kids learn about puberty. Most parents still avoid the topic, most teachers are still uncomfortable talking about it, and most kids still make up "facts" and believe myths.

All of us need to understand how our bodies work, and we need to feel comfortable talking about these normal and important changes. In this talk, we will focus on the body and any concerns your child might have (we will talk more about the psychological aspects of puberty and attraction in Chapter 5, Those First Feelings: Talking about Attraction and Love). We want to open the lines of communication and give young people permission to ask the questions they need to ask and get the resources they need to fully understand what's happening to them.

Preparing for the Talk

This talk will open the door for communication about a topic that, despite your child's potential denial, is very much on her mind. In this talk, you will let your child know that

- it's okay to talk about these kinds of topics.
- she can depend on you for support if she feels confused about what's happening to her body.

- she can depend on you to share information on how male and female bodies change during puberty (including all aspects of reproduction and sexual maturation).
- you have expectations about how she takes care of her health and hygiene.

What You Can Expect from this Talk

After this talk your child will

- be able to define puberty.
- be able to explain how puberty, reproduction, and sexual responsibility are related.
- understand the importance of taking care of her skin, hair, and health during puberty.
- know where to go for help if she has problems associated with puberty.

The Changing Body

This chapter explains how the body changes during puberty—a topic that will become more important to your child the closer he gets to it. Certainly, a conversation about puberty is less embarrassing for a fourth-grader than for an eighth-grader smack dab in the middle of it. But a parent should start the conversation as early as he or she can.

When I started my period, it wasn't a great surprise to me. My mom had been explaining everything to me on and off for about a year. My best friend's mom didn't tell her anything about puberty, and I found out later that my friend had basically come unglued—she thought she was dying.

—Nina, mother of three, Denver, Colorado

My father sat me down and explained everything about how a baby is made. I was about five. He explained it in terms I could understand, and I was fascinated. To this day I can remember the very words he used.

—Jeffrey, New York City

Puberty may be one of the more difficult topics to talk about because your child may already have developed some feelings of shame about her body. Unrealistic standards of attractiveness for both girls and boys and images of unattainable perfection abound in our culture. Your values may be very different from the mainstream culture's, but the media's pervasiveness makes it unlikely your child will be unaffected. America's mass media culture has young-looking models acting and looking extremely sexy, but the same kids who are the market for these sexy clothes and products are denied comprehensive sexuality education in their schools. Your child may tell you that he is getting sex education in health class, but he's more than likely getting the bare minimum on reproduction and physiology. And it's often served up with frightening statistics and information on sexually transmitted diseases, especially AIDS, designed to scare kids into being abstinent until marriage.

Your child may rebuff your first attempts to talk about puberty with, "Please! I know everything already!" However, it's highly unlikely she "knows everything" no matter what school she goes to. Even in the perfect sex-ed class, she'll never get the kind of conversations that she needs from you. Unless she's heard it from you, she doesn't know your values. It's vital to understand that normalizing puberty is something that is best done by an under-standing and accessible parent. You are the official sex educator in your child's life and you have your work cut out for you. Here are some issues to think about.

Different Families: Different Values

Each family has its own unique idea about how kids should learn about puberty—and this is a good time to think about what goes on in yours. Some families think it's the job of the school or reli-gious institution to discuss sexuality. Other families assume their boys will get the information they need from their coach, while still other parents think that no one should talk with their children about sexuality or about anything having to do with body parts. Others are ambivalent about how their children will learn about sex. Where does your family fit on this continuum? Consider the perspectives of the following parents.

When my son was in fourth grade, I remember him coming home one day—he had obviously had some sort of sex education class at school. He proudly announced to me that he knew what sperm was and where it came from. It came from his two balls under his penis. But his sperm weren't ready to make babies yet. They were just half-full and it was going to take some years for them to fill up.

—Naomi, mother of three, Seattle, Washington

When I was in fifth grade, my buddy Phillip called and said I had to run over to his place to see something important. When I got to

*Phillip's, he took me into his mom's bathroom and showed me a box.
It was filled with sanitary napkins. Phillip acted like he had discovered
some sexual secret. I had no idea what it was or why it was a big deal.*
—Elliot, father of two, Yakima, Oregon

*I snuck into my mom's room and looked through her bathroom cabi-
net. I found what I thought at the time was a diaphragm. I thought I
had really learned something. But years later I realized what I had really seen was a bunion pad!*
—Elaine, mother of three, Minneapolis, Minnesota

*When I was in sixth grade my mom came into my room, handed me a
small booklet, and rushed out. The cover of the pamphlet said, "A Father and Son Talk about Sex." I opened it to the only picture I could
find, which showed a man's face with whiskers next to a woman's
face. The text underneath read, "Husbands, always remember to shave
before you kiss your wife so you do not hurt her tender skin." The rest
of the book read like a medical manual and didn't really make much
sense to me. My mom and I never discussed the booklet. Since my
school didn't offer sex education, that pamphlet was all the formal sex
education I received growing up.*
—Nick, New York City

Influence of the Media

Television shows and commercials are filled with buff young bodies of both sexes. Obviously, TV doesn't present a realistic view of
young people and how they really look during puberty. A sensitive
program with a sanitized view of the issues young people face during puberty may surface from time to time. But you can bet that

the stars won't have pimples or awkward-looking bodies. For a pudgy boy with acne or a girl with a flat chest, positive TV role models aren't easy to find.

Marketing to the teen population is a sophisticated business. When baby boomers were kids there were one or two magazines marketed to teens—mostly girls. Today, young men and women have dozens of magazines and thousands of web sites vying for their money and attention. The cumulative effect is staggering: thirteen-year-olds judge themselves by nineteen-year-olds' bodies.

Pressure from Peers

If your child is physically different from the pack, your child may suffer. Kids who start puberty earlier or later than their peers can be labeled misfits or freaks. Kids can be very cruel and have a hard time passing up a chance to belittle others. For many, school is not a psychologically safe place. In the locker room and showers, the kids who look different suffer indignities. Waiting for the school bus or hanging out at lunchtime, kids struggling through the awkwardness of puberty can be teased mercilessly.

I was at a Catholic girls' school. I had started my period at nine and had already developed large breasts. I was teased by my classmates for years and felt terrible about my body. My mother didn't want me to wear a bra, so I just wore an undershirt. No other adult ever talked with me about it. I felt there was no one to help me.

—Gayle, mother of two, Olympia, Washington

I never grew above five feet until my junior year of high school. I was the shortest kid in middle school. I was called an elf and a shrimp for years. I hated it. I didn't feel masculine.

—Rick, father of five, Chicago, Illinois

Giving Your Child the Big Picture

Average age of first signs of puberty in males: 10–12

Average age of first signs of puberty in females: 8–10

*(Source: Santrok, John W., Life-Span Development, 7th Ed.,
McGraw-Hill: Boston, 1999)*

To an adult, issues about a child's body image may seem poignant but hardly urgent. Adults can forget how all-consuming those concerns are during puberty. A child can obsess for days over one pimple, and for years over a small penis or breasts that won't grow. True or not, today's kids often feel that they're under much more pressure to conform to body types than their parents were.

Your job during this talk is to get a good idea of how your child is adapting to or has adapted to puberty. The parent provides enough information and compassion to ease her journey to and through adolescence.

In general, most parents don't talk with their kids about how the body works and how their children feel about their bodies. Parents need to explain that puberty comes with strong feelings—feelings that touch on our self-esteem, our overall feelings of worthiness.

—Lisa Perry, health educator, Seattle, Washington

Beginning with Bathing

Some of the earliest and possibly easiest discussions are about personal hygiene. As the body changes there are new maintenance requirements. Daily rituals such as showering, shampooing, using deodorant, and dressing in clean clothes need to be mentioned and sometimes enforced.

My son is a slob. If I left it up to him we wouldn't be able to open his bedroom door because there would be a mountain of dirty clothes. But he is also vain as a peacock. He spends hours and hours in front of a mirror looking at his face, his hair, and his body fat. I have helped him clean up his act by stressing how important personal hygiene is. I've told him that oily faces, wrinkled clothes, and body odor won't impress his peers. He is a perfectionist about his body, and this desire to be a cool guy is the one hold I have over his otherwise gross personal behavior.

—Lila, mother of four, Syracuse, New York

I wasn't ready when my daughter started her period. I knew I wanted to tell her about the menstrual cycle but thought I could wait until she was twelve or so. At age nine she was watching TV in the living room with my husband and me. She started bleeding right then and there. My husband asked what was wrong and I said, oddly enough, that she had cut herself. I look back on that incident and wonder what the heck I was thinking and how unfair I was to my daughter not to have prepared her for this inevitability.

—Ann-Marie, mother of three, Dallas, Texas

Different Perspectives

In some cultures, as soon as a girl can have a baby, or a boy can father one, they are married off. Biological, not psychological, capacity determines when they begin their sexual life.

In the U.S., there are many good reasons for delaying sexual activity, including preventing teen pregnancy and sexually transmitted diseases. But just because a child isn't sexually active doesn't mean she shouldn't learn about her body and how to stay healthy.

Some parents think that by ignoring young people's sexual maturation they can indefinitely delay their sexual activity. But hormonal changes are occurring anyway, and puberty usually means the beginning of intense sexual curiosity and a need for new kinds of emotional and sexual connection. In our desire to control our children's sexuality for their own good, we also may oversimplify their relationship to their bodies. Instead of acknowledging that they will naturally have sexual feelings, we label those feelings as "out of line" and any sexual behavior as "wrong." But these biological impulses are real, and labeling them as "immoral" or "unnatural" won't make them go away.

As a parent, you have family values about when, and if, it's appropriate for your son or daughter to become sexually active. You may also have strong feelings about when is the right time for your son or daughter to become a parent. No one is suggesting you change your values.

For us the simple truth is that when a girl begins menstruation and a boy produces sperm, these young people have the capacity to reproduce. This changes how we should be treating them, what they should know about themselves, and what the consequences of their behaviors are.

What Kids Need to Know about Their Bodies

Young people need to know when they are capable of reproduction. Some parents think that telling their child about the possibility of becoming pregnant or impregnating someone takes away their child's innocence and childhood. This is similar to the argument that teaching children about sex makes them sexually active.

> *I had pretty good sex education all through school. They taught us about reproduction, birth control, even drugs. But it didn't turn me into a sex maniac. It was years before I actually had sex with a woman. I was twenty before that happened.*
>
> —Ed, Atlanta, Georgia

> *I didn't get one bit of information about sex from either my school or my parents. When I was in third grade my older brother did tell me some stuff about sex which was totally inaccurate.*
>
> —Kate, San Antonio, Texas

Sex Can Be . . . Fantastic!

This may be stating the obvious, but it's important to acknowledge that sexual activity can be very pleasurable and among the most wonderful experiences a person can have. And it's one of the great perks of being an adult. Your child may have been bombarded with tons of public health messages about the dangers of sex, the potential epidemics that await them, and the future of poverty that awaits a teen parent. These messages have their place. But we encourage you to balance them by discussing the rewards that come with a healthy sexual relationship.

What Do You Think about Bodies and Sexuality?

Sooner or later a conversation about our bodies makes a transition into what we do with them, and that leads to issues of sexual behavior. (Well, you knew we had to talk about that eventually in *Ten Talks!*)

This can be awkward but it is very important. Your child may have done some sexual experimentation already. It is the rare child who feels comfortable enough about these behaviors to talk about them with a parent. Many children act so young and seem so innocent about the world that it is hard to imagine they are already interested in sex. But we know from research that many children are touching and being touched even before middle school. By middle school the number of kids venturing beyond kissing goes up, and some communities have been shocked to find out that many of their children have had genital touching or intercourse by eighth grade.

Even if your child has not been sexually active, he is surely beginning to think of his body as sexual. Some boys are working on developing their chests; some girls are starting to wear short skirts and tight, form-fitting tops. Even if they haven't used their bodies for anything but display, they may be starting to enjoy seeing their bodies as sexual. Children who feel very ambivalent about their sexuality or who are less sexually adventurous may still be talking about sex, or seeing it on TV, at the movies, or on the Internet. They may be wondering: Am I normal? Is my body good enough? What does this feeling mean? Should I want to do these behaviors?

I remember playing doctor with one of my friends when I was in first grade. I'm not sure they were sexual feelings, but it was certainly sexual activity.

—Jeffrey, New York City

61

It was a strange, warm feeling. I was drawn to Mark in ninth grade. I didn't know it was sexual. I just knew it felt good.

—Maureen, mother of two, Kansas City, Missouri

Last-Minute Checkups before the Talk

Think back to your experiences going through puberty.

- What did your parents tell you about puberty?
- What were your main concerns?
- How did you feel?
- Did you have anyone to talk with about your feelings?

How do you think your childhood experiences have affected the way you raise your child?

- To date, what have you explained to your child about puberty, human reproduction, and sex?
- Have you told her to expect all kinds of changing emotions?
- What books about puberty have you given your child?

Do you have any stories that you could share with your child? For example:

- How you dealt with your body's changes
- What it was like when you had your first sexual feelings. (You don't have to be graphic. This is just an opportunity to show how normal these feelings are.)

This is also a good time to consider pulling out some pictures of yourself as a child and as a teen. Show them you've been there!

Sensitive Issues

It's not uncommon for adults to have insecurities about their own bodies. You might not be the weight you wish to be, or in the physical shape you'd like to be, which might make you feel awkward about this particular topic. There might also be some things in your own experience with puberty that were more than normally painful. If you were abused in any way or if your own sexual history is one you wouldn't wish on your child, you might want to be careful not to unduly alarm your child.

If your child has special challenges such as severe acne or weight problems or has had some abuse in his past, it's important to take this into account. Take this talk slowly and allow your child to feel and voice his perfectly normal anxiety about body image. It's tempting to avoid this talk because you think it's too sensitive. On the contrary, your child needs to get this information about her body and its development from you.

> *The one topic I hear moms shying away from is masturbation. Especially when it's a mom trying to explain it to her son. I told my son that it's normal, but it's a private thing. Was he embarrassed when I mentioned it? Absolutely.*
>
> —Phyllis, mother of two, Jamestown, New York

What Are Your Family Rules?

Do you have family rules about unwanted touching and name-calling? As kids mature, their siblings and classmates can spot their vulnerabilities and make vicious sport of them. The talk outlined in this chapter highlights the following situations:

- A girl in the shower at school
- A boy in the shower at school
- A boy and girl shopping for personal hygiene products
- Kids calling other children names
- A mom and dad at the bookstore

Discussing these situations will give you an opportunity to discuss your family rules. How do you want your child to respond to name-calling? What are your rules about calling others names? Where can your child find help if she has concerns about her changing body? At the end of this talk, you will have the chance to review the rules with your child.

The Talk

Introduce the Talk

You are about to begin what may be one of the more sensitive talks. Be sure to read through all the terms, scenarios, and follow-up questions before starting. If you are part of a two-parent family you may both wish to review and discuss this chapter to make sure you agree on what values you want to communicate to your child.

Beginning this talk is as easy as saying, "What have you learned about puberty in school?"

As always, expect a less-than-enthusiastic "Oh, no." And follow that up with a tender smile and the following, "I need to talk with you for ten minutes." (We repeat, this talk is much easier with a fourth-grade girl who has not entered puberty than with an eighth-grade boy already in the throes of puberty. Use the language that will treat your child as maturely as possible.) You may be surprised and find that your child is excited about having the chance to discuss the topic of puberty with you.

"I'd like to see what you know about some stuff you most likely have covered in school. First question: What is puberty?"

A normal response might be, "I don't know." Or a giant groan.

You can offer up, "What have you heard about puberty?"

After you child responds—with either a definition or more groaning—you can move on to terms.

Review These Words

The terms in this section are words you may already have gone over with your child during a talk about puberty and sexuality.

Please review the entire list. Discussing all the terms with your child, of course, is optional. You know what's appropriate for your child's age and maturity level. Keep in mind that more than likely, even the youngest children have heard many of these words on TV or from peers.

Use your own judgment to decide which terms are suitable for your child. A fourth-grader may not need to know as many of these terms as an eighth-grader might. You may also want to add your own words, or supplement the list with an illustrated book on human anatomy from the library or bookstore.

Many parents would rather just hand this list of terms to their kids and say, "Ask me if you have any questions." This may be tempting and may even work with some kids. But imagine how counterproductive it would be if that's how teachers approached sex and health ed.

General Terms

brain: the largest sexual organ. It can coordinate how you feel with what you do.

body image: how a person perceives her own appearance. Puberty is a time when people can focus a lot on their bodies and on whether they look normal or attractive. (It's possible for some people who are very thin to look in a mirror and perceive their bodies as fat. Eating disorders such as bulimia and anorexia are quite common, especially among girls. If your child is not eating correctly or you have any suspicion that he or she is throwing up after eating, talk to your child about the situation. Don't hesitate to consult with your doctor immediately. These disorders can be life-threatening.)

conception: when a sperm fertilizes an egg and a fetus begins to grow.

contraception: a wide variety of ways to prevent pregnancy.

"down there": a way of referring to genitals when people are embarrassed to say the real terms.

family planning: making conscious decisions about when or whether to have children.

genitals: the inclusive term for male and female sex organs.

hormones: substances that are secreted by the pituitary and other glands and that are central to creating the biological differences between males and females. Each sex has both the female hormone, estrogen, and the male hormone, testosterone, but women have much more estrogen than males— and males have much more testosterone. These hormones are responsible for the maturation of sex organs and other characteristics of the male and of the female body.

puberty: the period of time when reproductive ability starts to develop, producing characteristics such as body hair, pubic hair, heavier sweat and body odor, menstruation and breast development in girls, and production of sperm in boys. This process starts at very different times for different people and has been known to start as early as age eight or nine and as late as the late teens. Sexual attraction to others may intensify.

urethra: in males, a hole at the end of the penis and the channel through which urine and semen travel. Females also urinate through the urethra, which is a small hole inside the vulva.

unintended pregnancy: a pregnancy that one or both people did not want to have happen.

Female Anatomy and Functions

clitoris: a little "button" at the front of the vulva that is extremely sensitive and is a sexual pleasure center. It is biologically equivalent to the head of a man's penis.

eggs: the female genetic material, which must be fertilized in order for the reproductive process to start. The egg is microscopically small. A woman who is fertile usually has one egg released every month that could be fertilized—if more than one is fertilized there can be twins, triplets, etc.

fallopian tubes: the tiny tubes that carry the female's egg and deposit it in the uterus, where under appropriate conditions it can grow into a viable fetus.

menstruation: also called a "period," the monthly cycle in females that occurs when the uterus sheds the buildup of blood that allows an egg to be implanted and fertilized and grow to be a fetus.

uterus: the female organ, often called the womb, that may receive a fertilized egg and that expands to carry the fetus.

vulva: the female genitals, including the vagina and the clitoris.

vagina: the passageway between the labia and the cervix, which is the opening to the uterus.

Male Anatomy and Functions

ejaculation: what happens when semen comes out of the male's urethra.

involuntary erection: this is primarily something that happens to boys and young men, and it refers to an erection that happens unintentionally. The male may be in a place that is inappropriate (having an erection when waiting in line for lunch and wanting it to go away).

nocturnal emissions: also known as wet dreams, these are ejaculations that occur in the night, usually during sleep. They may be associated with erotic dreams.

penis: the male organ used for intercourse, sexual pleasure, and urination.

scrotum: the male sex organ, often called "balls," where semen (a combination of fluid and sperm) is manufactured.

sperm: the male's genetic material, carried within the scrotum and surrounded by fluid. Sperm are microscopically small and shaped a little like tadpoles. Millions of sperm are present in each ejaculation and during heterosexual intercourse only one of them may fertilize the female's egg and start the reproductive process.

Why Is Talking about the Body Important?

Let your child tell you why she thinks talking about the body is important. Here are some additional reasons you might offer:

- The body is probably one of the things that your child thinks about most often.
- Understanding how her body works gives your child much more control over what her body does.
- Your child may have misconceptions or fears about the body, sexuality, and human reproduction that this talk can help clear up.
- Talking about the body and reproduction lets your child know that you are an "askable" parent.

The Stories

In the next part of the talk, you'll be reading short stories to your child and discussing them together. You don't have to read all of them. Pick the ones that you think are appropriate for your child. The stories are very simple. Feel free to embellish them, adding details that you think might make them more believable to your child. For example, some parents change the gender of the characters to make a story mirror their own families.

The Story about the Girls' Shower

Read this story to your child. It provides an opportunity to discuss how the body changes during puberty, how people change at different rates, and how diverse body shapes are.

"A girl is in the girls' locker room taking a

shower after playing a game of soccer. She notices other girls and how different all their body types are."

Ask this question of your child:

- What is the girl thinking?

Now that your child has completed this scenario, ask the following questions:

- Is the girl embarrassed or not?
- How might the girls' bodies be different from one another?
- Is the girl proud of her body? Why or why not?
- What would make the girl feel better about her body?
- Would anyone ever make fun of the girl in the shower? If so, why?
- Is the girl going through puberty? How would she know?

The Story about the Boys' Shower

Read this story to your child. It provides an opportunity to discuss how the body changes during puberty, how people change at different rates, and how diverse body shapes are.

"A boy is in the boys' locker room taking a shower after playing a game of basketball. He notices other boys and how different all their bodies are."

Ask this question of your child:

- What is the boy thinking?

Now that your child has completed this scenario, ask the following questions:

- Is the boy embarrassed or not?
- How might the boys' bodies be different from one another?
- Is the boy proud of his body? Why or why not?
- What would make the boy feel better about his body?
- Would anyone ever make fun of the boy in the shower? If so, why?
- Is the boy going through puberty? How would he know?

Clarify Your Family's Values

Discuss the following questions with your child as a way of sharing your values about their behavior.

Ask your child: "Do you think most people your own age feel good about the way their body looks?"

Child: No.

Parent: Why not?

Child: Because most people are ugly.

Parent response: I think most kids your age are good-looking. Kids can be very critical of each other's bodies. What do you think?

Child: I don't know.

Parent: I think it would be good to be more accepting of others and try to make them feel good about themselves, or at the bare minimum not to add to their feeling ugly. It's important to me to know that you respect others and know that there is more to people than what their bodies look like.

Ask your child: "What makes a person attractive?"

Child response #1: A girl should be thin.
Parent: Why is that?
Child: That's the way it is.
Parent: That's not really the way it is. It's not the way most people look. As a matter of fact, even the models in advertisements don't really look that way without the photo being retouched.
Child: At school the popular girls are thin.
Parent: That might be true now. But that won't always be true. A lot of girls will be seen as pretty without being thin.
Child: I don't know if that's true.
Parent: Think about it. What I think is that it's important for a body to be strong and healthy and that there are lots of ways to look and to be pretty.

Child response #2: A guy should be buff.
Parent: What's wrong with a natural build or a slim build?
Child: You don't want to be a wimp.
Parent: I don't think it's good to call people wimps. If by wimp you mean small, there's nothing wrong with a guy being small. Are there any guys you like who aren't built-up and buff?
Child: No.

Parent: There are lots of body types for guys. What's important is for a guy to be healthy and fit, but that doesn't mean he has to be a bodybuilder. I don't want you to feel that you have to be big to be attractive. You'll find there are a lot of ways to be attractive to others. Who you are on the inside matters most.

The Story about Shopping

Read this story to your child. It provides an opportunity to discuss how the body changes during puberty and how to take care of it.

"A boy and girl are classmates and have met by accident in the drugstore checkout line. The boy is holding his purchases: deodorant, shaving cream, and pimple medication. The girl is holding shampoo, sanitary napkins, and mouthwash."

Ask these questions of your child:

- What is the boy thinking?
- What is the girl thinking?
- What is the boy saying?
- What is the girl saying?

Now that your child has completed this scenario, ask the following questions:

- Why is the boy buying these products?

- Is there anything that the boy is buying that might make him feel embarrassed? If so, what would that be?
- Why is the girl buying these products?
- Is there anything that the girl is buying that might make her feel embarrassed? If so, what would that be?

If your child mentions the sanitary napkins as a source of embarrassment, this would be a good time to explain that it's natural for females to menstruate and for males to know about this normal process.

For some children, it might be a good idea to explain how common products such as deodorant, mouthwash, sanitary napkins, and shampoo might be used more often during puberty.

Clarify Your Family's Values

Discuss the following question with your child as a way of sharing your values about their attitudes and behavior.

Ask your child: "When a person goes through puberty the body goes through many changes. What kind of new health and skin care issues are important during puberty?"

Child response #1: I don't know.
Parent: Bodies start to smell different during puberty. It's normal to start using deodorant daily and showering daily. What is one special thing a girl has to think about?

Child response #2: A girl gets her period.

Parent: Right, she needs to buy special pads or tampons when she is bleeding.

Child: Bleeding?

Parent: Yes. It's an amazing thing that the female body does. If women didn't get periods, none of us would have been born. It's part of the female reproductive system.

Child response #3: I'm not sure.

Parent: Well, kids have to think about pimples and skin care, such as washing the face and buying acne cream. For severe cases we could visit a doctor and get special medicine.

The Story about Name-Calling

Read this story to your child. It provides an opportunity to discuss how it feels to be called names, the vulnerability that comes with going through puberty, your family rules about name-calling, and how people should be treated.

"A teenage boy and a teenage girl are at the breakfast table with their little brother. The little brother makes fun of his older brother's and sister's pimples."

Ask these questions of your child:

• What is the teenage boy thinking?
• What is the teenage girl thinking?

Now that your child has completed this scenario, ask the following questions:

- How would it feel to have jokes made about your skin?
- How might the older brother and sister respond to their little brother?
- How would it be different if it was kids at school, rather than the little brother, who were making fun of the boy's and girl's skin?
- Why do kids make fun of each other's skin, weight, or attractiveness?

The Story about the Bookstore

Read this story to your child. It provides an opportunity to discuss how people learn about the body and sexuality.

"Two neighbors, a mom and a dad, are at the bookstore. The mom has a boy in her family. The dad has a girl in his family. Both kids are entering puberty. The mom and dad are looking at books on puberty, sexuality, and how people plan a family."

Ask these questions of your child first:

- What is the mom thinking?
- What is the dad thinking?

Now that your child has completed this scenario, ask the following questions:

- What kind of book should the mom buy to help her talk with her son?
- What kind of book should the dad buy to help him talk with his daughter?
- What would the mother like her child to know?
- What would the father like his child to know?

Your Family's Values

Ask the following questions of your child as a way of sharing your values about how to make decisions about whether and when to have children. You may have strong feelings about how to plan a family. This is an opportunity for you to share your perspective. We are writing this section from the perspective that you can teach young people about family planning without encouraging sexual activity. We have included a number of potential responses from children to help you formulate your own views.

Ask your child: "What does it mean to plan your family?"

> *Child:* I don't know.
> *Parent:* It is making sure that you have a baby only if you really want to and *when* you really want to.

Ask your child: "How do people make sure that they don't have a baby until they are emotionally and financially ready?"

Child: I don't know.

Parent response #1: One way is for people not to have sex when they are young. People wait until they are financially able to support a family.

Parent response #2: If males and females have sex before they are financially and emotionally prepared to be parents, they use contraception until they are ready to start a family.

Ask your child: "Do you know what contraception looks like?"

Child: Yeah, I've seen it at school in health class.

Parent: Well, let me review what I learned about contraception. I've learned that people use various types of contraception, which we can talk about in detail, to try and make sure that they don't have an unintended pregnancy. (This might be a good time to discuss the kinds of contraception you approve of.) No contraception is 100 percent effective. So having sexual intercourse means that there is always the chance of pregnancy. That is one reason most parents do not want their children to have sex when they are young.

Ask your child: "What age do you think is the right time for someone to become sexually active?"

Child: I know kids who are having sex now.

Parent: I know that some kids have sex very young. It worries me that these kids may not have enough information to protect themselves from unplanned pregnancy. I hope that my kids would abstain from sex until they're older, are able to financially support a child, and are in a committed and loving adult relationship.

Ask your child: "Can you think of other reasons to be careful about sexual activity?"

Child: AIDS?

Parent: Yes. AIDS is a very serious and a life-threatening illness. It is the result of being exposed during sexual activity to a virus called HIV, which stands for human immunodeficiency virus. HIV is one of many sexually transmitted diseases (STDs). Sexually transmitted disease is an issue for sexually active people to discuss. Any person who is going to have sex needs to fully understand how diseases are prevented. Any time two people share body fluids there is the possibility that diseases can be shared. Some diseases are life-threatening and others, if left untreated, could lead to sterility (the inability to have a baby). It's very important for people to protect their future.

The Bare Minimum: A Quick Quiz for Kids

Ask your child the following two questions to assess her knowledge of the body.

1. Can you give me one example of how a person might know when she or he has entered puberty?

Sample answers:

• A female starts her period.
• A male starts growing hair on his face or body.
• A male produces sperm.

2. What is one house rule about getting information on planning a family and STD prevention?

Sample answers:
- You can always ask any question you have.
- You can always visit a doctor, nurse, or clinic to get information.
- You can always go to a bookstore or library to get information.
- We talk about major decisions.

Talk about Your Family Rules

Family rules can help address common problems that occur when a child enters puberty. Give careful thought, and be prepared for your child to ask about the reasons behind the rules. Some answers from parents across the country follow.

Ask your child the following questions:

1. What is our family rule about calling people names?
- We don't call people names, even as a joke.
2. What's a family rule about getting answers to questions about puberty if you don't want to ask a parent?
- There are some parent-approved adults that I trust to give you answers. (These might include grandparents, aunts, uncles, or trusted family friends who share your values.)

After the Talk

A Moment to Reflect

Take a moment to reflect on the talk you just had with your child.

- What surprised you about your child's perception of puberty?
- How do you feel about your ability to discuss puberty with your child?

- If you hit a brick wall of resistance, how can you make sure that your child has the information he needs? Do you have a relative or friend whom your child trusts who could help out?
- How much time did you spend listening?
- How do you think your child felt about the talk?

After the talk, many parents report a variety of feelings—from frustration at not being able to sustain a quality talk to a sense of accomplishment at introducing their concerns or at finding a good book on puberty that the child seemed to like. Some parents report realizing that their children may be involved in situations that they can't handle. Others are surprised at the maturity level of the children.

This talk has probably introduced a lot of ideas and topics—certainly more than can be dealt with adequately in ten minutes. Remember, for schools that do teach sex education, teachers usually cover this ground over the course of four years. The goal of *Ten Talks* is to serve as a catalyst for ongoing conversation and enhanced parent-child communication.

Ten Talks *as a First Step*

For some parents, this book is a gentle first step into talking about sexuality with their kids. For other parents, it's an adventure. We want to reinforce the point that sexuality is a huge topic—one that is certainly not taught over a five-minute or even five-hour conversation. There is a lot of detailed information to be shared over the next few years with a child entering and going through puberty. Regarding contraceptives: we have brought up the topic but have not offered information on the different kinds, nor on their effectiveness. We have also mentioned clinics, but we haven't talked about what happens there and the differences between going to a women's health specialist, a family planning clinic, or your family doctor. In other words, we have begun the conversation, but there is so much more to talk about. It's our philosophy that both males and females, whether they are planning on having babies or not, should be knowledgeable about all the aspects of family planning. As parents, you are in the best position to communicate your beliefs on these issues.

1 Picture = 1,000 words

Throughout *Ten Talks* we refer to finding more resources to help you explain topics, and this is very useful when it comes to explaining the body. One possible strategy: pick up an illustrated anatomy or sex education book appropriate for your child's age level and mark specific sections in advance.

Warning Signs

The talks may also reveal potential problems your child is facing or bring out other insights into your child's world. If you have picked up on any of the following clues you might want to get professional advice on how best to help your child. You might consider asking for professional help if

- your child is very much overweight or much too thin.
- your child repeatedly says she hates her body.
- your daughter is extremely upset over having a period.

- your child seems to be far more sexually aware and interested than any of his peers.
- your child uses a lot of sexual humor and gives you sly hints about his interest in sex.
- your child insists on dressing in a sexually provocative way.
- your child has a boyfriend or girlfriend and they seem to be sexually interested in each other.
- your child's friends appear quite sexually advanced.
- your child is in a relationship with someone much older.

In any of these situations, you may need to find out what is happening and discuss your concerns with your child on a deeper level. Whether there's actually any danger may depend on many variables, including your child's age, emotional maturity, and your family rules about being sexually active.

Finding Help

We believe the parent is the best source for sexual information and ethical guidance. But most parents are not nurses, doctors, sex educators, or family planning experts. For expertise and solid information, consider contacting your local family planning group, or public health department or doctor. Many hospitals have special health centers with specialists on teenage sexuality and health who are trained to work with young people. Many of these centers are extremely sensitive to parents' wishes. Some parent groups hold special workshops for parents and their children to learn about sexual health and responsibility.

Success Stories

You have made it through talk number two. Again, even a five-minute chat is an important beginning and opens the door to a series of ongoing conversations. A mom in Boise reported that what she thought would be a five-minute chat with her sixth-grade daughter about puberty turned into a two-hour talk. Her daughter was hungry for information, and the timing for the talk was perfect. A mom in Gaithersburg, Maryland, reported that during a five-minute talk with her fifth-grade son, he'd let on how nervous he was about entering middle school and about how small he was compared to other guys—things he'd never mentioned before.

Sample Talks

Between Parents and Children

Before you begin your first talk, you might want to read this sample conversation. The following are excerpts of actual talks between parents and children.

Discussing the Story about the Girls' Shower

Participants: a mom and her nine-year-old daughter.

Mom: A girl is in the girls' locker room taking a shower after playing a game of soccer. She notices other girls and how all their body types are different. What is the girl thinking? (Pause, then nervous laughter from daughter.) Now be honest, what is she thinking? (Pause.) What is she looking at?
Daughter: Hair?

Mom: You mean in her private areas? Well, what else is she thinking about?

Daughter: Her boobs.

Mom: Her breasts. Do you think the girl is embarrassed?

Daughter: Which one?

Mom: The girl in the locker room.

Daughter: Probably not.

Mom: You don't think she's embarrassed? How might the girls' bodies be different from one another?

Daughter: More hair and their boobs might be bigger.

Mom: Breasts, let's call them breasts. That would make Mom feel better. Do you think the girl is proud of her body?

Daughter: She might or might not be.

Mom: If not, why?

Daughter: Some girls may think that their bodies aren't really that great.

Mom: In what way?

Daughter: That their breasts are too big.

Mom: Anything else that might be of concern?

Daughter: Like, when they have their period. They might think that's icky.

Mom: What else?

Daughter: Or maybe how chubby they are.

Mom: Okay. How do you think a girl could feel better about her body? Like if she were chubby?

Daughter: By exercising and eating healthy foods, and there's nothing you could really do about the other two things.

Mom: Like the size of your breasts and stuff? You are what you are?

Daughter: Yep.

Mom: Would anyone ever make fun of the girl in the shower?

Daughter: Maybe.

Mom: Why?

Daughter: Because her body is different from theirs.

Mom: Why do you think girls make fun of differences?

Daughter: Either they're jealous of the other girl's body or they think their body looks stupid.

Mom: It looks strange or kind of scares them? Do you think this girl is going through puberty?

Daughter: Probably.

Mom: How would she know?

Daughter: If her breasts overlap.

Mom: Get bigger?

Daughter: Yeah. And they sag, sort of, hang down. And she'll probably get hair.

Mom: Where will she get hair?

Daughter: In armpits and private area and her legs.

Mom: What else might happen to her body? How about her feet and how tall she is?

Daughter: She'll probably get taller and her feet will get bigger.

Mom: Might she get pimples?

Daughter: Yeah.

Mom: Maybe her hair might get a little oilier?

Daughter: I was thinking her hair might change color a little bit.

Mom: Yes, you're absolutely right. Her hair could change color.

Lessons Learned from This Sample Talk

This mom and daughter have really covered a lot of the physical description of puberty. Mom has discovered that her daughter is well aware of these changes, and it sounds like she might not think all of them are good. She's also acknowledged that girls are capable of teasing a girl whose body is atypical from the rest of the peer group. There is a lot here for Mom to learn from and discuss further with her daughter. Future topics could include: family rules about teasing others and self-esteem.

Discussing the Story about the Girls' Shower

Participants: a mother and her twelve-year-old son.

Mom: There is a story I want to talk about. It's about a girl in the shower.

Son: I don't want to talk about that stuff.

Mom: Why?

Son: It's too embarrassing.

Mom: Okay, what about a story about friendship?

Son: Okay.

Lessons Learned from This Sample Talk

Mom has found out that her son is really uncomfortable talking about the story. She may find that he is uncomfortable talking about anything that has to do with sex—with her. She might want her husband or a male friend to approach these subjects. The son may not want to talk about "the story about the girl in the shower" for a number of reasons: talking about nudity or females' bodies or talking about intimate issues with his mom might cause discomfort. The mom did not push the topic. But she had a fall-back position that was less threatening—talking about friendship. Often it is a matter of timing and trust. If a family has never talked about issues related to sex, it makes sense to start with very non-threatening topics like friendship. Later a talk about females, body image, and issues around grooming and skin care can be explored.

Discussing the Story about the Boys' Shower

Participants: a mother and her fourteen-year-old son.

Mom: This is a story about the boys' shower. If you get embarrassed we can stop. It talks about the body. This is something you and Dad might talk about. A boy is in the boy's locker room taking a shower after playing a game of basketball. He notices other boys and how different all their types are. I guess body types. What is the boy thinking?

Son: He's thinking, "Wow!"

Mom: "Wow"? Why "wow"?

Son: Well he's seeing all the different body types and how different everybody is.

Mom: Is he embarrassed?

Son: I wouldn't be.

Mom: You wouldn't be?

Son: I don't care.

Mom: How might the boys' bodies be different from each other?

Son: Different ways. Thinner, fatter, some of them might have hair.

Mom: Body hair?

Son: Yeah.

Mom: Is the boy proud of his body, you think?

Son: I wouldn't care.

Mom: Do you think boys, in general, are pretty proud of their bodies? Are you proud of your body?

Son: Yes. I think so.

Mom: Why?

Son: I just am. I have a high self-esteem of myself.

Mom: What makes a boy feel better about his body?

Son: I don't know.

Mom: Do you think if he worked out and got muscles?

Son: Yeah. Maybe. Like if he got some muscles. And if he was better at doing stuff.

Mom: I don't understand what "stuff" is.

Son: Well, like basketball.

Mom: Do you think this boy is going through puberty?

Son: Maybe.

Mom: How would he know? (Pause.) How do you know you are going through puberty?

Son: Hormones and junk.

Mom: What are the changes that go on in your body?

Son: (He sighs.) You get hair, facial hair, and in different places on your body. And aches.

Mom: You get aches in your joints when you grow. Your feet are huge, right?

Son: Right . . . Emotions get stronger. You get more prone to get angry. The flood of emotions is more than it used to be. That's how it was for me. It's different for everybody.

Mom: How it was? How it is! (They both laugh.)

Son: How it is.

Mom: It affects people differently. The boy next door is tall and thin. You are a little shorter and stockier. Who knows? By the end of puberty, you might be tall and thin. You never know.

Lessons Learned from This Sample Talk

Mom finds out that her son is quite well informed about the physical and emotional changes in puberty. He is also pretty pleased with himself. He does talk about getting angry and she gets to say, subtly, that she's noticed. Finally, she gets to assure him that he's not through changing—and that's okay too.

Discussing the Story about Name-Calling

Participants: a mom and her nine-year-old daughter.

Mom: This is a story about name-calling. Oh, you rolled your eyes. You hate name-calling, don't you?

Daughter: Yes.

Mom: A teenage boy and a teenage girl are at the breakfast table with their little brother. You can pretend it's a little sister, all right?

Daughter: Okay.

Mom: The little brother makes fun of his older brother's and sister's pimples. This NEVER happens here. (Both are laughing at the sarcasm.) What do you think the teenage boy is thinking?

Daughter: "Shut up!" (Both laugh again.)

Mom: Okay. What do you think the teenage girl is thinking?

Daughter: "This is not a good guy."

Mom: Do you think she is a little upset by what her little brother has said?

Daughter: Yes.

Mom: Do you think she might be hurt?

Daughter: Yes.

Mom: How would it feel to have jokes made about your skin?

Daughter: I don't know because no one has ever said anything about my skin.

Mom: Well let's take it another step then. How would you feel if someone made fun about your body?

Daughter: Then I would feel very angry and annoyed at them. Because it would be just unfair.

Mom: Of them to make fun of you?

Daughter: Yeah. They're making fun of my body, but it's my body and it's not theirs.

Mom: Do you think this is how the older brother and sister might respond to their little brother? What might they say?

Daughter: I think the teenage boy might say, "Oh, be quiet."

Mom: How would it be different if it was kids at school, rather than the little brother?

Daughter: It would be way different. The kids at school, they would keep on calling them names. When they got tired of one name they'd go to another name and stuff.

Mom: Okay. Why do kids make fun of each other's skin or weight or how pretty or ugly someone is?

Daughter: Two different reasons. One is because they are jealous of something else that they have, and they just found something else to make fun of. Let's say someone can throw really well but they might be entering puberty too soon, so they make fun of that. The other is that they just hate that person. They just don't like them at all.

Lessons Learned from This Sample Talk

This confident, articulate child has taught her mother a lot about the "name-calling culture" at home and school. Mom has also learned that her child is a junior psychologist and can figure out other people's emotions well. She should gain confidence in her daughter's ability to withstand peer nastiness.

Discussing the Story about the Bookstore

Participants: a mom and her nine-year-old daughter.

Mom: We are going to talk about a story about a bookstore. Two neighbors, a mom and a dad, are at the bookstore. The mom has a boy in her family. The dad has a girl in his family. Both kids are entering puberty. The mom and dad are looking at books on puberty, sexuality, and family planning. Do you know what family planning is?

Daughter: No.

Mom: Family planning is ways that, if you had sex, you could keep yourself from getting pregnant. Now, the mom is the one who has the boy in her family. What do you think the mom is thinking while she's looking through these books?

Daughter: "I can't believe my son is growing up this fast."

Mom: What kind of book should the mom buy to help her talk with her son?

Daughter: A book about young men going into puberty.

Mom: What kind of book should the dad buy to help him talk with his daughter?

Daughter: A body book, maybe, for girls.

Mom: Like the one you have?

Daughter: Yeah.

Mom: What does that book have in it? What kind of changes does it show?

Daughter: The way things change.

Mom: The parts of a woman that would change? It talks about some other things. Do you remember?

Daughter: Pads and tampons and things.

Mom: It even talks about things like brushing your teeth and keeping clean, right? Does it have a section on pimples too?

Daughter: Yeah, it's called acne.

Mom: That's right. Is it a good book for either parent to buy?

Daughter: Yeah.

Mom: What would the mother like her son to know?

Daughter: That it's okay to go through puberty. And the way the body works.

Mom: Maybe not be scared of it? To ask questions if they need to?

Daughter: (Nods yes.)

Mom: Yes. What would the father like the daughter to know? (Long pause.)

Daughter: That it's okay.

Mom: It's okay to what?

Daughter: Go through puberty and stuff.

Mom: Do you think the daughter could be worried that as she grows up, her dad would like her less?

Daughter: Yes.

Mom: Why do you think that?

Daughter: She might and she might not. It depends on whether she thinks her dad loves her right now or not. Because if she doesn't think her dad loves her now, she'll probably think he'll like her even less when she grows up. But if she thinks he likes her now, then she'll think he'll love her just as he does now.

Lessons Learned from This Sample Talk

In this intimate exchange, the mom and her daughter get to agree on what would be good sources of information about the body. Mom may have inadvertently created some insecurity in her daughter about "growing up," or she may have sensed this fear in her daughter and diminished it by bringing it up and discussing it. The daughter seems to think out loud and realize puberty won't change things. In future talks the mom can bring up the topics of self-esteem and attractiveness.

3

Personal Space

Talking about Boundaries

*When I was a kid we didn't use the term "boundaries." But I think
my dad tried to help me understand the concept. He said, "Boys like
girls with shiny chrome and no dents. So keep your chrome clean."
Thinking back—the message from my dad was not the clearest.*
—Agnes, mother of two, Oklahoma City, Oklahoma

*My problem is not that my daughter does not understand
boundaries. My problem is that I don't think she wants to use them.
She is fifteen and keeps going out with older guys and I keep saying
I don't approve. We are in a constant battle over what boundaries I
want her to have and which ones she wants to have. We just can't
agree and she is driving me nuts.*
—Didi, mother of four, Seattle, Washington

*All of us have shields to protect us. Like the force field they use in
Star Trek.* —Matt, fourth grade student, Washington, D.C.

A girl is standing in line waiting for a school bus and a boy
comes up behind her and pulls her bra strap.

A boy is taking a shower after gym class when some older classmates enter the locker room and knock him down and swat him
with wet towels.

A girl is listening to music in her room with a new boy from
school. Suddenly the boy grabs her and starts to kiss her.

What the stories above have in common is that in all three situations, a person's boundaries were crossed. Some people might say that having a bra snapped, being swatted with towels, and being kissed unexpectedly are just part of growing up. When these situations are described to kids, some of them say that girls like getting boys' attention; getting your bra snapped could be a good thing. Some boys say that locker room roughhousing is a fun part of hanging out with the guys and no big deal. Few boys say that they should ask before "making a move," and one boy said, "Since the girl had the boy in her room, it was a sign that she wanted to kiss and maybe more." Of course, there are other ways to look at all of these situations; some might call them sexual harassment, abuse, disrespect, or even forms of violence.

It's complicated, but what boundaries do is give us control over who touches us and how we are touched. Each of us deserves the right to choose how we are treated—physically and emotionally. Many of us had experiences at home and at school where our boundaries were disrespected to one degree or another. Almost all of us have stories about unwanted touching of some kind. This talk will help you talk with your child about her boundaries—and how to respect others'. We believe that having boundaries and respecting the boundaries of others is the fundamental building block of all healthy relationships.

Preparing for the Talk

This talk opens the door for ongoing conversations about boundaries, how to defend them and how to respect others' boundaries. In this talk you will help your child know that

- she can choose who gets close to her.
- he can choose who touches him.
- she can choose how and where she will be touched.
- he can refuse to be touched.

What You Can Expect from This Talk

After the talk your child will

- understand how to set personal boundaries and control how she is touched.
- understand the importance of respecting other people's privacy, body, and emotional rights.
- understand your family rules about setting and respecting boundaries.

How Do You Define Boundaries?

Each family has its own unique idea about what is permissible—and this would be a good time to think about what goes on in yours. In some families people walk into each other's bedrooms without knocking, thinking it's no big deal. In other families, privacy is a core value and no one ever would think of entering someone else's room unannounced. Even opening someone else's magazine first would be considered inappropriate. Where does your family fit in on this continuum? Consider the perspectives of Peter and Betty.

I grew up where we knocked before going into someone's bedroom. I was surprised to see that my friend's family went into each other's rooms—even the bathroom when it was occupied—without knocking.
—Peter, father of two, Syracuse, New York

My daughter Cathy feels she must have total privacy, even for the most mundane phone conversations with her friends. The rest of us don't see anything special about talking on the phone within earshot of others. Cathy is the same way about her physical privacy: if I catch a glimpse of her before she has her bra on she is very upset. Her older sister has no issues about being seen undressed by me.

—Betty, mother of two, Portland, Oregon

Influence of the Media

If your child is like most children, he or she watches a lot of television and videos and goes to movies. This programming shows relationships where boundaries are disrespected and crossed constantly. Take a look at almost any adventure film from the 1950s through today and you see the leading man making advances on the leading "lady"—who may say "no" but who means "yes" (at least to the conceit of the screenwriters). Today's programming shows a grab bag of unwanted and wanted sexual advances, and cartoonish and realistic aggression. Violence is common, especially by males against females. At best, TV offers mixed messages about respecting others and being respected. Strong clear messages about boundaries need to come from parents. You need to take some time—if you haven't already—to review the programs your child watches to see what behavior is being modeled.

Pressure from Peers

At every school level, there are peers and adults who do not respect personal boundaries—sometimes intentionally, sometimes unintentionally. Young males in particular can be aggressive and assume the right to disregard other people's boundaries. Not too long ago this might have been dismissed with "Boys will be boys!" Now the media's focus on school safety and violence, as well as the frequency of harassment lawsuits, have changed attitudes about what is and what isn't appropriate behavior at school.

Pushing, shoving, touching, and unwanted fondling are, unfortunately, very common. Girls and boys learn early on that harassment and small acts of violence happen—and while we now have laws and policies in place to defend people's boundaries, these may not be effective on a day-to-day basis. Most kids don't know that they have the right to resist or get help if they want to put an end to harassment and violence.

Ask your child if pushing, shoving, unwanted hugging, or snapping of bra straps is going on in their peer group. We think that you will find considerable unwanted touching involving boys with boys, girls with girls, boys with girls, and girls with boys. Your child most likely is getting the message that at school, especially during unsupervised times, boundaries are not respected.

Giving Your Child the Big Picture

Reported sexual assaults where the victim was female and under 18 years of age: 61%

Reported assaults that were committed by a friend, acquaintance, intimate partner, or family member: 75%

Reported sexual assaults where the victim was male: 5%

(Source: American Medical Association Report, 1999)

Younger children may need some other descriptions of boundaries to fully understand the concept. You may substitute the word "limits" for "boundaries." Tell your child that limits are useful everywhere in the world. Limits help create civilized, sensitive, and peaceful interaction. For example, even friendly countries have very specific borders. Wars can happen when people don't respect these boundaries. Respect usually brings peaceful collaboration—like the relationship between Canada and the United States. But, when boundaries are tested or ignored, it can be seen as a challenge. The same kind of challenge occurs when you tell somebody to stop pushing you or hugging you and to back off—and they don't. Diane and Beth describe how they both came to talk to their children about the concept of boundaries:

As part of my homework for a parenting class, I asked my daughter if she knew what a boundary was. She said she learned the word when she was studying the fifty states. When I asked if she knew about the term "personal boundaries," she said it means "people have a bubble around them."

—Diane, mother of two, Rockville, Maryland

My first-grade daughter was mad at a boy and pinched his penis, causing him pain. I had to tell her why that was unfair. I told her that was a place that you don't touch another person. It was the beginning of my talk about respecting other people's boundaries, though we didn't use the word "boundaries."

—Beth, mother of four, Seattle, Washington

Points of View

Both adults and children have to remember that there is a lot of room for misunderstanding about boundaries. Some people expect affectionate physical contact from relatives, while others do not. Today's diverse world requires that we think about respecting other people's customs and let them know our own comfort level. Two parents look back at their boundary issues during their childhood:

> *Family gatherings were the worst. When I was growing up my parents would pinch me to show what a cutie I was to visiting relatives. I never liked it and when I grew older it was humiliating.*
>
> —Judith, mother of two, Chicago

> *When I was a kid our family always spent Sunday dinner at my grand-parents'. We were part of a very big extended family. My aunts and uncles all wanted to kiss me and I didn't like it. I especially didn't like having to kiss my uncles.*
>
> —Mario, father of three, New York City

Different Families: Different Values

Everyone defines boundaries in his or her own way. Here are some behaviors that may be experienced differently depending on a person's background.

Two people are standing a few feet apart and talking.

Some people feel the need to stand three to four feet away from someone when they are chatting, while others are comfortable with half that distance.

One person is touching another person's belongings.

Some people feel that using someone's hairbrush or going through someone's backpack is acceptable, while others find those behaviors rude and unhealthy.

■

Two people are talking. They are casual acquaintances. One is telling a very personal story.

Some people feel comfortable discussing personal feelings or experiences, while others consider such matters private.

Last-Minute Checkups before the Talk

It helps to understand your own feelings about boundaries before you talk to your child.

- When you were a child, was it understood that people had to knock before going into your room?
- Could you put something in a cabinet in your room and be assured that no one would go looking for it?
- If you wrote in a journal or diary, did you know it would be totally private?
- Did your parents give you as much privacy as you wanted?

How do you think your childhood experiences have affected the way you are raising your child?

- Under normal circumstances, do you go through your child's room, closets, cabinets and drawers looking for clues about her life?

- If you want to know who your child's friends are, do you think you should eavesdrop on their telephone conversations?
- Under normal circumstances, do you think it is appropriate for you secretly to go into your child's computer to read his or her personal files?
- Would you pressure your child to kiss your relatives?

This is a complicated set of questions, because there are times when checking up on your child's private life is what a good parent has to do. For example, if you suspected your child was using drugs or was being preyed upon by an adult, it would be appropriate to look for evidence of the problem. But under normal conditions the same detective work might look like disrespect for your child's boundaries.

Make sure your values are consistent with your actions. Children learn as they model adult behavior. If the adults in your house respect boundaries then the child can observe that and learn. If there are adults who talk about respecting boundaries but do not do so themselves, the child will experience mixed messages.

Your child already may have had some important boundaries challenged. Even if your child is only in first grade, she may have a crush on someone or someone may be infatuated with her. Unwanted sexual attention can be very upsetting, especially if the child doesn't know how to interpret the behavior or has no idea how to stop it. Consider the experiences of Raphael and Patty:

When I was a little boy, there was a girl who would always throw my cap away. She was always knocking it off my head. My mom said she did it because she had a crush on me. I was just mad at the time. I didn't understand it.

—Raphael, father of one, Missoula, Montana

When I was nine, a boy in my school told me he wanted to "stick his thing in my thing." I didn't know what he was talking about, but I knew that it was something I shouldn't do. Looking back, I can see how disrespectful he was. I wish I had understood what he meant. I could have had a response ready in a way that made me feel good.

—Patty, mother of two, Seattle, Washington

One of the first things children have to learn is how to respect the boundaries of family members and friends. It's a skill that will help them establish boundaries when they become infatuated with someone or someone becomes infatuated with them. As a child grows older and becomes sexually attracted to someone, he may want to revise his personal boundaries. Do you remember how you felt when you had your first crush? Most likely the last thing you wanted was any type of space between you and the object of your infatuation! Our own experiences underscore the importance of giving our children the skills to navigate sexual relationships as soon as possible.

Last-Minute Checkups before the Talk

Think back to your experiences with setting boundaries and respecting others' limits.

- What did your parents tell you about boundaries?
- What were your main concerns?

- How did you feel?
- Did you have anyone to talk with about your feelings?

How do you think your childhood experiences have affected the way you're raising your child?

- To date, what have you explained to your child about boundaries?
- Have you told her to expect that some kids and adults might try to "cross" her boundaries?
- Does she know what to do if she feels that her boundaries have been disrespected?

Do you have any stories about boundaries that you could share with your child? For example:

- How you dealt with a person who tried to touch you against your wishes
- What it was like when you stood up for yourself, or when you didn't

What Are Your Family Rules?

Do you have family rules about boundaries? The talk outlined in this chapter highlights the following situations:

- A boy barges into his sister's room.
- A girl gets her bra snapped at school.
- A boy is harassed in the locker room's shower.
- A boy tries to kiss a girl.

Discussing these situations will give you an opportunity to discuss your family rules. How do you want your child to respond to people who don't respect him and try to harass him in any way? What are your rules about harassing others? Where can your child find help if she has concerns about harassment or violence? At the end of this talk, you will have the chance to review the rules with your child.

The Talk

Introduce the Talk

All right—you are almost ready to have the talk about boundaries with your child. To fully understand the *Ten Talks* process, make sure to read the rest of this chapter first. You may find the sample talks at the end of this chapter particularly helpful.

Find a time for an uninterrupted ten minutes or more—with some children a talk may easily fill an hour. The talk could be done in the house, on a walk, or in the car—whichever suits you best and seems like it would be most successful. A talk about boundaries can be very personal and we recommend that you have the talk one-on-one with your child.

Tell your child you need to borrow him for a few minutes. Begin by asking your child, "What does the phrase 'setting personal boundaries' mean?"

If your child has an appropriate response, proceed to the next chapter. If not, offer some examples like: "Boundaries are your way of controlling who can and who cannot touch you, when they can or can't touch you, and how they touch you. Boundaries can also include controlling how people talk to you, how close they can come to you, how they respect the things you own and care about, or your privacy in general."

You can use examples about boundaries between countries, or in sports ("going out of bounds"), or any other examples you can think of to help make the point.

Review These Words

Please review the terms in this section. Discussing all of them with your child is optional. You know what's appropriate for your child's age and maturity level. Keep in mind that more than likely, even the youngest children have heard these words on TV.

boundaries: a physical boundary is the area around a person that sets rules for how and when that person wishes to be touched. An emotional boundary sets the rules for how a person wishes to be spoken to and treated.

feeling violated: when someone breaks your boundaries in a serious way. A person may say something to you, touch you, or threaten you in a way that makes you feel unsafe.

harassing: bothering or threatening a person physically or verbally; disrespecting a person.

ignoring boundaries: behaving in such a way as to disregard how other people wish to be treated, physically and emotionally (i.e., hitting or calling someone cruel names).

sexual harassment: when a person treats another person in such a way, physically or verbally, using sexual words or actions, that it hinders the victim's ability to learn in school. Sexual harassment also impacts negatively the victim's performance in the workplace.

school safety: programs and policies developed in schools to prevent harassment and violence.

private space: places where you deserve to be alone (like the bathroom or in your bedroom).

public space: a room or area (like a park or school) that many people share.

respecting boundaries: when people understand your right to have personal boundaries and honor your wishes by touching you in ways that you approve.

too close for comfort: when a person is standing so close to you that you feel uncomfortable.

Why Is Talking about Boundaries Important?

Ask your child whether she thinks talking about boundaries is important. Here are some reasons you might offer. Talking about boundaries

- lets people know how you wish to be treated.
- tells people what you want and don't want to share with them (i.e., an article of clothing or a CD).
- sets a standard for behavior (for example, that it's not okay to push someone or call someone names).
- lets other people know what you consider private (i.e., listening in on a phone call).

The Stories

In the next part of the talk, you'll be reading short stories to your child and discussing them together. You don't have to read all of them. Pick the ones that you think are appropriate for your child. The stories are very simple. Feel free to embellish them, adding details that you think might make them more believable to your child. For example, some parents change the gender of the characters to make a story mirror their own families.

The Story about Families and Boundaries

Read this story to your child. It provides an opportunity to discuss how family members set boundaries, and what to do when boundaries are not respected.

"A girl is in her bedroom getting dressed when her brother needs something from her room. The brother barges in without knocking, something he has done before."

Ask these questions of your child:

- What is the sister thinking?
- What is the brother thinking?
- What does the sister say?
- What does the brother say?

Now that your child has completed this scenario, ask the following questions:

- Is the sister embarrassed or upset?
- Does she wish her brother had knocked? Why or why not?

- Is the brother embarrassed?
- Does he wish he had knocked? Why or why not?
- Why does the brother keep doing this?
- What would make him stop?
- Are the sister's boundaries being respected?
- If the sister doesn't like him coming into her bedroom without permission, what should she do?
- If it was the sister barging in on her brother, would the situation be different?
- If it was a parent coming in without knocking, how might the situation be different?
- What would be the best thing to do if you were in a situation like this and your boundaries weren't being respected?

Clarify Your Family's Values

Discuss the following question with your child as a way of sharing your values about boundaries. We have included potential responses from children to help you formulate your own responses.

Ask your child: "When a person is in his bedroom and wants privacy, can he expect others to give it to him?"

Child's response #1: Yes.
Parent: It's good to hear that you feel your boundaries are respected. Do you respect the boundaries of others?

Child's response #2: No.
Parent: Why not?
Child: Kids never get privacy.

Parent: Never? What kind of privacy would kids like to have?

Child: I don't know.

Parent: Let's talk about the rules we have for privacy in our home.

Child: I'd like a lock on my bedroom door.

Parent: Let's talk about the rules we have for privacy in our home and why you want a lock.

Child: What house rules? Since when do we have those rules?

Parent: We are going to review some house rules that I want to put in effect. And we're going to discuss the consequences for breaking the house rules. Breaking house rules is breaking a commitment to the family and to me. It is very serious. And there are always consequences to breaking a commitment. (Review your house rules and the consequences for breaking them. Some parents like to post these on a wall for the child to see.)

Note to parent: Suggest ways to enhance privacy that you find acceptable. If your child wants some changes that you do not approve of, such as a lock on a bedroom door, suggest a compromise, such as a sign saying, "Knock before entering."

The Story about Disrespecting Boundaries

Read this story to your child. It gives you an opportunity to discuss how people can respond when their boundaries aren't being respected.

"A girl is standing outside school when a boy she knows from class passes her and

snaps the back of her bra. She is surprised. Everyone laughs."
(Note: for younger children you may use the example of a boy
pulling the girl's hair instead of snapping her bra if you think that
example would be more appropriate.)

Ask these questions of your child:

• What is the girl thinking?
• What is the boy thinking?
• What is the girl saying?
• What is the boy saying?

**Now that your child has completed this scenario, ask the
following questions:**

• Is anything unusual happening in this situation? If so, what?
• What might happen if the girl complains to her friends about
  having her bra snapped?
• Are the girl's boundaries being respected? If not, why not?
• Why would the boy want to snap the girl's bra?
• How would the situation be different if the girl knew the boy
  well?
• How would the situation be different if it was a girl who
  snapped a boy's underwear?

Clarify Your Family's Values

Discuss the following question with your child as a way of sharing
your values about boundaries. We have included a number of po-

tential responses from children to help you formulate your own responses.

Ask your child: "What do girls think about having their bras snapped?"

Child: That's just something that boys do. You can't stop them.

Parent: I think the girl has more power than you think. Can you think of a way she could stop the boy?

Child: No.

Parent: Could she report this to her teacher?

Child: She won't tell the teacher.

Parents: Why not?

Child: If she told the teacher and the boy got in trouble, he wouldn't like her anymore.

Parent: How important would it be to the girl to be liked by the boy?

Child: I don't know.

Parent: Do you think all boys or girls would feel the same way about being liked?

Child: Yes.

Parent: You may find that boys and girls all feel very different about unwanted touching. Do you think it is more important to fit in than to say how you feel?

Child: A girl likes it when a boy that she likes gives her attention.

Parent: Sometimes girls just act like they like it when they really don't. Could a girl be afraid to show her true feelings? Could a boy be afraid to show his true feelings if he was the one being picked on?

The Story about Boundaries and the Boys in the Shower

Read this story to your child. It gives you an opportunity to discuss how people can respond when their boundaries aren't respected.

"A boy is taking a shower after gym class. A bunch of older students enter the shower area and start making fun of the boy. One of the bigger guys knocks the boy to the ground and swats him with a wet towel."

Ask these questions of your child:

- What is the younger boy thinking?
- What is the older guy thinking?
- What is the younger boy saying?
- What is the older guy saying?

Now that your child has completed this scenario, ask the following questions:

- How often does something like this happen?
- What would happen if the boy complained to the coach?
- Are the boy's boundaries being respected? If not, why not?
- Why would the older guy want to harass the younger boy?
- How would the situation be different if this happened between two girls?

Clarify Your Family's Values

Discuss the following question with your child as a way of sharing your values about boundaries. We have included potential responses from children to help you formulate your own responses.

Ask your child: "What do boys think about when they are harassed by older guys?"

Child: That's just something that older guys do. You can't stop them.

Parent: Can you think of a way he could stop the harassment?

Child: No.

Parent: Could he report this to his coach or teacher?

Child: He won't tell anybody.

Parent: Why not?

Child: If he told the teacher or coach and the older guy got in trouble, then the younger guy would get beat up later.

Parent: How can a student report harassment or violence and not get in trouble with other students?

Child: I don't know.

Parent: If no one ever reports violence, then how do the bullies ever get stopped?

Child: They don't get stopped.

Parent: There are students and teachers and parents who do want all bullying to end. Let's look at your school's safety rules and see what they say to do.

The Story about Setting Boundaries on the Couch

Read this story to your child. It provides an opportunity to discuss setting boundaries with people you might be attracted to.

"A girl knows a boy from school. She likes him a lot. She wants to kiss him. The boy wants kissing and more. One day they are watching TV when he starts to touch her in places that make her uncomfortable. The girl just wants to kiss."

Ask these questions of your child:

- What is the girl thinking?
- What is the boy thinking?
- What is the girl saying?
- What is the boy saying?

Now that your child has completed this scenario, ask the following questions:

- In this situation, whose job is it to set boundaries?
- When the girl sets a boundary, should the boy respect it or question it to see if the girl is really serious?
- What might happen if the girl says, "I only want to kiss"?
- How would this situation be different if it was the boy who wanted to set boundaries and the girl who did not respect them?

Clarify Your Family's Values

Discuss the following question with your child as a way of sharing your values about boundaries. We have included potential responses from children to help you formulate your own responses.

Ask your child: "When a person likes someone and wants to kiss, can he or she expect to set a boundary and only kiss?"

Child's response #1: I don't know.

Parent: One thing doesn't really have to lead to another. There is no timetable that says first you do this, then you do that, and then you have to quickly proceed to the next stage. You can and you should do only what you are comfortable with. A person who really likes you will respect your boundaries and let you make up your own mind about what you want to do. If they really like you, they will accept your decisions.

Child's response #2: Girls usually do what the boy says.

Parent: I think it's important for girls to stand up for themselves. And for a boy not to try to control what a girl does. These days girls can be appreciated if they are strong and confident. Girlfriends have to be treated like other friends.

Child's response #3: Girls always say "no" but they mean "yes."

Parent: Most girls, like most boys, say "no" and mean it. While there might be some people who say "no" but really mean "yes," you have to be very sure that the person you are with is really giving you a clear answer about what she wants. And if you think someone is unsure, you should wait until she's sure. Otherwise, you both could do something you would be sorry for. It could spoil the whole relationship. Someone who felt she was forced into doing something she hadn't intended to do could go to her parents, the principal, or the police and blame you for forcing unwanted sexual behavior.

Child's response #4: Boys don't do things girls don't want.

Parent: That's not true. Sometimes boys are mistaken about what they think a girl is telling them. Boys may act on what they think the girl's body language or dress suggests to them. Just because a girl is on a couch with a boy in a dark room doesn't mean she's allowing him to do anything he wants. Even if she looks sexy, that doesn't give anyone the permission to touch her.

Child's response #5: Girls shouldn't be kissing if they don't want more.

Parent: Kissing is fun all by itself. It doesn't have to lead to anything else but kissing. Kissing is pleasurable for most people, and often it is a sign of how much one person likes another. It doesn't have to progress to anything more sexual.

Child's response #6: Sometimes things happen but it's nobody's fault.

Parent: I don't want to be harsh, but that's a cop-out. If people do something they don't feel right about, they are still responsible for that act.

Child's response #7: Boys are usually hounded by girls.

Parent: I know that can be true in some cases. But a boy can say no. If some girl wants to put a boy in situations that he is not comfortable with, he has the right to say no.

The Bare Minimum: A Quick Quiz for Kids

Ask your child the following question to assess her knowledge of the term "boundary."

Can you give me one example of how a person might set a boundary with someone else?

Sample answers:
- Asking a person to stop touching you
- Asking people to knock before they enter a bedroom
- Asking a person not to open your diary or computer files
- When being kissed, telling the kisser that this is not an invitation to touch below the waist
- Asking someone to stop making rude remarks
- Asking someone to stop asking personal questions
- Asking someone to stop pushing or poking

Talk about Your Family Rules

To clarify your family rules, ask your child the following three questions.

1. What is one rule about respecting boundaries that we have in this home?
   Sample answers:
- We always knock before entering someone's bedroom.
- We always knock before entering a bathroom.
- We ask permission before looking in someone's purse, wallet, or backpack.
- We ask permission before going through someone's desk for something you need.

- We do not open someone else's private journal or mail.
2. What's our rule about reporting harassment at school?
   Sample answers:
- All incidents are reported to teachers or a school staff person.
- If I'm not sure whether to report something or not, I'll always tell you.
3. Do we ever allow hitting or harassing of others?
- No hitting of others is allowed except in self-defense to get away from someone.
- No name-calling is allowed.

After the Talk

A Moment to Reflect

Take a moment to reflect on the talk you just had with your child.

- What surprised you about your child's perception of boundaries, harassment, and violence?
- How do you feel about your ability to discuss boundaries with your child?
- What do you think your child may not want to talk about?
- How much time did you spend listening?
- How do you think your child felt about the talk?

After a talk about boundaries, many parents report feeling surprised by how much everyday harassment and violence their kids observe on their way to school, on breaks, and on the way home. Often these everyday acts are not described by the child as harassment or violence—kids just call it "life."

Warning Signs

The talks may also reveal potential problems your child is facing, whether in the role of the victim or the victimizer. There is cause for concern if you hear from the school or other parents or child care providers that your child

- is touching other kids inappropriately.
- is being touched inappropriately.
- is afraid of another child.
- is submissive to another child.
- feels bossed around by a boyfriend or girlfriend.

In any of these situations, you need to find out what is happening. If, after your discussion, you feel your child needs more than you can accomplish in discussion, go see a school counselor or therapist, or look further into one of the many resources available in your community.

Finding Help

It is important for your child to know that he can get help when he needs it. Most schools have policies that prohibit boundary-breaking, although the enforcement of such anti-harassment and anti-violence policies varies from school to school. Getting a child to admit that he needs help is not always easy. But if you think that your child needs help with setting his own boundaries or respecting the boundaries of others, consider counseling with a school social worker, therapist, or someone from your religious organization. Often a short-term visit can do a world of good. And if you have a good relationship with your child's grandparents or other extended family members, tell them what's going on with your child and seek out the kind of support your child and you might need.

Success Stories

Congratulations! You have made it through talk number three! If you managed at least a five-minute talk that included basic definitions, consider it an unqualified success. A mom in Seattle reported that her fourteen-year-old daughter had accepted as "normal" being called sexual names at school. During the talk, the mom let her know that name-calling isn't something she—or any student—should have to endure.

Remember that future talks may get easier as you become more familiar with the format of the book and your child's style of communication.

Sample Talks

Between Parents and Children

Before you begin your first talk, you might want to read this sample conversation composed of excerpts of actual talks between parents and children.

Discussing the Story about Families and Boundaries

Participants: a father and his eleven-year-old daughter.

Dad: A girl is in her bedroom getting dressed when her brother needs something from her room. The brother barges in without knocking, something he has done before. What is the sister thinking?

Daughter: The sister is thinking he is very rude and he shouldn't have done that in the first place.

Dad: What is the brother thinking?

Daughter: He's not thinking about his sister, he's just thinking on getting that toy.

Dad: What does the sister say?

Daughter: "What are you doing? Can you please get out of my room now?"

Dad: What does the brother say?

Daughter: He's saying, "Let me just get it really quick and then I'll get out of your way."

Dad: Is the sister embarrassed or not?

Daughter: The sister is very embarrassed. She knows now that her brother will barge in and he might tell his friends something like, "my sister wears a bra" or something like that.

Dad: Does she wish her brother had knocked? Why or why not?

Daughter: Yes, for one reason, if she were mean and were hiding things from him or, two, out of respect, you should knock on someone's door.

Dad: Is the brother embarrassed?

Daughter: Let's see. He's probably mainly embarrassed unless he just picked up his game and left, then he wouldn't have been.

Dad: Does he wish he had knocked? Why or why not?

Daughter: He probably does wish he had knocked 'cause if they are getting older, like they're in puberty, he probably wouldn't want to see anything.

Dad: Why does the brother keep doing this?

Daughter: He's unorganized, so he's always putting his stuff in a different room, like he's trying to find his socks and he's trying to find them to get ready for school.

Dad: What would make him stop?

Daughter: Maybe if he keeps things in his room all neat and organized.

Dad: Are the sister's boundaries being respected?

Daughter: No, not really in this situation.

Dad: If the sister doesn't like him coming into her bedroom without permission, what should she do?

Daughter: In a magazine I saw a card-sign that said, "STOP I'm Studying."

Dad: "Do Not Disturb" in other words?

Daughter: Or a note that says he can come in only at certain times.

Dad: Keep out?

Daughter: Yeah.

Dad: If it were the sister barging in on her brother, would the situation be different?

Daughter: The situation would be a lot, lot different because the brother might be having a friend in his room and they're talking and there might be something he didn't want her to see (she laughs).

Dad: If it was a parent coming in without knocking, how might the situation be different?

Daughter: It would be different 'cause, well, the parents are the ones who gave the child birth, so they know everything from the head to the toe.

Dad: From the hooter to the tooter? (He laughs.) What would be the best thing to do if you were in a situation like this and your boundaries weren't being respected?

Daughter: If you're talking about a child, put up a sign. If you're talking about an adult, sit down and have a conversation with them.

Lessons Learned from This Sample Talk

This is a great example of using the talk to help a child understand that she can maintain boundaries by using some simple tools (like putting up a sign). She needed a little reinforcement to understand her right to privacy—and she got it. Future talks can continue to support her desire for privacy and respect from family members and schoolmates.

Discussing the Story about Disrespecting Boundaries

Participants: a father and his nine-year-old son.

Dad: A girl is standing outside school when a boy she knows from class passes her and snaps the back of her bra. She is surprised. Everyone laughs. What is the girl thinking?

Son: That she just got very embarrassed.

Dad: What is the boy thinking?

Son: That he's funny.

Dad: What is the girl saying?

Son: She says, "Stop it," and runs away.

Dad: What is the boy saying?

Son: He probably would have made fun of her.

Dad: Is anything unusual happening in this situation? If so, what?

Son: It's unusual for a boy to walk over and snap a girl's bra. You don't do that when you walk into school.

Dad: No they shouldn't. That's rather personal. What might happen if the girl complains to her friends about having her bra snapped?

Son: Her friends would probably tell her to come with them and they'd do something to that guy, like make fun of him.

Dad: Are the girl's boundaries being respected? If not, why not?

Son: They're not because that's her personal stuff and that's just rude.

Dad: You don't do that. Why would the boy want to snap the girl's bra in the first place?

Son: I guess because he's funny and he likes the girl.

Dad: It seems like a mean thing to do. How would the situation be different if the girl knew the boy well? Like they were best buddies.

Son: The girl might think the boy's just having fun and playing around.

Dad: How would the situation be different if it was a girl who snapped a boy's underwear?

Son: He would get really mad and push her or something.

Dad: You don't touch people's personal clothing, you just don't do that.

Lessons Learned from This Sample Talk

It's good that the son knows that there are different reasons a boy might snap a bra strap but even better that he knows it is rude. Dad has learned that his son respects that kind of boundary. Future talks can explore how boundaries might change as people get older, and how to find friends who share similar views about boundaries.

It's important to note how perceptions differ between grades. In middle school a bra snap may mean one thing while in elementary school, where most girls do not even wear a bra until close to fifth grade, it may be viewed as a rare occurrence.

Discussing the Story about Disrespecting Boundaries

Participants: a father and his eleven-year-old daughter.

Dad: A girl is standing outside school when a boy she knows from class passes her and snaps the back of her bra. She is surprised. Everyone laughs. What is the girl thinking?

Daughter: She's thinking that boy is very rude or he better start running 'cause she's about ready to go over and tell a teacher.

Dad: What is the boy thinking?

Daughter: Depends on the type of the boy. Maybe they're really close friends. Maybe he's playing around, that's his way of, kind of, flirting with her.

Dad: What is the girl saying?

Daughter: "Hey! What are you doing? That is RUDE!"

Dad: What is the boy saying?

Daughter: "Hey, we're just having fun. Have a good time. Don't be worried."

Dad: Is anything unusual happening in this situation? If so, what?

Daughter: It's very unusual, 'cause that is just SO RUDE for a guy to come up and pull your bra. That's like if a girl went and pulled his underwear, for goodness sakes.

Dad: What might happen if the girl complains to her friends about having her bra snapped?

Daughter: If they were really close friends they'd probably be shocked and worried, but if they weren't, they'd probably laugh.

Dad: Are the girl's boundaries being respected? If not, why not?

Daughter: NO WAY. That guy should not be on her like he owns her. That's her own private property. She pays money for that.

Dad: He better back off. Why would the boy want to snap the girl's bra in the first place?

Daughter: Trying to show off, probably.

Dad: How would the situation be different if the girl knew the boy well?

Daughter: It would still embarrass her and he'd probably say "sorry," but he'd say he was playing around.

Dad: So her feelings wouldn't be as bad if it was someone she knew well?

Daughter: If it was a friend from school?

Dad: Yeah.

Daughter: It would still be embarrassing.

Dad: How would the situation be different if it was a girl who snapped a boy's underwear?

Daughter: It would probably hurt. He'd say, "HEY, that stings a little!"

Dad: What's good for the goose is good for the gander?

Lessons Learned from This Sample Talk

The daughter expressed her right to privacy and how she could react to a violation. She got approval from her dad. She is empowered even further by this conversation. In future talks Dad can check in on his daughter's progress.

Discussing the Story about Boundaries and the Boys in the Shower

Participants: a father and his nine-year-old son.

Dad: A boy is taking a shower after gym class. A bunch of older students enter the shower area and start making fun of the boy. One of the bigger guys knocks the boy to the ground and swats him with a wet towel. What is the younger boy thinking?

Son: That he wants to cry and run away.

Dad: Those guys are being bullies, aren't they? What is the older guy thinking?

Son: That he's being very funny and he's really hurting him.

Dad: He's really mean. What is the younger boy saying?

Son: "Aww, stop doing it."

Dad: What is the older guy saying?

Son: Probably, "Now I'm going to push you down and hit you with a towel" and he'll keep doing it.

Dad: He'll keep doing it, threatening him with "try to get up, try to get up."

Son: "And if you don't get up, I'll hit you with a towel again."

Dad: How often does something like this happen?

Son: Not that often. You don't see it much.

Dad: When you get to middle school?

Son: When you get to middle school it will happen five or six times a month, but usually it's not going to happen.

Dad: What would happen if the boy complained to the coach?

Son: The older boys would get suspended off the team.

Dad: They'd get in trouble. Are the boy's boundaries being respected? If not, why not?

Son: No, because he's trying to take a shower and he's in the nude and they're making fun of him.

Dad: Why would the older guy want to harass the younger boy?

Son: Because he's much bigger and he knows he's much stronger.

Dad: And he's a bully.

Son: Yeah.

Dad: Bullies are not nice people. How would the situation be different if this happened between two girls? If a bigger girl did that to a younger girl?

Son: The girl would probably tell the coach.

Lessons Learned from This Sample Talk

This talk was excellent. The son revealed to his father how he feels about people being hit and his sense of justice. The dad may want to let his son know that in the real world, bullies may get away with harassment and violence because some coaches look the other way. And sometimes a bully who gets reported will seek retaliation on the person who reported him. The dad can, in future talks, discuss how he wants his son to deal with violent situations, whether he is the victim or the observer.

Discussing the Story about Setting Boundaries on the Couch

Participants: a mother and her seventh-grade son.

Mom: This is a story about two kids kissing. In this story the girl likes the boy and enjoys kissing but does not want to go further. The boy does.

Child: That's just something that boys do. You can't stop them.

Mom: I think the girl has more power than you think. Can you think of a way she could stop the boy?

Child: No.

Mom: What about if the girl said she didn't think that was funny and that she would like the boy to respect her feelings? Aren't girls entitled to that boundary?

Child: If she told him to keep his hands to himself he wouldn't like her anymore. A girl likes it when a boy that she likes shows that kind of attention.

Mom: I think it does show that he is interested in the girl, but he has not gotten her permission to show his interest in that way. Is there a way a boy can show his interest in a more respectful way?

Child: I don't know.

Mom: What is the girl saying?

Child: "Maybe later."

Mom: What is the boy saying?

Child: "Let's do it now." (Laughing.)

Mom: In this situation, whose job is it to set boundaries?

Child: The boy.

Mom: When the girl sets a boundary, should the boy respect it or question it to see if the girl is really serious?

Child: Question it.

Mom: The girl might be afraid that if she sets a boundary, such as saying kissing is all she wants to do, that she may lose the boy as a boyfriend. Should the girl fear losing the boy for this reason? Why or why not?

Child: Yes, she should be afraid of losing the boy.

Mom: How would this situation be different if it was the boy who wanted to set boundaries and the girl who did not respect them?

Child: That never happens.

Mom: You might be surprised.

Child: Can I go now? (He gets up.)

Mom: Yes.

Lessons Learned from This Talk

This is a very important talk. Mom has found out that her son has learned somewhere that boys are supposed to get their way and that women's desire to set boundaries should be challenged. He appears to have strong, set ideas about gender roles, and he will need some serious talks to safely navigate male-female friendships or dating. He seems to feel that girls should "deliver." The mother reports that the entire conversation about boundaries took less than a few minutes and that her son was acting like he had to leave the whole time, although he had nowhere to go and nothing to do. He did not want to talk about these issues in depth. Future topics to discuss could include: respecting others, sex roles, and the consequences of disrespecting others' boundaries.

Discussing the Story about Setting Boundaries on the Couch

Participants: a mother and her fifteen-year-old daughter.

Mom: Here is a story I want your opinion on. A girl knows a boy from school. She likes him a lot. She wants to kiss him. The boy wants kissing and more. One day they are watching TV when he starts to touch her in places that make her uncomfortable. The girl just wants to kiss. What is the girl thinking?

Daughter: The girl is thinking, "I'm physically attracted to this boy." She might want a relationship, but she's not willing to go as far as the guy is at that point and time.

Mom: What is the boy thinking?

Daughter: Depending on his maturity level, he might want to fool around or he might be trying to express his affection for her too fast and too soon.

Mom: What is the girl saying?

Daughter: She wants a relationship with the boy, but she's not willing to take it very far.

Mom: What is the boy saying?

Daughter: He's saying he wants a relationship, but he wants it to be more physical.

Mom: In this situation, whose job is it to set boundaries?

Daughter: It's both of their responsibilities because they both need to talk about it and decide what they are both comfortable with, but, in this situation, the guy needs to respect the girl's feelings if this relationship is going to work.

Mom: When the girl sets a boundary, should the boy respect it or question it to see if the girl is really serious?

Daughter: I think he should definitely respect what she says.

Mom: What might happen if the girl says, "I only want to kiss?"

Daughter: If the guy was worth being with, he'd say that it was fine. They could go as slow as she wanted. But if he wasn't a good enough guy to be with, then he might leave her.

Mom: How would this situation be different if it was the boy who wanted to set boundaries and the girl who did not respect them?

Daughter: It probably wouldn't be much different except it's not as common for girls to do that.

Mom: What did you think of this talk?

Daughter: It's something that you see every day on TV and stuff like that and everyone has their morals, so it was interesting.

Lessons Learned from This Sample Talk

The daughter shared a lot of information with her mother about ethics, morals, and boundaries. The daughter seems to have a good understanding of how things work between boys and girls who are dating. She understood that some guys leave girlfriends who don't go as fast as they would like. Future talks can focus on how to find quality guys who share similar values (or as the daughter said, "morals").

4

Friends for Life

Talking about Healthy Relationships

My son had a kid in his class who was selling pot in eighth grade. He told me about it but wouldn't tell me who it was. He was so loyal to this boy I couldn't convince my son to let me intervene. He said he would not "rat on a friend."
—Patrice, mother of two, Seattle, Washington

My daughter's best friend was so thin I thought she was anorexic. It turned out she was bulimic too and trying to convince my daughter that this was a cool way not to gain weight. I was terrified of this girl's influence over my daughter but I didn't know what to do.
—Beatrice, mother of two, San Antonio, Texas

There were three boys in my son's inner circle and they did everything together. Suddenly they stopped including him and he was crushed. —Debra, mother of two, Portland, Oregon

Friendships are at the center of most children's lives. A few kids are happy loners, but most kids want to be accepted and if they are not, they are miserable. Their concern starts early and becomes intense during middle school, where, unhappily, cliques are usually tight and cruel. Who is popular? Who is unpopular? Somehow everyone in the class knows who is in, out, cool, or geeky. High-status kids are insecure about keeping their position; low-status kids usually know it and face it with bravado or misery. Even kids who manage to escape all this rating and ranking become unhappy if they can't find at least one or two really close friends who make them feel worthy of friendship. The quality of these friendships and the ability to be a good friend may be the most important aspects of your child's day-to-day life.

This chapter explains the role friendship plays in life, the difference between a true friend and a false friend, and how having and being a good friend is important to a person's well-being. This sounds straightforward, but it can be hard for children to comprehend. Most of them are so hungry for acceptance, they may cling to a friend—even one who demonstrates bad behavior. It can be frustrating and scary for parents to see their child hanging out with someone who demonstrates risky behavior or unethical conduct. It is easy to derail these undesirable friendships when a child is very young, but the older a child gets, the more he will vigorously defend his right to hang out with whomever he wants to.

As early as possible, children should be taught that friendships have to be evaluated according to some standard, and that some friendships are good and supportive, while others are not healthy and should not be continued.

Children also have to be given some rules about how to be a friend and what kind of conduct they are expected to demonstrate with both same-sex and opposite-sex friends. They need to know what healthy friendships look like: that these are friendships that teach, and demand, trust, respect, and loyalty.

Preparing for the Talk

This talk opens the door for ongoing conversations about finding, keeping, and in some cases retiring friends. In this talk you will let your child know

- what makes a relationship a good friendship.
- what it takes to be a good friend and have a healthy relationship.
- that a person you think is a friend may not be.
- that there can be more important issues at stake than loyalty to a friend's wishes.
- that there are family rules about how friends are to be treated.

What You Can Expect from This Talk

After this talk your child will

- be able to distinguish between a healthy and unhealthy relationship.
- know when he is being a good friend.
- know when he should not be loyal to a friend in order to honor your family rules and values.
- know how to apply the basic rules of friendship to romantic relationships.

How Do You Define a Healthy Relationship?

Relationships should be an easy topic to talk about because your child has already had some experience finding, keeping, and possibly fighting with and losing friends. As your child grows, relationships can become more complicated and textured.

Each family has its own unique idea about what a friend is—and this would be a good time to think about what kinds of friends you have and how you have role-modeled friendship. Some family members call a casual acquaintance a friend. Other family members would not think of calling someone a friend unless they had known the person for a long time and had shared many intimate thoughts or experiences. Where does your family fit in on this continuum?

My husband and I have very different ideas about what a best friend is. I have girlfriends I talk with almost every day, and he has two "best friends" who live in the same city we do and he sees them maybe four times a year, maximum.

—Eve, mother of four, Portland, Oregon

I used to be the kind of person who had a lot of acquaintances until I realized what I really needed were real friends. Now I have a handful of very intimate friends I would trust with my life, but no acquaintances.

—Kevin, father of two, New York City

Influence of the Media

Relationships are a common theme on television and in movies. But often, these portrayals of relationships, whether platonic or romantic, create unreal expectations about the elements of healthy relationships. TV dramatizes relationships—shows are often about betrayal, rejection, or a kind of loyalty or heroism that few people experience.

In situation comedies, the message transmitted is that it's great to be in some special types of relationships. In these shows it's difficult to differentiate between the casual friends, the pals, the intimate trusted friendships, the eccentric buddies, and the lovers.

TV sometimes provides good moral lessons about loyalty and trust. But it also serves up a surplus of artificial crises with little intimate conversation. Often the humor is based on the inability to communicate. How often are friendships tested by real crisis? How often do people in daytime soap operas and nighttime dramas stay in the unhealthiest of relationships?

These programs offer mixed messages, making it hard to know what our children are taking from them. Of course, one way to find out is by asking them how healthy the relationships are they see in the movies or on TV. Or you can ask them about their favorite programs: Why are the friends on *Friends* friends? Take a popular show and ask your child how the people on that show demonstrated true friendship. Were there any things in the show that real friends wouldn't or shouldn't do? Can your child think of TV programs with friendships that model what they would want in a friend? Have her tell you what appeals to her in these shows and what she thinks the messages are. It will help you know if a specific program is good for your child and if the show's messages about friendship reflect your values.

Pressure from Peers

Most children worry about being accepted. One of the ways they "know" they are okay is if they are adopted by a group of friends whom they admire. No matter how many friends your child has, she'll probably do almost anything to keep them. The child who has only a couple of good friends may be even more afraid of disrupting those friendships for fear he will be alone in the world. Still, as important as friendship is, the standards for conduct are hazy. Kids may not know when they have a true friend—or when they are being undermined.

Ask your child who is friends with whom at school. Ask your child what the standards for friendship are and try to get a sense, before you start the talk, of what kind of pressure he feels to be friends with certain people. Ask if there are kids who don't have any friends at school and what happens to them. School can be a very intimidating and threatening place, and having a friend at school can mean the difference between feeling good about life and feeling awful.

Giving Your Child the Big Picture

Poll after poll shows that most people's number one ambition is to marry someone who will be their "best friend." The idea of a best friend is so strong that it starts almost as soon as kids can talk and it is transferred into their ambitions for a lifetime partner. The deep need for a best friend sometimes keeps a person from seeing the reality of how a given friendship is working.

It may puncture the vision of lifetime friendship, but it is helpful to tell children that it is unusual for most friendships to go the distance to adulthood. People change and friendships adjust. Kids need to know that their friendships will change over time and that it is not dishonorable to withdraw from a friendship you're unhappy with. It may be necessary to modify a friendship if the two of you start to have different ethics and values about life. We can teach our children that it's important to learn to support a friendship, but it's also important to know when a friendship needs to end and new ones need to begin.

Some people call this "retiring a friend." Sometimes you change, sometimes the friend changes, sometimes you learn something about the other person that makes that friendship no longer attractive. When a child's friendship ends, she may take it as proof of her own unworthiness. She may also think she'll never make another close friend. Assure your child that you appreciate how important these friendships are and that evaluating friends is a normal and ongoing process.

One of my kids' friends was always physically aggressive with him—bullying him in front of others and pushing him around. My son referred to him as his best friend. I asked him, "Are you sure he's your best friend?" I think it might have got my son thinking about what a best friend is supposed to be.

—Bonnie, mother of three, Ithaca, New York

From my kids' perspective, their friendships appear immortal. I have to remind myself that their relationships should not be dismissed as something fleeting or trivial.

—Lorna, mother of three, Syracuse, New York

Buddies vs. Intimate Relationships

There is a lot of room for misunderstanding about friendship. Some people think that if you start up a conversation on the Internet, you suddenly have a new friend. Other people call a person a friend only if they've known the person for years. And a few people demand such a high level of attention, loyalty, and service that they may have only one or two people who meet their high standards for what a friend should be. It's very possible that one person might call someone a friend, while the other person would be surprised to hear it. Some people have different categories for relationships: some people fit in the "friendship" category, and a relationship that is romantic is in another category called "mate." If we look back at ourselves, we can see how our own ideas about friendship have changed from when we were in middle school or high school.

Up until I was in middle school I used to think of about everyone I knew as a friend. The word "friend" really meant "classmate."
—Rita, mother of two, Seattle, Washington

When I entered high school I had a group of friends and we all thought of ourselves as buddies. But I felt alone because I never let them know something very important about me—I was attracted to other guys. Maybe, rightly or wrongly, I thought my buddies would not accept me.
—Robert, Orlando, Florida

Everyone defines friendship in a different way. But it seems that in general, boys and girls evaluate friendships in different ways. Here are some insights from parents who comment on how males and females perceive friendship.

Relationships require maintenance. Girls usually require a lot of inter-action, by phone and in person, or they do not think of the person as a good friend. Boys may see each other a lot in informal ways in their usual hangout but usually don't require a lot of communication to feel close.
—Jenni, mother of two, San Antonio, Texas

I think that intimacy means sharing personal information. Most girls don't feel close unless they tell each other secrets and can confide in each other about classmates and their looks and love interests. Most boys seem to be different. My son doesn't share confidences or secrets with his male friends.

—Susie, mother of three, Memphis, Tennessee

Sometimes boys can feel uncomfortable if a male friend is truly unburdening himself and talking honestly about his vulnerabilities. It baffles me why my son and his male friends don't seem to be able to have talks about feelings.

—Emma, mother of one, Seattle, Washington

If boys feel the need to share personal information, they often turn to females. In fact a lot of the long, soulful telephone conversations in middle and high school are between male and female platonic friends.

—Tonya, mother of two, Portland, Oregon

Healthy Relationships and Sexuality

Pretty early on in your child's life his friends may begin sharing "facts" about sex and models for sexual tactics. As early as fourth grade, children talk about sex together. And while most parents are extremely uncomfortable with the thought, it is common for sexual experimentation to occur between same- and/or opposite-sex friends. These can be insignificant events or powerful influential experiences. We need to think about how friends talk about sexuality and influence each other's sexual behavior. We need to know more about what is happening between friends so that we can advise our children, interpret advances or situations they have observed, and be available for advice or help.

Much of the early sex talk I heard was rumors. Kids traded versions of information about sex they have heard, or things they have seen on television or the Internet. And some children passed around some very unkind rumors about one another.

—May, mother of three, Yakima, Washington

Kids talked about what they see or what they think they've seen. They were not sympathetic to some students who were ahead (or behind) the curve of what was sexually acceptable in their peer group.

—Lynn, mother of two, Denver, Colorado

I had a good male friend in high school who fixed me up with a friend of his. I didn't know he had told his friend that I would "put out." This guy thought I was easy and was genuinely surprised when I resisted and cried. Fortunately, he let me go—but the real shock was that my friend set me up like that in the first place.

—Sharon, mother of three, Chicago, Illinois

When Relationships Become Sexual

This talk can include a discussion of friendships that turn sexual. As a child grows older and becomes sexually attracted to others, we want him or her to know how to handle that and how to apply the standards of friendship to that relationship, too. It's important to ask the question, "Does this person have the qualities I look for in a friend?" Realistically, when your child experiences infatuation, the rational thinking process may take a backseat to passion and excitement. But getting your child to talk about friendship and to identify the qualities found in a good friend will serve your child for a lifetime. Starting out, your child might not even imagine that a date could be expected to show the same honesty and loyalty as a platonic friend. But it is our job as parents to integrate the values and ethics of friendship into the context of relationship so that our children know that romance does not exempt a person from ethical and responsible behavior.

Different Families: Different Values

Different families have different values about friendship. To some, a friend is someone to do things with. To others, a friend is someone to share intimate thoughts with and to depend on emotionally. How is someone a good friend? This question is very important when you are faced with a friend in crisis. Consider the following situations and the variety of ways to respond as a friend.

A young woman has a boyfriend who calls her names and hits her. The woman tells her best friend about the abuse.

What does a good friend say at a time like this? Some parents encourage their children to support friends in need, while others say it's best not to get involved in other people's personal lives. Consider the variety of potential responses. Some friends would tell the woman to leave the boyfriend; others might tell her to have him arrested. Some friends might not want to get involved at all—even offering advice might feel like an invasion of privacy. Others might ask the young woman whether she provoked him. If the young woman who was hit has no intention of leaving her boyfriend, a friend might ask the young woman to seek counseling. If the friend knows that the young woman comes from a family where the parents were abusive to one another, a friend might also want to point that out.

■

A young man is very depressed and unhappy. He drinks a lot to deal with his painful feelings. His friend doesn't question his drinking.

Being a good friend to someone who is abusing alcohol or other drugs isn't easy. Some parents identify alcohol and drug abuse as a serious problem that should be discussed between friends. Some parents would tell their children that encouraging a friend with an alcohol problem to seek help is very caring, noting that if a good friend doesn't help a friend with alcohol abuse, then who will? Other parents would say that broaching the topic of alcohol abuse is crossing a personal boundary.

■

Two young people have been in a relationship throughout high school. Now in college, they are engaged but not getting along the way they used to. One asks the other to go to couples counseling to see how to improve their relationship. The other says no.

When you are engaged to someone it should mean that there is a deep friendship. And even the best friendships can hit serious roadblocks. The question presented here is, how do friends help one another solve a serious interpersonal problem? Some parents would say that counseling is useless and they should just decide if they love each other or not. If not, they should break up. Some parents would want these young people to go to counseling to see if they are still right for each other. Some parents might say that a refusal to go to couples counseling does not speak well for the relationship.

Last-Minute Checkups before the Talk

This is a good time to think about your first relationships and friendships in elementary, middle, and high school. Think back to your childhood to share your experiences.

- When you were a child, did you consider yourself popular?
- Did you have friends that you could trust and best friends who didn't disappoint you?
- Would you have done just about anything a close friend asked, even if it meant disobeying your parents' wishes?
- Did you do things that you later regretted because of a friend's suggestion?
- Did you ever stay in a relationship that you felt was unhealthy?

As a parent, do you feel your child has healthy relationships?

- Have you asked your child about her friendships and how they are going?

Do you have any stories that you could share with your child? For example:

- A friendship that meant a lot to you when you were your child's age
- Something that happened between you and a friend that told you it was time to end the friendship
- Something that told you that it was time to get out of an unhealthy relationship

- A time you had a friendship that turned into a romantic relationship or a romantic relationship that really needed to be a friendship, but wasn't

What Are Your Family Rules?

Do you have family rules about friendships and relationships? If not, this is a good time to think about them. This talk highlights the following activities:

- A friend excludes another friend.
- A boy hears a friend being spoken of unkindly.
- A girl is not sure if she can trust a friend with a problem.
- A boy is not sure if he can trust a friend with a problem.
- A friend influences his friend to break a family rule.

The idea is to talk about what kinds of behaviors your child expects of friends. The stories allow you to discuss a range of topics, including peer pressure, trust and intimacy, self-esteem, ethics, and honesty, and the influence friends have on one another. Discussing these situations will give you an opportunity to share your family rules about friendships, acceptable behavior between friends, and what one can and should expect from friends.

The Talk

Introduce the Talk

You are almost ready to have the talk about relationships with your child. You might want to review the stories in this chapter and the sample talk to make sure you are comfortable with talking about this subject. Remember, your goal is to listen as well as to speak. You want to find out what your child's opinions and values are and give your child a clear picture of family values, guidelines, and rules.

Find some time to be alone with your child. If you had trouble convincing your child to talk last time, consider experimenting with the setting and time of the talk.

Ask your child for a few minutes and present the question, "What makes a person a good friend?"

Some kids are going to say, "I don't know." You can add, "Do you like your friends?" "What do you like about them?" or simply, "What is a friend?" Follow up with, "What is it that makes your friend someone who is fun to spend time with?"

Even if you just get a response like, "My friend is fun," it's a good beginning. Go over the following terms to see if you and your child share similar definitions.

Review These Words

Please review the terms in this section. Discussing all of them with your child is optional. You know what's appropriate for your child's age and maturity level. Keep in mind that more than likely, even the youngest children have heard these words on TV.

acquaintance: someone you have met a few times, or see quite often, but have not gotten to know very well. An acquaintance may or may not be someone to whom you feel close enough to go to for help.

betrayal: when someone you trust misleads you, lies to you, or in some other way is disloyal. A betrayal is a broken commitment, whether spoken or unspoken.

buddy: someone you can hang out with but who is more like an acquaintance than a friend.

false friend: someone who pretends to like you, but in reality is not loyal or trustworthy.

friendless: having no friends.

friendship: a relationship based on trust and shared interests and experiences. A friend's interest in you and loyalty are constant and predictable. A friend is someone you feel good being around and who likes being around you.

intimacy: a feeling of closeness between close friends or romantic partners. People who are intimate usually tell each other private things that are very important to them that they tell very few other people.

loyalty: a commitment to a friend. A loyal friend protects his friend's feelings, interests, and reputation. A loyal friend would never desert a friend in a time of need or say something bad about a friend.

platonic friend: someone you like but do not think of in a romantic or sexual way.

trust: a feeling that you can count on the other person to do what they say they will, and to be who they seem to be.

Why Is Talking about Friendship Important?

Ask your child whether she thinks talking about friendships is important. Here are some reasons you might want to offer. Talking about friendships

- gives you the skills to make close and reliable friendships.
- helps you spot unhealthy relationships.
- helps us clarify our family rules about how we treat people and how we deserve to be treated by others.
- helps point out that the same standards used for friendship in a platonic relationship should also be applied to a romantic one.

The Stories

In the next part of the talk, you'll be reading short stories to your child and discussing them together. You don't have to read all of them. Pick the ones that you think are appropriate. The stories are very simple. Feel free to embellish them, adding details that you think might make them more believable. For example, some parents change the gender of the characters to make a story mirror their own families.

The Story about Including and Excluding

Read this story to your child. It gives you the opportunity to discuss how friends treat one another.

"Two boys have been neighbors and friends for years. They are spending some time together at the park and spot a new boy, another classmate. One of the boys invites the new boy to come over to his house to have dinner and watch a video. He doesn't invite his old friend and neighbor."

Ask these questions of your child:

- What is the new boy thinking?
- What is the boy who was not invited over thinking?
- What is the boy who excluded his friend thinking?

Now that your child has completed this scenario, ask the following questions:

- Is it polite for a person to invite someone over to his home in front of others who are not invited?
- How can we make an invitation without making others feel excluded?
- How does it feel to be excluded?
- Do friends need to be sensitive to their friends' feelings?
- Is there anything wrong with two people wanting to spend time together without others?

Clarify Your Family's Values

Ask the following question of your child as a way of sharing your values about friendship. We have included a number of potential responses from children to help you formulate your own.

Ask your child: "When you are going to do something with a friend and you want to invite another person to join the two of you, should you ask your friend if it's okay to invite the third person?"

Child: I don't know.

Parent: It's usually a good idea.

Child: My friends don't care if others join us.

Parent: Are you sure? How about if your friend was looking forward to spending some time alone with you or wanted to talk about something important and private?

Child: We don't talk about stuff like that.

Parent: All friendships are different. Some people enjoy having lots of friends around all the time. Other people like to spend time one-on-one, rather than in groups. Sometimes when people want to talk about serious things they prefer to confide in one special friend in private. What kind of person are you?

Ask your child: "When a new person is added to a group of friends, can someone in the group feel jealous?"

Child: I don't know.

Parent: Sometimes people can feel bad when they think they might be losing their place as a person's best friend. Have you ever felt this way?

Child: No.

Parent: Friends are really important and if it looks like a person is losing a friend, it's upsetting. But sometimes when someone gets a new friend it's just a temporary change or not really a change at all. Anybody new to the group might be the most interesting person around for a while. Then things might settle down and return to normal.

Ask your child: "Do you have a friend who got upset with you when you got friendly with someone else? Or do you know someone who was dropped as a friend by someone else?"

Child: Yes, I know kids who were dumped by other people.

Parent: The idea of dumping someone sounds like someone was put in the trash heap. Good friends don't dump one another. If you see someone do that to someone else, then that person could do that to you. Maybe that's a person who doesn't know how to be a good friend.

Ask your child: "How do you want to be treated as a friend?"

Child: I'm not sure what you mean.

Parent: I think you deserve someone who keeps in touch with you and explains if they don't see you when they normally do. A friend doesn't talk about you behind your back and sticks up for you if someone says bad things about you. A friend is someone you can trust with secrets. Friends are dependable and show up when they say they will. They keep commitments. Have I forgotten anything?

Ask your child: "How do you treat a good friend?"

Child: How should I?

Parent: Well, all the things that you want as a friend are the things that you should do for someone else. Treat people as you want to be treated. It's the Golden Rule.

The Story about Loyalty and Friendship

Read this story to your child. It gives you the opportunity to discuss the role loyalty plays in friendship.

"A teenage boy and a teenage girl have been friends for many years. One day at school the boy hears some guys talking about the

girl. An older guy is telling some friends about how the girl is having sex with lots of guys. The friend knows this is not true but does not know if he should say something to defend her."

Ask these questions of your child:

- What is the teenage boy (who is the friend to the girl) thinking?
- Is he defending his friend? Why or why not?
- What is the guy who is spreading the false rumors thinking?
- Why would this guy be saying such things about the girl?

Now that your child has completed this scenario, ask the following questions:

- Does this kind of situation happen at school? If so, how often?
- What happens if the boy stands up for his friend?
- What happens if the boy does not stand up for his friend?
- Should the teenage boy tell his friend what was being said about her?
- Have you ever been in a situation like this? If so, what did you do?

The Story about a Girl Trusting a Friend

Read this story to your child. It gives you a chance to discuss how true friends can trust one another.

"A teenage girl has a serious problem. (You can make up any problem that seems serious and realistic.) She needs to talk to someone about it. She has some people whom she spends time with but doesn't know if she can trust them with her personal problem. She is not sure her friends will help her. She's about to meet with one friend but is not sure what to say. She is feeling very stressed."

- What is the girl thinking?
- What is the girl saying?
- What is the friend thinking?
- What is the friend saying?

Now that your child has completed this scenario, ask the following questions:

- How can the girl decide what to do?
- What's the worst thing that could happen if she discussed her problem with her friend?
- What's the best thing that could happen if she discussed her problem with her friend?
- How can a person know if a friend can be trusted to keep personal information private?

The Story about a Boy Trusting a Friend

Read this story to your child. It provides an opportunity to discuss how true friends can trust one another.

"A teenage boy has a serious problem. (You can make up any problem that seems serious and realistic.) He needs to talk to someone about it. He has some people whom he spends time with but doesn't know if he can trust them with his personal problem. He is not sure his friends will help him. He is about to meet with one friend but is not sure what to say. He is feeling very stressed."

- What is the boy thinking?
- What is the boy saying?
- What is the friend thinking?
- What is the friend saying?

Now that your child has completed this scenario, ask the following questions:

- How can the boy decide what to do?
- What's the worst thing that could happen if he discussed his problem with his friend?
- What's the best thing that could happen if he discussed his problem with his friend?
- How can a person know if a friend can be trusted to keep personal information private?

Clarify Your Family's Values

Ask the following question of your child as a way of sharing your values about healthy relationships. We have included a number of potential responses from children to help you formulate your own.

Ask your child: "What do you think about passing on rumors about someone's sexual behavior?"

Child: That's just something that people do.

Parent: I know that other people spread rumors, but what do you think you should do?

Child: I don't know.

Parent: What would happen if you said, "She's my friend, don't talk about her that way when she's not here to defend herself"?

Child: If I stand up for her, the group might turn on me and start telling rumors about me.

Parent: But wouldn't you want a friend to stand up for you even if it caused some people to be cruel to her?

Child: I can take care of myself and so can my friends.

Parent: Maybe some people can "take care of themselves," but some people really suffer for it. People can feel hurt or embarrassed or angry when they're the subject of rumors. Rumors can hurt a person's life. In fact, if someone at school tried to damage your reputation by spreading stories about your sex life, it might be time for me to visit the school principal. You have legal rights at school. And I would want to protect you.

Child: I would never want you to start something like that.

Parent response: I wouldn't want to do something like that either, but that's what's happened at some schools when things got out of hand. I understand that you might want to find a way to report on someone but remain anonymous. I felt that way when I was in school. What's important is that school is supposed to be a safe place to learn and feel good about yourself. Our family rule is that if anyone spreads a rumor about you, I want you to tell me about it. I also think that a good friend doesn't spread rumors and stands up for their friend's reputation.

The Story about a Friend Influencing a Friend

Read this story to your child. It gives you an opportunity to discuss how friends can help each other be honest and keep commitments.

"A teenage girl told her mom that she is going to the library to study with her boyfriend. The boyfriend convinced his girlfriend to instead go to a party. At the party, there are no adults and almost everyone is either kissing or heading into bedrooms and closing the doors. The girl knows her parents would not approve of her being there."

Ask these questions of your child:

- What is the girlfriend thinking?
- What is the boyfriend thinking?
- What is the girlfriend saying?
- What is the boyfriend saying?

Now that your child has completed this scenario, ask the following questions:

- What should the girl do?
- What should the boy do?
- Why would the boyfriend try to convince his girlfriend to come to this kind of party knowing that she would be breaking her word to her mother?
- In this situation, is the boy being a good friend to the girl?

Clarify Your Family's Values

The following question helps you share your values about how a friend can influence a person to break family rules.

Ask your child: "If a friend wants you to do something that you know is against the house rules, how can you disagree with your friend without hurting the friendship?"

Child: I don't know.

Parent: You can tell your friend that you would like to do what she's suggested, but if you break the house rules the consequences would be so great that it wouldn't be worth it. Or you can suggest an alternative to what your friend suggested. You can say that you made a promise and, just like you keep your promises to your friend, you keep your promises to your parents. You want me to be the kind of person who keeps promises, right?

Child: Maybe.

Parent: You can say, "No," and tell them that a good friend doesn't put pressure on people. You can say, "I'll know what you think of me by how you support my right to make my own decision."

Child: I don't talk that way with my friends.

Parent: You can tell them that you have already been caught breaking the rules once and the consequences were huge. You don't want to deal with the consequences from your parents.

The Bare Minimum: A Quick Quiz for Kids

Ask your child the following questions to assess her knowledge of healthy relationships.

1. Can you give me one example of somebody being a good friend?
   Sample answers:
- A person calls or comes over regularly and shows you that she enjoys spending time with you.
- A person stands up for you at school when you are being picked on.
- A person makes you feel good about yourself when you are together.
- A person cares about your feelings (especially if you lost the game or got a bad grade).
2. Can you give me an example of somebody being a false friend?
   Sample answers:
- Someone who is nice to your face but talks about you behind your back.
- Someone who is nice to you only when she wants something from you (like getting invited to a party, getting on a sports team, or borrowing money).
- A person who does not do for you what you do for them. You always give and they always take.
3. How can you tell if you are in an unhealthy relationship?

Sample answers:
- Because you feel bad when you are with the person. He makes you feel less confident about yourself.
- Because you don't really believe she stands up for you all the time.
- Because you aren't sure your friend really likes and admires you.

Talk about Your Family Rules

What is our family rule about unacceptable behavior from friends?

Sample answers:
- If they hit me I immediately leave and get help if I need it. I tell you what happened and we decide together what we should do about it.
- Sometimes people do a certain amount of joking, but if someone is serious and calls me a bad name, or keeps on calling me something I don't like, I stop being friends with that kid.
- We don't stay friends with people who lie, especially about important things.

What is our family rule about how we treat our friends?

Sample answers:
- We are loyal to our friends. We defend them . . .
- We treat our friends as we would wish to be treated.
- We never take our friends for granted.

- We do not break an appointment with a friend except in an emergency.
- If we have had to disappoint a friend, we apologize.

After the Talk

A Moment to Reflect

Take a few moments to reflect on the talk you just had with your child. How do you feel about it? You've given your child a lot of information about relationships, the healthy and unhealthy kinds. More than likely your child has friends and this talk may give them an opportunity to review those relationships. It's possible that she may see that the person she thought was her "best friend" is actually not much more than a casual buddy or maybe even a false friend. On the other hand, she may not relate this talk to her real life, so you need to reinforce the messages about friends by observing your child and her friends—looking at behaviors that do or do not live up to your standards for a friendship. When you see examples of kindness or cruelty, talk with your child as soon as you can.

Warning Signs

The talks may also reveal potential problems about your child's friendships.

If your child has no close friends or is being victimized by someone he calls a friend, that's a serious situation. There may be cause for concern if your child

- never brings friends home.
- is never invited to a friend's home or to play with others.
- appears depressed for more than a few weeks.
- constantly tries to avoid going to school or complains of being all alone there.
- always seems to defer to a boyfriend or girlfriend.
- always seems to dominate a boyfriend or girlfriend.

In any of these situations, you need to find out what is happening. If, after your discussion, you feel your child needs more help than you can offer alone, go see the child's teacher and ask how your child is doing in the school environment. See if your child has a friend at school or fits into any group at all. You might consider asking the school counselor for advice or for a referral to a child psychologist.

Finding Help

If your child doesn't have any serious psychological difficulties but still isn't having any luck forming the kind of friendships you would like him to have in school, you may be able to help him form friendships outside of school. Kids can create some quality friendships by joining a youth group at church or temple, becoming involved in a sports league, or going to a summer camp that is organized around the things they like the best. A serious student might have a whole new place in the peer group at a computer camp; a child who is a talented musician has many fine music camps to choose from, some of which award scholarships. Sometimes it's just a matter of supporting your child until the next grade level or new school year provides a new start.

It is important, as parents know, that your child not only has friends but also has friends that meet your family values about behavior and character. Keep reinforcing the "good friend/false friend" distinction so that a child who has few friends or no friends knows that a good friend is worth waiting for. Acknowledge also that sometimes there are long periods of time when just having casual acquaintances or buddies is enough. Sometimes it takes a long time before people form intimate, trustworthy friendships. Cultivating and maintaining quality friendships (including romantic relationships) is a lifelong process.

Success Stories

Congratulations again! You have made it through another talk. No matter how well a talk goes, you have accomplished a lot by raising questions and concerns. At the very least you have made certain distinctions about friendship that your child will remember and you have had the chance to share your values on the standards for friendship in your household. A mom in Portland talked about how the talk helped her daughter understand that some of the kids she'd been calling "friends" weren't being very nice at all. The daughter admitted she hadn't looked at those friendships too closely, and she and her mom agreed that it might be better to spend time alone, or with family, than with false friends.

Sample Talks
Between Parents and Children

Before you begin your first talk, you might want to read this sample conversation. The following are excerpts of actual talks between parents and children.

Discussing the Story about Including and Excluding

Participants: a mother and her eleven-year-old son.

Mom: Okay, here is a story. Two boys have been neighbors and friends for years. They are spending some time together at the park and spot a new boy, another classmate. One of the boys invites the new boy to come over to his house to have dinner and watch a video. He doesn't invite his old friend and neighbor.

What is the new boy thinking?

Son: "Hey, a new friend. Maybe he can come over and we can have a good time."

Mom: What is the boy who was not invited over thinking?

Son: He's thinking, "Why should he be my friend? He left me out. What kind of friend is he?"

Mom: What is the boy who excluded his friend thinking?

Son: "Why did I do that? Now we aren't going to be friends. I should have done something."

Mom: Like what?

Son: I don't know. (He laughs.)

Mom: Is it polite for a person to invite someone over to his home in front of others who are not invited?

Son: No. He should have called him on the phone or told him privately.

Mom: How does it feel to be excluded?

Son: Not very good.

Mom: Do friends need to be sensitive to their friends' feelings?

Son: Yes they do. It's only the right thing to do.

Mom: Is there anything wrong with two people wanting to spend time together without others?

Son: No.

Mom: Anything else you want to say about this subject?

Son: No.

Lessons Learned from This Sample Talk

The mom and son had a productive, brief talk about being polite. The son appears to share the same values as his mother about including and excluding people. Future talks can focus on how friendships might change as he gets older and on how to find friends who share similar values about respecting others' feelings.

Discussing the Story about Loyalty and Friendship

Participants: a mother and her eleven-year-old son.

Mom: A teenage boy and a teenage girl have been friends for many years. One day, at school, the boy hears some guys talking about the girl. An older guy is telling some friends about how the girl is having sex with lots of guys. The friend knows this is not true but does not know if he should say something to defend her. What do you think the teenage boy is thinking?

Son: Gee, why are those boys saying that about her. If someone said that about one of my friends I wouldn't accept it.

Mom: What would you say to these guys? Remember, these are older guys, like, you are in sixth grade and these are eighth-graders.

Son: Sometimes you really don't know what to do (Pause) 'cause they could kick your butt any time. But, to be nice about it, say, "That's not nice. Why would you talk about her like that?" And they'd say, "Mind your own business." And I probably would.

Mom: The story says you know it's not true.

Son: I know. It's not right to say lies, but you really can't go up to them and start bossing them around. But you can say something. You can say what you need to say.

Mom: So you would defend your friend?

Son: Yeah.

Mom: With your words?

Son: Yeah, work it out orally.

Mom: And if they threatened you?

Son: I'd tell someone.

Mom: So you'd defend her, say it wasn't true, she never did that. What would you say, exactly?

Son: "Hey, why are you saying that? She didn't do that with all those guys. I don't think that's cool. Lying isn't going to get you anywhere."

Mom: Okay. What is the guy who is spreading the false rumors thinking?

Son: He thinks he's funny. He doesn't care.

Mom: Why would this guy be saying such things about the girl?

Son: Maybe he knows her or her older sister, maybe. Or maybe he's looking for trouble.

Mom: Do you think it has anything to do with him?

Son: Maybe if she does have an older sister and they got into a fight, instead of starting rumors about her, he's starting them about the younger sister.

Mom: Could something have happened between the girl and him? Something that would make him spread false rumors about her?

Son: They may have had a fight.

Mom: So he would be doing this for what reason?

Son: Get revenge.

Mom: Does this kind of situation happen at school?

Son: Yeah. Lots of times. Not about having sex with guys, but there's gossip about other people.

Mom: This happens a lot?

Son: Well, not a lot. It's a nice school.

Mom: False rumors like this sometimes are spread?

Son: Yeah. Some people say stuff occasionally, "Oh, yeah, did you know that such-and-such slapped her and called her names?" and what really happened was that he was trying to calm her down and work it out with her and he didn't like her anymore, but he was trying to work it out but then he told a friend something misleading.

Mom: What happens if the boy stands up for his friend?

Son: Most likely he'll get pushed around, but, you know, they may just ignore him and walk away.

Mom: What happens if the boy does not stand up for his friend?

Son: It could turn out miserable. If her parents hear, her friends hear, maybe if she has a boyfriend and he hears.

Mom: What could it do to her reputation? Remember what I told you about me when I was your age and a rumor got started and it wasn't even true? How would you feel if you heard a rumor and you didn't open your mouth because you were afraid?

Son: I'd be sad and put down by myself, because we are friends and I'd feel ashamed of myself.

Mom: Should the teenage boy tell his friend what was being said?

Son: No, no, no. Well, if she's real understanding and she wouldn't get mad, you'd tell her.

Mom: Doesn't she have a right to know? Maybe she'd want to go confront the guy about it.

Son: She might want to confront him or get her mom to confront him. I wouldn't tell you because it doesn't have to do with me, it's her.

Mom: This may be one of those things that you are old enough to try and handle on your own at this point. Not that you can't ask your parents if you ever want to, but when you are a teenager, sometimes you have to handle things on your own. You probably wouldn't want your mom to call her mom unless this was really getting out of hand.

Have you ever been in a situation like this?

Son: Sort of, when one friend said something about another friend, and I said, "What are you doing?"

Mom: So you tried to help out a friend?

Son: I tried to.

Lessons Learned from This Sample Talk

Mom takes a long time to discuss this situation with her son because she really wants to reinforce his defense of his friend. He tells her his limits (he doesn't want to take any punishment), but she helps him look at his conscience and his options. He seems to call upon his better self. Future talks can address his ability to find friends who share his values about friendship and loyalty.

Discussing the Story about a Girl Trusting a Friend

Participants: a mother and her ten-year-old daughter

Mom: "A teenage girl has a serious problem. Maybe it's a problem like, she started to talk to someone on a chat room on the Internet and now that person wants to meet her. She needs to talk to someone about it. She has some people whom she spends time with but doesn't know if she can trust them with her personal problem. She is not sure her friends will help her. She's about to meet with one friend but is not sure what to say. She is feeling very stressed." What is the girl thinking?

Daughter: She's thinking she wants to talk to a friend but she's a little scared, but she still wants to do it. She might get in trouble.

Mom: What is the girl saying when she meets her friend?

Daughter: The girl is saying she wants to meet her friend on the Internet, but she's not sure if he's a robber or crook or anybody bad and, if she did do it, it's not real safe to do it. But she wants to do it really badly even if she knows it's wrong.

Mom: What is the friend thinking?

Daughter: You shouldn't do it because it's not very safe, and also it's really important to stay away from people you meet on the Internet. They could be very bad, you just don't know. They might try and hurt you.

Mom: What is the friend saying? You were just saying what the friend was thinking. Is that what she's saying too?

Daughter: Yeah.

Mom: How can the girl decide what to do?

Daughter: She should listen to her friend's advice and listen to other people, like different people who are friends, and her siblings, and ask advice from her parents.

Mom: What's the worst thing that could happen if she discussed her problem with her friend and what's the best thing that could happen if she discussed her problem with her friend?

Daughter: The best is that she'll listen to her friend and not do it at all and she will be in good hands, and if she needs more advice she should ask her friend or her siblings.

Mom: What's the worst thing?

Daughter: If she could meet the person on the Internet and she could get in big trouble, if the person is trying to murder her.

Mom: How can a person know if a friend can be trusted to keep personal information private?

Daughter: If your friend tries to tell information and spread rumors about you and is not honest about anything, then that's not a good friend. If they are honest and trustworthy and respect you in the way you want to be treated, then that's a good friend.

Lessons Learned from This Sample Talk

Mom and daughter have discussed how to seek advice from a friend, and Mom has checked in on her daughter's values about meeting people she doesn't know. The daughter has shown Mom that she knows the difference between a real friend and a false friend. Future talks can reinforce the daughter's standards as she develops new relationships.

Discussing the Story about a Friend Influencing a Friend

Participants: a mother and her fifteen-year-old daughter.

Mom: A teenage girl told her mom that she is going to the library to study with her boyfriend. The boyfriend convinces his girlfriend to go to a party instead. At the party, there are no adults and almost everyone is either kissing or heading into bedrooms and closing the doors. The girl knows her parents would not approve of her being there. What is the girl thinking?

Daughter: Either the girl knows what she's getting herself into and she wants it, or she might be feeling guilty because she knows her parents are trusting her to do the right thing and she's not doing it.

Mom: What is the boyfriend thinking?

Daughter: The boyfriend probably isn't thinking about the consequences at this point. He's just thinking about having a good time.

Mom: What is the girl saying?

Daughter: The girl wants to stay at the party but her conscience is getting in the way.

Mom: Yes, but what is she saying?

Daughter: I guess, "Yes," she wants to be there.

Mom: What is the boyfriend saying?

Daughter: That he wants to be there too.

Mom: What should the girl do?

Daughter: Well, depending on her morals, she might figure she'll have fun and her parents don't need to know, or she might have her guilt get the best of her and she might leave.

Mom: What should the boy do?

173

Daughter: The boy should be more aware of what he's asking her to do because it could mess up their relationship, because, if the parents found out, they wouldn't trust him in this relationship anymore.

Mom: Why would the boyfriend try to convince his girlfriend to come to this kind of party knowing that she would be breaking her word to her mother?

Daughter: Because he knows the girlfriend's parents don't approve of him having that kind of physical relationship at that age, so the boyfriend wanted to be sneaky about it.

Mom: In this situation, is the boy being a good friend to the girl?

Daughter: No. He's putting pressure on her to do something that would potentially get them in trouble.

Mom: What do you think about this talk?

Daughter: I think we should talk about the perspective of the boy's parents.

Mom: So it's important to talk about what the boy's parents are thinking of this situation also?

Daughter: Yes. If it's against his rules as well, then you might change the way you answer these questions, because then they are both breaking the rules and they are both taking risks and sacrifices for each other, so that is different.

Lessons Learned from This Sample Talk

A very interesting talk. The daughter questioned the assumptions her mom was making: that only one kid was "on trial." Mom should keep her ears open—her daughter thought of the "risks and sacrifices" they were both making, which is a fairly romantic "Romeo and Juliet" idea that Mom might want to discuss. The daughter knows there could be sexual reasons for breaking the rules and so another good dialogue about being "sneaky" and "what is a good boyfriend" and what do teens "owe" their parents would help Mom and daughter better understand one another.

5

Those First Feelings

Talking about Attraction and Love

I remember my first big intense kiss. I was fifteen. I was sure that I was in love and I wanted to get married on the spot.
—Dean, father of two, Seattle, Washington

I always thought infatuation was love. It took me way into my thirties to understand the difference.
—Anne, mother of one, Syracuse, New York

I loved this boy so much in fifth grade—or at least I called it love. He had a baseball cap and he gave it to me and I slept with it every night for years. —Maria, mother of three, Denver, Colorado

The dictionary says that a kiss is "a salute made by touching the lips pressed closely together and suddenly parting them." From this, it is quite obvious that, although a dictionary may know something about words, it knows nothing about kissing.
—Hugh Morris, "The Art of Kissing," 1936

Attraction! That mysterious transformation when your heart beats faster and the whole world lights up. We may think of attraction as an adult phenomenon, but think back and you'll remember that it happens very early, sometimes as early as kindergarten. Your child may already have had a crush on someone, have had someone have a crush on him, or have had a genuine and mutual romantic relationship. And if these things haven't happened already, they're bound to happen sooner or later. Now is the time to start a conversation about them.

In this chapter, we will help you to understand your child's emotional needs and give you a chance to impart some wisdom and house rules about acting on feelings of attraction and love. By now, your child has had talks with you about many important aspects of sexuality: character, boundaries, friendship, and healthy relationships, just to name a few. But now we need to put these issues in the context of love and longing—a big challenge!

In this talk you will help your child understand that she has

- the ability to understand the difference between lust and love.
- the ability to recognize infatuation in himself and others.
- the right to be attracted to someone.
- the right to be affectionate with someone.
- the responsibility to respect the choices and attractions of others.
- the right to feel good about, and in control of, the timing and conditions of sexual behavior.
- the responsibilities that come with sexual behavior.

Preparing for the Talk

This chapter explains how attraction and sexual desire emerge in a young person's life and what information each child needs as she begins to have sexual feelings. Young people need some guidance about how to handle these new feelings. This talk will help your child

- recognize feelings of sexual attraction.
- accept other people's choices of partners.
- decide what boundaries he wishes to have when he is in a relationship.

What You Can Expect from This Talk

It helps to keep in mind what we want you to achieve with your talk. You can add your own objectives, but here are ours:

- To define attraction, sexual attraction, and love
- To illustrate the difference between attraction and love
- To learn how to recognize when someone is interested in you in a romantic or sexual way
- To teach a young person how to recognize and handle her own romantic or sexual feelings
- To encourage respect for other people's needs and desires
- To emphasize everyone's right to say *no* to sex at any time

Background Information about Attraction

We have a special word for attraction when it is experienced by the young—we call it infatuation. In the old days we called it "puppy love." This term is used because we know that, like puppies, the feeling is cute, pure, and uncomplicated. And that, like the puppy stage in a dog's life, it won't last. But feelings of attraction aren't trivial to a child who is experiencing them. In this talk we wish to give all due respect to the intensity of a child's emotions during "first loves." As parents, we must prepare our children for the future and share values and perspectives to help them better navigate these emotional ups and downs.

I started dating again, which can be very strange when one is past forty. I have crushes, but I have the experience of decades to counter the infatuation. This makes a big difference. As a teen, with no experience to fall back on, I was bowled over by infatuations.

—Simone, mother of three, Syracuse, New York

My daughter asked me what the difference between attraction and love is. I said that I viewed attraction as a wonderful experience and mutual attraction can be one of the most powerful feelings a person can experience. It's based on visual chemistry, an excitement in the other person's presence, and often sexual arousal. Love is that deeper sense of connection when feelings of tenderness, commitment, and even sacrifice combine with attraction.

—Judith, mother of two, Portland, Oregon

My first crush was so deep that it scared my parents. I was in seventh grade and all I could think of was this one guy. He asked me out to a movie and my parents wouldn't let me go. I was desperate. I snuck out of the house and went anyhow and then they really grounded me! He finally gave up on me. I was so depressed they ended up taking me to a counselor.

—Amy, mother of one, Orlando, Florida

It was like a roller coaster ride. I remember vividly the emotional highs and lows of my first big crush. I was a freshman in high school, more than twenty years ago, and I remember it like yesterday. She was a senior and very popular. She didn't know I existed.

—Nora, Seattle, Washington

I remember what it was like to be near her my freshman year of high school. When she came through the halls my whole body was at attention. My hands would sweat when she talked to me. I knew she wouldn't take someone like me seriously—she dated the older guys, the guys with cars. But twenty years later, I still think about her every once in a while.

—Rich, father of two, Kansas City, Missouri

He was my best friend. He would have been shocked that I felt more for him than just friendship and I would never have put him in that position. He never knew. But for years, he was the model of everything I wanted in a man. Hard to believe that I could feel so sure at thirteen, but I knew.

—Judy, mother of one, Portland, Oregon

Different Families: Different Attitudes about Attraction

Some children start pairing off even before kindergarten and their parents may find it "cute" that they hold hands and hug each other. Someday those kids may find themselves sexually attracted to each other. But what age is the right age for them to express it? The answer varies from family to family. Some believe a middle school child should be allowed to date. Others think high-schoolers should be given condoms and birth control pills, while other parents expect their children to ignore their peer pressure and avoid romantic relationships.

But as children get older their natural attraction toward one another eventually can become sexual in nature. And sometimes this happens much younger than a parent is comfortable with supporting. Some families do not allow their child to even consider dating until late high school. Others give their children lots of freedom to have private time with a boyfriend or girlfriend, trusting that nothing much will happen. There are some parents who assume their child will have increasingly more sexual experiences with peers, starting in middle school. The following stories from parents illustrate the diverse perspectives:

I was desperately hoping that my daughter would be at least sixteen before she had sexual intercourse. But that was not the way it happened. Her brother dragged her to the kitchen one morning and said to her, "Tell Mom." She squirmed and giggled nervously. I knew something important had happened. Her brother kept pushing her to tell me something. Finally he said, "Tell her what you did with Mike." I immediately asked my daughter, "Did you have sex with Mike?" She denied it several times before admitting it. I felt sad. She was only fourteen.

—Mara, mother of two, San Antonio, Texas

A double standard existed in my family. The girls were forbidden to explore any aspect of sexuality and the boys were actually encouraged to "get some experience."

—Dyana, mother of two, Memphis, Tennessee

My sixteen-year-old son has never told me exactly what he does with girls, but he gives me clues that he's sexually experienced. I think he generally has good sense and I've insisted that he use condoms and not trust women to use birth control no matter what they tell him. I don't want him becoming an unwed father. I've explained that if he gets a girl pregnant, then he will be responsible for that baby for eighteen years. I guess I expected he would be sexual by the time he was sixteen and I think he's being sensible about it.

—Shirelle, mother of two, Atlanta, Georgia

My daughter's life is very busy and structured. She can't go out with a boy alone, only in groups. We might change this after she becomes a junior in high school, but we don't see any reason to change it now. It seems to be working. And she does seem to have developed some nice friends—both girls and boys.

—Pat, mother of two, Portland, Oregon

My fourteen-year-old daughter looks like she's eighteen. She's very beautiful and seems to attract older guys. There was a twenty-year-old who wanted to go out with her. Carmen could not understand what the problem was. I looked at that guy and saw the problem immediately. He was nice and polite, but I'm not going to let a twenty-year-old guy be alone with my fourteen-year-old daughter!

—Alice, mother of three, Dallas, Texas

Influence of the Media

In many ways, TV is the sex educator of our nation's children. Most TV programs are about love, sex, and attraction, not usually in that order. Sitcoms present "loving" couples who in real life would be dysfunctional families. Most of the characters on TV soap operas have the kind of emotional turmoil in their lives that in real life would be unbearable. Talk shows present a parade of abusive husbands, unfaithful wives, and love triangles gone bad. And of course rarely are there any negative consequences shown for sexual behaviors—how often does a character in a sitcom or soap opera get unintentionally pregnant and have a baby? Or have a sexually transmitted disease? It would be a miracle if our children did not have a distorted vision of how "attraction" and "love" fit together.

Pressure from Peers

Kids get an enormous amount of peer pressure to "go out" with someone. This happens so early that it can take a parent's breath away. At some schools, kids start pairing off in sixth grade, and by eighth grade many children feel terrible if they don't have a boyfriend or girlfriend. Of course, from a parent's vantage point, all of this may seem like too much, too soon.

In seventh grade it seemed every one of my son's friends was playing musical chairs with a different girl every week—it seemed the boys' popularity was directly related to how popular they were with girls. Boys were only supposed to have one girlfriend at a time or else they were labeled a "player." And being a player was bad—at least in my son's peer group. My son took these girlfriend relationships very seriously, whether he was in them for weeks or for months.

—Tess, mother of two, Seattle, Washington

My eighth-grade son told me he had a girlfriend. He wanted to bring her to the movies and a school dance. He talked about her for weeks. Finally, when I asked him about this girlfriend, it turned out he had never told her she was a girlfriend, and I suspect she never knew.

—Beatrice, mother of two, Gaithersburg, Maryland

My daughter began a serious relationship in eighth grade that scared us silly. The boy was two years older and it was obviously getting intimate. He was related to her best girlfriend. They all hung out in a group. When we tried to break this thing up, she got hysterical, saying we were trying to ruin her entire social life. It was hard to end this because her friends would cover and lie for her.

—Michelle, mother of two, Portland, Oregon

My thirteen-year-old daughter met a guy at camp. They talk every night on the Internet. She considers him her boyfriend. And I love that. He lives 3,000 miles away.

—David, father of three, El Paso, Texas

Giving Your Child the Big Picture

Attraction is normal, necessary, and wonderful. From a strictly biological point of view, attraction is the way reproduction gets accomplished. But attraction is also a blessing because it is part of the emotional bonding process. It can also be pure and simple lust.

Now love is something else altogether. If attraction is the physical and visual chemistry that arises between two people, love is the deeper emotion that sometimes goes along with attraction and sometimes doesn't. Much has been written about the differences between males and females and their experience with love. A real difference in our culture seems to be that, in general, males are more easily able to separate sexual behavior from the need for any deeper feeling, while females would much prefer sexuality and love to be in the same package.

Indeed, many women cannot or will not have a sexual relationship unless the emotional connection is strong and there is a promise of commitment. Girls need to hear that boys know that girls prize commitment. The result is that some males will sometimes promise more commitment than they can deliver. Later on, girls get more savvy about the difference between love and lust, but in the beginning the difference isn't so clear and shallow promises are easy to believe.

Male and female sexual conduct has been changing and the roles can be reversed. I've seen females who are very sexually aggressive and have a great interest in sex without any attachment to emotion. On the other hand, there are males who would not consider having any kind of sex without having an emotional commitment.

—Brenda, mother of two, Chicago, Illinois

I felt a certain twinge of guilt when I lectured my daughter about not having sex early. She knew my sexual history and knew that I was sexual before marriage. And I had a baby at seventeen, way before I was economically independent. But I felt it was okay to say, "I want you to do as I say not as I did." I tried to explain what I learned from my experience and how I want a different life for her.

—Laura, mother of three, Seattle, Washington

My kids are very bold. The first time I tried to talk about sex the first thing out of my fourth-grade daughter's mouth was, "When did you have sex?"

—May, mother of two, Boise, Idaho

I'm a realist. I understand that my children may not wait until marriage before having sex, but I do want to help them understand the importance of being in a long-term committed relationship before having sex. The conversation about sex is more complex than just saying, "Wait till you are engaged."

—Tim, father of five, Chicago, Illinois

If I were to be totally honest, I have a double standard. The way I feel now is that when it comes to my teenage kids being sexual—for my daughter, never! For my son, anytime. My wife says I'm old-fashioned, but that's my true feeling.

—Casey, father of two, Lafayette, North Carolina

Same-Sex Attraction

Some parents know that same-sex attractions will exist, while others would rather deny the possibility. The fact is, however, that a small but significant number of males and females will know that their attraction is to same-sex, not opposite-sex, friends and acquaintances. They may not verbalize this to friends, to you, or even to themselves. But it's something for every parent to think about. If your child voices any concern or interest in this topic, be supportive of those questions. We must teach our children tolerance so that some other child's life is not made miserable by name-calling, harassment, or violence. We must teach tolerance so our kids know that any question they have about sexual orientation is okay and that we love them for who they are. More and more schools have policies in place to prevent harassment and violence against students (whether it's because of race, gender, or sexual orientation). Of course the enforcement of these policies varies from school to school.

The issues of attraction and love are the same for people whether they are attracted to people of the same or opposite sex. There are so many children who suffer intolerance from peers—and even parents—who spend an enormous amount of their adulthood dealing with that hurt. Our goal is to have open and honest talks that support healthy ways of being sexual and forming committed relationships, no matter what the child's sexual orientation turns out to be.

I was finishing breakfast with my son, who was a freshman in college, when he said he wanted to talk with me. I knew something serious was coming because he never said he wanted to talk. He said that he had fallen in love with someone. I asked what her name was. He said, "Tom." I sat there for a minute not saying anything. It seemed like hours. Then I said, "I know how hard it can be to find a good woman." Looking back, it wasn't the most enlightened response.

—Mario, father of three, New York City

I was very confused. My daughter had a boyfriend from middle school until she was a senior in high school. Then she broke up and was suddenly spending all her time with her best friend, Marie. Finally she told me that Marie and she were not just friends but they were girlfriends. She said that she was in love with Marie the same way she had been with her boyfriend. I wasn't sure what to think or do. It took me some time before I could talk candidly with my daughter about her relationship. I don't know why, but it bothered me that my husband thought it was no big deal.

—Lois, mother of two, Seattle, Washington

My seventeen-year-old nephew was dressing in bright colors, painting his nails, and not playing any of the sports he used to. His mom was concerned that he might be gay. I realized that my sister was confused about the difference between sexual orientation and sex roles—as I'm sure most people are. I told her that just because he might not be acting traditionally macho does not mean he is gay. I also explained that there are lots of guys who act very masculine and are gay. She decided to let her son dress as outlandish as he wants, but she told me that she was not comfortable asking him anything about his attractions.

—Emily, mother of two, Gaithersburg, Maryland

The first time I facilitated a workshop for parents on "talking to your child about sex" there were lots of questions about sexuality. The first question from a mom was, "What is heterosexuality?" There was a lot of confusion about the terms "heterosexual," "homosexual," and "bisexual" mixed with lots of myths about same-sex attraction. There is a lot of information about sexual orientation, sex roles, and workplace and school policies protecting people who are not heterosexual that needs to get out to parents so they can feel comfortable discussing it with their kids.

—Lisa Perry, health educator, Seattle, Washington

Different Families: Different Values

Here are some behaviors that may be experienced differently depending on a person's background and beliefs:

A young man is talking, smiling, and laughing with a young woman. She is returning his interest.

Research shows that males are most likely to interpret female friendliness as a demonstration of sexual interest. Females, on the other hand, are likely to see male sexual interest as just friendliness! This means there's a good chance of each person misinterpreting the other's intentions.

■

A couple is going together and they have begun kissing. The boy starts to touch her breasts, but she resists.

Females are less likely to think that one sexual behavior has to lead immediately to another. Males are much more likely to think that once two people are going out, their new status as "a couple" requires a higher level of sexual involvement.

Last-Minute Checkups before the Talk

Most of us hold strong values about love. This is a good time to think about your childhood experiences with love.

- How did your parents explain attraction and love to you?
- When did you experience your first attraction?
- In elementary, middle, or high school, did you tell your parents about any romantic interests or activity?
- When you were a young person, did you only have romantic and sexual relationships your parent approved of?
- When you were a young person did you understand the difference between sexual attraction and love?
- When you were a young person, did you ever have a romantic or sexual experience that you felt you shouldn't have had?

How do you think your experiences have affected the way you are raising your child?

- How have you explained attraction and love to your child?
- Have you explained same-sex attraction to your child?
- Have you talked about your values and whether your child should have sex before marriage?
- Do you believe that your child should not have sex until he or she is eighteen? (Is this what you did?)
- Do you believe that your child is not likely to be interested in

sex before the age of sixteen? Or eighteen? (Would this be similar to your childhood experience?)

- Do you believe that your child, if he or she were to be sexually
active before age sixteen, should be punished, grounded, or
continually monitored to keep him or her from sexual activity?
(Was this your parents' approach?)

This is a good time to think about the attractions, crushes, infatuations, and loves you had through elementary, middle, and
high school. Do you have any stories that you could share with
your child? For example:

- The first time you kissed
- The first time you fell in love
- An early attraction you felt for someone that turned out to be
wrong for you, and how you discovered that
- How you felt the first time you broke up and how you got
over it

Sensitive Issues

This may be the most difficult talk in the book because it raises
such strong feelings. Both you and your child may be afraid of
what you might learn in this talk. If any of the following scenarios
is difficult for you, don't feel that you have to do them all. You can
always come back to this talk another time. Just don't put it off forever! It may seem premature to discuss sexual relationships with a
fourth-grader more interested in baseball scores than dating. But
remember, your child sees people kissing, dating, and even having
sex on TV every day. Your child also has a private life, and it prob-

ably includes things you don't know about. Who better to provide guidance and clarification than you?

What Are Your Family Rules?

Do you have rules about when young people can be alone and un-chaperoned? Or about when people can become sexual? If not, this is a good time to think about such rules. The talk outlined in this chapter highlights the following situations:

- Two young people meet and are attracted to one another.
- Two young people are kissing.
- Two young people are in the backseat of a car when things get sexual.
- Young people think about going to a dance.

Discussing these stories will give you the opportunity to share your family rules. What would you want your child to do in such a situation? What are your expectations? Before the talk, think about what rules you want to communicate to your child. At the end of the talk, you will have the chance to review the rules together.

The Talk

Introduce the Talk

You are almost ready to have the talk with your child about attraction. Take a deep breath. Begin by telling your child, "I'd like to talk with you about attraction and love." Be prepared for your son's jaw to drop and your daughter to ask whether you are on drugs, although some kids will be enthusiastic.

You can explain to your child, "Attraction can be more than something physical. Sometimes people are attracted to someone because of their personality, sense of humor, or intelligence."

Explain to your child that there are a lot of terms to understand when talking about attraction and that you are going to review them together. If this talk makes you nervous, admit it. Tell your child that if there is anything in this discussion that makes him uncomfortable, you will try to be sensitive to those feelings. Tell him that these discussions will not require any personal information unless he wants to offer it. The focus of this talk is to consider questions, rather than having to come up with answers.

Review These Words

Please review the terms in this section. Discussing all of them with your child is optional. You know what's appropriate for your child's age and maturity level. Keep in mind that more than likely, even the youngest children have heard these words on TV.

abstinence: not having sex.

attraction: a desire to get to know someone. It can be a feeling of wanting to get to know someone as a friend, or it can be a more powerful need to want to touch, kiss, or be intimate with the person. Being attracted to someone is not necessarily a comfortable feeling. It can feel strange.

boyfriend or girlfriend: usually implies a steady dating relationship with someone involving a certain level of commitment; boyfriends and girlfriends usually are expected to be sexually and emotionally loyal and to not be involved with anyone else romantically.

celibate: usually used to refer to people who have decided to refrain from having any sexual activity.

chastity: a state in which someone has made a religious or moral commitment to not have sex.

crush: usually refers to the feeling of being very physically attracted to someone. This occurs most often in the early stages of getting to know someone. People often confuse a crush with being in love.

double standard: a judgment that you apply to members of one sex that you don't apply to members of the other. For example: if a boy has a lot of sexual experience he is considered a "stud." If a girl has the same experience she may be called a "slut."

homophobia: an irrational fear of people who are homosexual.

hooking up: slang for having sex (from kissing to intercourse).

infatuation: intense feelings of attraction. You think of the other person all the time or a lot.

love: when used in the context of a romantic relationship, a feeling of deep closeness, respect, and desire for companionship. Love usually includes strong feelings of protectiveness and commitment to continue the relationship.

monogamy: being sexually faithful to a partner.

obsession: an unhealthy state of mind when infatuation gets out of hand. Some people cease to be able to function in school or work. They may start to call or write or stalk the other person.

player: someone who is dating or having sex with more than one person at a time.

prejudice: a deep bias against a group of people. Some people are prejudiced against affection between members of different races or any show of affection or love between members of the same sex.

sexual harassment: showing sexual interest even when someone has told you to stop. If harassing behavior takes place at school and interferes with a student's ability to learn, it is against the law—even when it occurs between young children in elementary, middle, or high school.

slut: a term, usually meant as an insult, that is applied to females who are or appear sexually active.

sexual orientation: the sexual preference expressed by the person. Most people are heterosexual—attracted to people of the opposite sex. A small percentage of people are homosexual—attracted to people of the same sex. Some people are bisexual, meaning attracted, to some degree, to both males and females.

virgin: a term used to describe people who have never had sex. Historically it meant people who have not had sexual intercourse.

Why Is Talking about Attraction and Love Important?

Here are some reasons sexual attraction is a good thing to think about and understand:

- It's a very powerful emotion that people need to understand.
- People need to know that if someone desires them physically it may not mean anything about love or commitment.
- People often confuse attraction with love, so it's good to understand the difference.

The Stories

In the next part of the talk, you'll be reading short stories to your child and discussing them together. You don't have to read all of the stories. Pick the ones that you think are appropriate. The stories are very simple. Feel free to embellish them, adding details that you think might make the story more believable. For example, some parents change the gender of the characters to make the story mirror their own families.

The Story about Attraction

Read this story to your child. It gives you the opportunity to discuss how sexual and physical attraction feels and the powerful pull it can have on a person.

"A teenage girl and boy are at a party, sitting together at a kitchen table. They have just met. They are very attracted to each other."

Ask these questions of your child:

- What is the girl thinking?
- What is the boy thinking?
- What is the girl saying?
- What is the boy saying?

Now that your child has completed this scenario, ask the following questions:

- How long have the girl and the boy been talking? (Minutes or hours?)
- How do they show their interest in one another?
- How might these two people know they are attracted to each other?
- What do they want to do with the rest of their time at the party?

Clarify Your Family Values

Ask the following question of your child as a way of sharing your values about attraction. We have included a number of potential responses from children to help you formulate your own answers.

Ask your child: "When two people are attracted to one another, it can be a great feeling. Should they be left alone for that attraction to run its course?"

Child: Sure.

Parent: It might be fine for two people who like each other to spend time together talking. But I might want an adult to be present.

Child: Why?

Parent: Sometimes when two people are attracted to one another, they may want to be sexual. Depending on their age, their parents might not be ready for them to do that.

Child: You are so old-fashioned!

Parent: Well, call it whatever you want. My values are that parents supervise young people. Being old enough for attraction does not automatically mean being old enough to be sexually active.

The Story about the First Kiss

Read this story to your child. It gives you an opportunity to discuss how people decide whom to kiss, when to kiss, and how powerful the experience of kissing someone can be.

"A teenage girl and boy are sitting in a parked car kissing each other for the first time."

Ask these questions of your child:

- What is the girl thinking?
- What is the boy thinking?
- What is the girl saying?
- What is the boy saying?

Now that your child has completed this scenario, ask the following questions:

- How long had the girl and boy known each other before kissing? (Minutes? days? months? years?)
- Do their parents know what they are doing?
- What do they want to do with the rest of their time together tonight? Why?

Clarify Your Family's Values

Ask: "How long should people know each other before they kiss?"

Child: I don't know.

Parent: I think you should be friends with someone before kissing.

Child: Why?

Parent: Because kissing is being sexual. And that should be done only with someone who really likes you and respects your boundaries.

Child: Kissing is no big deal.

Parent: I think it is a very big deal. Kissing creates more sexual feelings and often leads to more sexual activity. Those choices need to be made carefully. If you want to kiss someone and start a relationship, I want to meet that person before there is any kissing.

The Story about the Backseat

Read this story to your child. It gives you an opportunity to discuss how people make decisions about when to become sexual.

"The teenage girl and her teenage friend are in the backseat of the car. They have been kissing a lot but not doing anything else. They feel a powerful sexual attraction to one another."

Ask these questions of your child:

- What is the girl thinking?
- What is the friend thinking?

- What is the girl saying?
- What is the friend saying?

Now that your child has completed this scenario, ask the following questions:

- How long ago was their first kiss? (How much time has passed? Minutes, days, months, or years ago?)
- What is their relationship? If it's been years, could they be married or engaged?
- Are they sexually involved with anyone else?
- Do they have different ideas about the kind of relationship they want?
- Have they talked about what they want to do if they want to do more than kiss?
- What do they need to talk about before having sex?
- If they decide to have sex, how will the teenage girl feel afterward?
- If they decide to have sex, how will the friend feel afterward?

Clarify Your Family's Values

Ask your child: "What do people need to know about each other before they have sex?"

Child: I don't know.
Parent: Do they need to know each other's names?
Child: Yes.
Parent: Do they need to know how they feel about each other?
Child: I don't know. I guess . . .

Parent: How should they feel about each other?

Child: I don't know.

Parent: Should they like each other?

Child: Sure.

Parent: I have very strong feelings about when young people are ready to be sexual and what kind of relationship they should have *before* they become sexual.

Parent's response #1: In our family, I believe that choosing to be sexual with someone is a very important decision. I think people not only need to like each other but also to care deeply about one another. They should care about one another's welfare and be best friends. If I could design the perfect situation it would be that they were committed to each other and knew that they had each other's love, respect, and trust before they had sex. They would have discussed important health matters, like protecting each other from STDs and unplanned pregnancy. If people aren't able to have this kind of talk then they are not ready for sexual activity.

Parent's response #2: In our family, I believe that only adults should be having sex. There is no way that young people are mature enough to protect, respect, and love each other in the way they should. I believe that if you have intercourse this early in life, it will lead to disappointment and perhaps unplanned pregnancy or STDs.

Parent's response #3: It's our religious beliefs that should be respected and followed. (This is an excellent time to discuss your religious beliefs.)

My daughter knew I was a teenager when I started having sex, and it's made my talk about waiting for the right guy difficult. I don't want to sound like a hypocrite, but I've talked about decisions I've made that were harmful and things I wish I could have done differently. My daughter was very mature for her age, and I worried about her getting pregnant in high school. And, thank god, she didn't.

—Deb, mother of three, Portland, Oregon

My parents were my role models. They waited until they were married to have sex and were very involved in the church. They raised my brothers, sisters, and me with tons of love. I knew from very early on that sex was special and not something to do carelessly. I met my wife through my church. We waited until we were married until we had sex. It was great. And now I have a son who I know will share those values—they're really positive.

—Daniel, father of one, Idaho Falls, Idaho

Once I got over the shock of my older son being gay, I realized that I needed to talk about my values about love and respecting others. I made sure that both my sons knew how I felt about being thoughtful, patient, and caring about their relationships with women and men.

—Adele, mother of two, Seattle, Washington

The Story about the Dance

Read this story to your child. It gives you the opportunity to discuss self-image and attraction.

A poster has been put up at school announcing a dance on Friday. Several students walk up to look at it.

Ask these questions of your child:

- What are some of the boys thinking?
- What are some of the girls thinking?

Now that your child has completed this scenario, ask the following questions:

- If a boy or girl are attracted to someone and would like to go to the dance with that person, how can they let them know?
- Do any of the students want to go to the dance, but are reluctant because they think no one will dance with them?
- How do most students feel about dances?
- Do some students have fun at dances?
- Do some students have a lot of anxiety concerning dances?
- What does it mean when you dance with someone?
- If a boy or girl are attracted to someone and they see that person dancing with someone else, how does the person watching feel?

The Bare Minimum: A Quick Quiz for Kids
Ask your child the following two questions to assess her knowledge of attraction and love.

1. Can you tell me the difference between attraction and love?
   Sample answers:
- Attraction is often physical without any romantic feelings. Love is a deep feeling about the whole person and that person's welfare.
- Attraction is common. Love is rare.
- Attraction can be instant. Love takes time to develop fully.

2. Would someone who loves you pressure you into having sex?
Sample answers:
- If you love someone, you want to respect the person's boundaries.
- If you love someone, you are patient.
- Being in love means wanting the best for the person you are in love with.

Talk about Your Family Rules

This is an opportunity to review your family rules. Ask your child the following questions:

1. What is our family rule about kissing?
Sample answers:
- Kissing is something that is reserved only for a special person.
- Kissing is something you do only with someone you know well and trust.

2. What is our family rule about when a person is ready to be sexual?
Sample answers:
- Having a sexual relationship can be one of the greatest experiences in life and choosing the right person is very important.
- We have specific values in this house. We respect and follow those values.
- We have specific religious beliefs about being sexual. We follow those.
- This is one of the most important decisions a person can make. It needs to be made with advice from a trusted adult. If for some

reason you feel you can't talk with me about this, please talk with the other adults that I trust (name specific people, a trusted family friend, or someone from your religious community).

- Being sexual with someone may impact everyone in this family. It is something very special that must be taken very seriously.
- There are serious consequences for breaking the family rules about being sexual.

3. Who can you talk with about relationships and attraction if you aren't comfortable talking with me?
   Sample answers:
- If for some reason you couldn't talk with me, you will talk with (name another adult family member, friend, or representative from your religious group) so that you can get some adult advice.

After the Talk

A Moment to Reflect

You've opened very important lines of communication with this talk. Even if your child said almost nothing during the talk or was argumentative the entire time, you have done well. You have made important distinctions between attraction and love, and you have begun to lay out your values and family rules about when and with whom sexual activity should occur. You've shown your child the way sexual feelings and attraction can turn into sexual behavior. Your child has been given the chance to think about what she wants in a relationship. Good job!

Warning Signs

This talk may reveal some problems that your child is facing. If a child reacted very strongly to this conversation, she may be feeling guilty or threatened by your interest. If your child was very angry and refused to talk with you at all (after a few repeated attempts on your part), make a deal that he needs to talk with someone. Give him some options, such as a family member or trusted friend. Use your own judgment, but it's been our experience that, in general, a very strong negative reaction means that a child has something to hide. Back off if you need to, and try this talk another time.

There may be cause for concern if your child

- stays out late and you don't know where she is.
- is hanging out with kids much older than he or she is.
- has friends who are sexually experienced.
- is often caught lying about whom she spends time with and how the time is spent.
- is giving you hints about a brother's or sister's sexual behavior.

Finding Help

If you find out that your child is sexually active but doesn't want to talk frankly about it, you may want to get the help of someone trained to talk with young people about sexual health.

Your choices depend on how you feel about your child's behavior and what you want to do about it. If you feel that your child's behavior results from low self-esteem or running with the wrong crowd, you might want to make an appointment with a school counselor or child psychologist. Sometimes a trained professional can get to the root of your child's behavior. If you think you have a well-adjusted child, you might consider taking him to a clinic or program where he can learn about contraception and its limits and risks. There are some discussions that may be too graphic and personal for some parents. There is nothing wrong with delegating those sorts of conversations to a wise and well-trained health professional.

Success Stories

If you made it though this talk, congratulations are in order! If parents got medals you would be getting one now. Remember, even a five-minute talk about sexual attraction and the related family rules is an excellent beginning. One mom in upstate New York said that, at first, her teenage son adamantly refused to talk about his sexual feelings. But it was really just a matter of timing. A few days later, he brought up the topic in his own fashion, asking, "Why'd you want to talk about that stuff, anyway?" Persistence pays off!

Over the coming weeks, months, and years your values can be reinforced. You will find that Chapter 10, What We Believe: Talking about Your Family's Values will help you review and integrate all the lessons of the book. Chapter 10 is designed as a summary that will help make clear what it is that you think is best for your child.

Sample Talks

Between Parents and Children

Before you begin your first talk, you might want to read this sample conversation. The following is based on excerpts of actual talks between parents and children.

Discussing the Story about Attraction

Participants: Mom and her eleven-year-old son, a sixth-grader.

Mom: A teenage boy and girl are at a party, sitting together at a kitchen table. They have just met. They are very attracted to each other. What do you think the boy might be thinking?

Son: He's thinking, "She might like me and want to do something."

Mom: Do something, like what?

Son: Make out or more.

Mom: What do you think the girl is thinking?

Son: She's thinking the same thing or maybe nothing at all.

Mom: What would you be saying to the girl?

Son: If I were the boy?

Mom: Yes.

Son: Um. I'd start talking slow and work my way up. I wouldn't just jump in with something.

Mom: What would you say?

Son: "Hi, I'm Mark. What's your name?" Start a friendly conversation.

Mom: What do you think she would say?

Son: She'd probably answer back.

Mom: How might the boy and girl know they are attracted to each other?

Son: Well, if she sounds nice or he does, to each other, it's usually a good sign. But if she's snotty or he's snotty back when she's trying to talk, those are some signs.

Mom: How do you know before you even speak to each other? What are the things you pick up on?

Son: Body motions, stuff like that.

Mom: Any expressions or anything? Facial expressions.

Son: Yeah, smile, or a frown if they're mad at you.

Mom: You know you're attracted to one another when you have that eye contact.

Son: Yeah. There's that special thing you feel.

Mom: That special thing you feel? Do you know what that is?

Son: I don't know how to say this, but it's sort of like when you have fun together, feel good together.

Mom: That special thing you feel, that special attraction that you feel in your head and stomach.

Son: You get butterflies in your stomach, get nervous.

Mom: You recognize that feeling?

Son: Yeah.

Mom: What do they want to do with the rest of their time together tonight?

Son: If they are older, probably make out or something. If they're younger, maybe a kiss or talk awhile.

Mom: Maybe get to know each other a little bit? Would they jump right into the kissing part?

Son: Some people, yeah.

Lessons Learned from This Sample Talk

The parent brought into the conversation many of the unspoken ways people can communicate with one another. Making a pre-teen aware of this can be extremely helpful as they enter adolescence. Talking about "how" a young man feels with a sixth-grade son is a major achievement. How many people would say their sixth-grader would have experienced this type of emotion and understand the relationship between these emotions and sex drive? This parent knows a lot more about her son's sexual development now since he's shown signs of being emotionally and physically attracted to girls.

Discussing the Story about the First Kiss

Participants: a father and his thirteen-year-old son.

Dad: The teenage boy and girl met at a party. Now they are sitting in a parked car at night kissing each other for the first time.

Son: That sounds very sixties.

Dad: Either that or they are in somebody's house.

Son: This sounds like a movie.

Dad: A movie? You can decide how long this boy and girl have known each other. Were they kissing right after the party? Or was it a few days or weeks or months or years later?

Son: Hours.

Dad: Remember, they are kissing for the first time somewhere. We'll leave the place to your imagination. What is the boy thinking?

Son: The boy is thinking, "Finally."

Dad: Hmm. No, that's probably right. Is he thinking that he really likes this or that he really likes her?

Son: Yeah.

Dad: What would the girl be thinking, do you think?

Son: "Finally." The same thing.

Dad: Do their parents know what they are doing?

Son: No.

Dad: I would say not. What do they want to do, meaning the boy and girl, with the rest of their time together, tonight, after they have kissed?

Son: Spend it together. Make the most of it.

Dad: Meaning what?

Son: Being together, not just go home.

Dad: Like go out?

Son: Go out for a date or something.

Dad: But not necessarily do more hugging, kissing, groping?

Son: Might.

Dad: You know the more you start to get into it, the harder it is to stop and you have to be able to stop. It used to be, they always thought the boy was the one to be pushy, but that's not necessarily true anymore. Any comments you'd like to make on this one?

Son: No.

Lessons Learned from This Sample Talk

Dad has learned that his son is probably sexually active or at least sexually interested. Dad had some time to give some thoughts about "stopping" (once you've started kissing), and future talks can expand on the concept of pacing, timing, and patience. Future discussions can focus on kissing, petting, or other sexual customs in his son's peer group. The son seems pretty open to talking with his dad, and Dad listens well.

Discussing the Story about the Backseat

Participants: a mother and her eleven-year-old son.

Mom: A teenage boy and girl are in the backseat of the car at night. They have been kissing a lot but haven't done anything else. But they are feeling very attracted to one another. They feel a powerful sexual attraction to one another. How long do you think they have been going together?

Son: A long time. Usually you wouldn't jump right into it, all hot, when you just met.

Mom: So they wouldn't be interested if they just met?

Son: I think they'd have known each other awhile and are good friends.

Mom: What is the boy thinking?

Son: They are really into it? He's probably thinking he'd want to have sex. Or he may be thinking, "This is great but this is as far as I want to go tonight."

Mom: Okay. What is the girl thinking?

Son: She's thinking, "I'm not going to risk having sex because I could get pregnant and I wouldn't want that to happen at fifteen or seventeen." Or, she could be thinking, "This is a great experience."

Mom: Sometimes you're feeling love, like you're really loving each other.

Son: Probably the guy would say, "Do you want to have sex?"

Mom: You think he's actually saying that?

Son: I don't know if he's actually saying it, but he's thinking it and he's expressing it.

Mom: What kind of things do you think a boy would say to a girl in this situation?

Son: He'd probably charm her.

Mom: So what might that be?

Son: He'd say, "You look nice."

Mom: Might he say how he feels about her?

Son: He might say, "You'll be protected," and "Don't be worried."

Mom: Would he say how he feels about her?

Son: Yes, he might say, "I like you really, a lot," or, "You know, we should just end this." But that wouldn't be nice, to be with someone that long and break up.

Mom: What would the girl say at this point?

Son: She might say, "Stop. Don't push me any further." Or she might be saying, "Let's get it on."

Mom: Do you see them as married or in a committed relationship?

Son: Not married, not at fifteen or sixteen, but they know each other 'cause they've been going out awhile.

Mom: So they are in a committed relationship?

Son: Yeah.

Mom: Are they engaged or have they talked about any kind of commitment to one another?

Son: No. Right now they're just thinking, "This is great."

Mom: So they do have a commitment?

Son: Yeah.

Mom: Exclusively, or do they date other people?

Son: They aren't cheating on each other. They're dating, They go to movies with each other.

Mom: Are they sexually involved with anyone else?

Son: No. Well, they could be. But if it were me, no.

Mom: What kind of relationship does each of them want to have?

Son: A good one. They don't want to cheat on each other or break up or anything bad like that.

Mom: Are they in love?

Son: Of course.

Mom: Do they have different ideas about the kind of relationship they want?

Son: They both want a sturdy relationship but, then, the boy might be thinking, "This is great!" and the girl might be thinking, "I like him *but* I like John more." And she may want to leave him. But, well, they could also be thinking, "This is great. I really want to go with you," and like that.

Mom: What do you think about moving beyond kissing? What needs to be present before moving to the next level?

Son: You have to be ready for it. I mean, anyone can have intercourse, but you're not ready, your hormones couldn't handle it. And it's not that safe.

Mom: What about the safety? Here it is, the next question. Have they talked about what they want to do if they become sexual?

Son: If he has sex with her and she gets pregnant, it's not as safe because you don't know if she can handle it, being pregnant.

Mom: Aren't there things you would be talking about to prevent that?

Son: Protection.

Mom: Which would be?

Son: A condom.

Mom: What would that protect you against?

Son: Getting somebody pregnant.

Mom: I mean are there other physical things you need to be conscious of before you have sex with someone? Maybe diseases?

Son: Yeah, AIDS, HIV.

Mom: Those were things you weren't even thinking about. If you are sitting there, honestly, in a car, possibly ready to have sex with somebody, that is something you have to talk about.

Son: Yeah, probably.

Mom: So have they talked or do they just go ahead and have sex?

Son: They aren't thinking much right now, they want to go right into sex because, but, that's not right. You have to know what could happen.

Mom: Right.

Son: Everything that's possible to happen. You can't just jump the gun and be, like, "Uh oh, what happened?"

Mom: Exactly. That's something you want to think about before you're in a passionate, hot state where you may not be thinking clearly. If they decide to have sex, how will they feel afterwards?

Son: Great. Relieved.

Mom: Relieved that the first time is over with?

Son: Or that this is how it feels, so you aren't wondering, "How does it feel?"

Mom: So you think it will be a great feeling?

Son: Yes.

Mom: How do you think she'll feel afterwards?

Son: "Wow, that was fun." Maybe even, "Let's do it again." Or, "Uh-oh, I don't want to do this anymore. Once is enough."

Mom: Why would they feel like that?

Son: They may be worried that they may get caught or it may not be as safe as they want it to be.

Mom: So it could go either way, how they feel?

Son: Either way.

Mom: What do you think if they decide not to have sex, how might they feel?

Son: Relieved.

Mom: Would it be positive?

Son: If they decided not to. One might feel, "Man, this is bad" and get all mad. Or you can think, "That is the safer idea." If you are the boy and the girl says, "No," then you should respect her and say, "I understand how you feel. Maybe we can try some other time."

Mom: It could go both ways, the boy may say, "I'm not ready for this," and the girl might want to. Right?

Son: Yeah, but it's usually the boy who wants to.

Mom: Why?

Son: I don't know.

Lessons Learned from This Sample Talk

This boy appears to have a good idea about all the emotional possibilities that would be part of a first sexual encounter. His mom can see he's interested but also ambivalent. If sexual intercourse didn't happen, the reaction would be "relieved." She can use the conversation to help reinforce the idea that sex doesn't have to happen and that everyone needs to stay aware of unhappy consequences. The son knows it would feel good physically, but he also knows it could lead to regret. The mom could see from this discussion that her son is well informed and sexually interested.

The mom kept asking her son why he thought boys were more interested in sex than girls. The son didn't know why he thought like that, but he was sure he was right. He did say, later, that "Girls are faster, while boys are more immature." This attitude can be explored in future talks.

Discussing the Story about the Dance

Participants: a mother and her fourteen-year-old son.

Mom: Some students see a poster about a dance at school. What are some of the boys thinking?

Son: It depends what grade they're in.

Mom: They're in all grades.

Son: Okay, the sixth-graders are like, (in high voice) "Oh, cool, a dance." The seventh-graders are like, "I'll see if anyone else is going." The eighth-graders are, "I don't think I'm going to go."

Mom: What are some of the girls thinking?

Son: "Oh, a dance. Pretty cool."

Mom: All the grades?

Son: Yes.

Mom: What are some of the boys saying?

Son: "Cool, a dance."

Mom: What are some of the girls saying?

Son: Same thing.

Mom: If a boy or girl are attracted to someone and want them to go to the dance, how can they let them know?

Son: You both go to the dance and dance.

Mom: Do you ask each other ahead of time?

Son: Not in middle school, you don't. Not unless you're going to the prom or something.

Mom: Do any of the students want to go to the dance but are reluctant because they think no one will dance with them?

Son: Probably. There's always somebody.

Mom: You mean there's always somebody who thinks nobody will dance with them?

Son: Yeah.

Lessons Learned from This Sample Talk

This talk illustrates how the son perceives the maturity level of boys as a thing that changes with every grade level, while the girls' attitudes remain constant. The mom might want to explore the situation of being the guy "nobody will dance with." The son might be feeling this way.

6

Keeping Commitments

Talking about Trust and Honesty

*I'm always amazed at the messy lives some people create by their
inability to tell the truth. It is very difficult to keep track of lies
when they get beyond a certain number.*
—Jan, mother of two, Jamestown, New York

*I remember when I was told my first big lie by my boyfriend. How he
and his "just a friend" Amy slept in the same bed but "didn't do
anything."* —Mary, mother of one, Seattle, Washington

*A lot of our public health problems with AIDS and other STDs are
really a problem of ethics and people not being honest with
themselves and their partners.*
—Mary Ellen, mother of two, Memphis, Tennessee

Among the essential character traits, honesty ranks high. We all
depend on our friends being who they say they are and doing
what they say they are going to do. If we don't know whether
they'll keep our secrets or pick us up when they say they will, we
know we are in an unstable relationship. It may take your child
years—or longer—to learn the importance of trust in a friendship.
With this talk, you'll have the chance to speed up that process.

We want our kids to be honest and to know that they deserve
honesty from others. And we know that nowhere is it more important to put honesty to work than in intimate relationships. We

all deserve to have friends who are real friends and who act for, not against, our best interests. We all deserve to have romantic partners who tell us the truth so that we can make decisions that are fair for all concerned. We want our children to know that the basis for love and friendship is trust—to give and receive honest information, support, and feedback.

Preparing for the Talk

This talk also will give you the chance to talk about what being honest and trustworthy means to you and how it impacts every relationship, both platonic and romantic.

In this talk you will help your child understand that

- trust and honesty are essential in all relationships.
- friends you can't trust aren't really friends.
- you should expect no less trust and honesty in a romantic relationship than you would in a friendship.
- there are family rules about being honest and consequences for being dishonest.

What You Can Expect from This Talk

After the talk your child will

- be able to define trust and honesty.
- know the difference between a "small" lie and a "big" lie.
- understand how all relationships suffer greatly when trust is broken.

- understand how peer pressure from friends might lead to pressure to lie to parents.
- know what to do when trust is broken.

How Do You Define Trust and Honesty?

We use words like "trust" and "honesty" a lot, but what do they really mean? Do we really believe people should be totally honest 100 percent of the time? What each person considers a lie may vary based on their personal beliefs and values. Few of us learned to make clear distinctions in the households in which we grew up.

We need to examine our own feelings about what level of honesty and consistency that we think is necessary in our own family life as a preface to thinking about the lessons we're teaching our children. Take a look at the list below. Which of these behaviors do you think are acceptable or unacceptable behaviors for your family?

- Telling your son you will take him somewhere and then canceling because something "more important" came up.
- Telling your child that Uncle Fred can't come because he is sick, when Uncle Fred really has a hangover.
- Telling your child his room is his private space, but secretly going through it every once in a while to make sure nothing harmful is going on.
- Listening in on a child's phone call to find out what she and a friend are up to.
- Telling your child that you like a friend of his when you really don't.

Of course there are times when it might be appropriate to protect people's feelings by telling a "little, innocent" lie. How do you feel about these examples?

- Telling your ninety-five-year-old great aunt that she looks fabulous.
- Pretending not to notice that your friend has put on fifteen pounds since you last saw her.
- Looking at your child's artwork and pretending you know what it is.
- Offering to throw a party for a dozen eleven-year-olds and saying, "It will be no trouble at all."
- Telling a friend that the dish her child broke is no big deal—when it really is.
- Masking your disappointment when your child forgets to give you a birthday card.

The Challenge to be Honest

In all relationships, especially committed loving relationships, it's a challenge to be 100 percent honest all of the time. The daily work of being in a relationship presents a challenge for honest communication. How much should we edit our thoughts and feelings? Should I protect my friends from some things but not other things? Do I keep some feelings inside? How do I decide what to reveal and what to keep to myself? As young people grow and their relationships become deeper, honesty will become an issue. When young people are ready to explore intimate friendships, the ability to balance honesty with tact will become an even more important skill.

Here are some important things to think about before your talk:

• Being honest with yourself

It is sometimes hard to be honest with yourself. For example, how do you really feel about the people you call your friends? It is important to take a good look at your behavior and see how well it matches up with your true feelings.

• Being brave enough to confront lies

It is hard to confront a friend who you think has been dishonest. It is even harder to face up to the possibility that a partner is being unfaithful. It is important to learn the skill of finding out the truth and dealing with it.

• Being secure enough to face the possibility of rejection

Both adults and children may hesitate to show their feelings for someone when they fear that those emotions may not be returned. It is an important skill to say what you feel and risk rejection. It is important to know that while failure or rejection may take place, expressions of interest also allow for connections to be made.

Speaking truthfully is a vital skill in family life, work, and in all relationships. It is important to think about how you feel and your ability—and the ability of your child—to say "I feel scared," "I feel angry," and "I need help." For me, this kind of candor has taken lots of practice and sometimes courage.
—Sarah, mother of two, Gaithersburg, Maryland

My ten-year-old daughter kept making up excuses why she couldn't see her "best friend," Sara. When I talked with her about it, it was clear that she didn't like her best friend anymore. She felt relieved to know that friendships change—and eventually she went out and found some new friends.

—Jen, mother of three, Seattle, Washington

Influence of the Media

Want a course in dishonesty? Turn on the afternoon soap operas. On daytime dramas, relationships are ripe with betrayal; deception is to be expected. Talk shows are no better. A favorite topic is "the secret I haven't told you." In front of a bloodthirsty audience, one member of a couple reveals something that will break a partner's heart. Think about your favorite TV shows. How many characters are having affairs, or lying to their spouse or partner?

How do we teach our children about trust and honesty in relationships with such messages being broadcast twenty-four hours a day on hundreds of channels?

I've got to admit that I love the soaps in the afternoon. But after watching some with my teenage daughters, I realized that basically all the characters are lying, untrustworthy sex maniacs.

—Karen, mother of two, Portland, Oregon

I used to think of the TV as just another piece of furniture in the living room. Clearly, it is a very powerful machine transmitting messages to my kids. And the majority of these messages do not reflect my values. Which is why we have rules about when and what can be watched.

—Al, father of two, Rockville, Maryland

Different Families: Different Values

Everyone interprets behavior in his or her own way. Here are some behaviors that may be experienced differently depending on a person's background.

A girl is looking forward to going to the movies with her best friend on Friday. On Thursday afternoon the best friend calls to say that she got a date with a guy and needs to cancel her movie plans.

Some parents might say that friends sometimes take second place to a date. Others would say that friends should always keep commitments to other friends. What do you think?

■

A junior in high school comes home from a party where he has been drinking. His mom asks, "Have you been drinking?" He says no.

Some parents would laugh this off as part of being a teenager. Others would say that the teen's lying is worse than his drinking. What do you think?

■

A girl goes to spend the night at her friend Anna's. When she gets there, she is surprised to find that Anna's parents are gone and an older brother is watching X-rated videos with his friends. The girl knows that staying over without any adults present and watching X-rated videos would mean breaking two big family rules. She doesn't tell her parents when she comes home the next day.

Some parents would say that this situation is not their daughter's fault. Others would say that she has betrayed their trust. What do you think?

■

A girl is mad at her boyfriend. She goes out on a date with another guy. She reasons that since it's only a date and she's not going to do anything sexual, then she is being faithful and doesn't have to tell her boyfriend.

Some parents might say that a dinner with a new friend is okay. Others might say that being faithful means being sexually and emotionally committed. What do you think?

■

A seventeen year old tells his two closest friends that he's had sex with his girlfriend. He promised his girlfriend that he would not tell anyone about what they did.

Some parents might call this predictable male behavior. Others might say that he has betrayed his girlfriend's trust. What do you think?

■

A senior in high school tells his worried mom that he is not having sex with girls. The mom knows that lots of his peers are already sexual. He promises to talk to her before he "has sex with girls." The son is actually having a relationship with another guy. The mom doesn't know that her son is attracted to other males.

The son tells himself that he isn't actually lying because his mom asked if he's having sex "with girls," which he isn't. But his mom wants to know about her son's sexual activity and whether he is being safe and responsible. What do you think?

Last-Minute Checkups before the Talk

Before you talk with your child, try to remember what your parents taught you about trust and honesty when you were growing up.

- Did a parent ever talk to you about the importance of trust and honesty?
- Did they tell you to look for trustworthiness in all your relationships?
- Did they provide a role model for trustworthiness?

As a parent, what are you teaching your child about trust and honesty?

- Do you encourage her to be honest with her feelings?
- How do you let your child know that you welcome candor and honesty?
- Do you talk to your child about how to find friends who are trustworthy and honest?
- How do you provide a positive role model for candor and honesty?

Do you have any stories you can share with your child about friendships, how you were honest in a difficult situation, or how you confronted someone who was lying? For example:

- The time a friend lied to you and you found out about it
- The time you told an "innocent" lie to protect someone's feelings
- The time you felt betrayed in a relationship

Sharing your stories lets your child know how you feel about honesty and trust and what they meant to you when you were growing up.

What Are Your Family Rules?

Do you have family rules about being honest, along with clear consequences for not telling the truth? If not, this is a good time to think about them. This talk highlights the following situations:

- A child asks her mom to tell a "small" lie on the phone.
- A mom spots her daughter kissing when she is supposed to be doing homework.
- A girl sees her boyfriend kissing someone else.
- A guy misleads an Internet "friend."
- A man and woman are tempted to break a commitment.
- A young man has an important health issue to reveal.

These stories give you the chance to talk about the importance of having friends who are honest and trustworthy. But the stories and questions are open-ended, allowing your child to reflect on a range of topics, including the things friends do to protect one another, peer pressure, and any other problems or concerns. Depending on your child, the talk could even include issues of alcohol and drug use and sexual relationships. And remember, the stories also give you an opportunity to share your family rules about the situations described.

The Talk

Introduce the Talk

To start this talk you could say, "I'm reading a chapter on honesty and I've got some questions for you. How honest do you think most people are?"

Your child may offer anything from "People lie all the time!" to "I'm always honest!" You can offer the following: "Every person is different. One person's small, innocent lie is another person's big lie."

Review These Words

Please review the terms in this section. Discussing all of them with your child is optional. You know which are appropriate for your child's age and maturity level. More than likely, even the youngest children have heard these words on TV.

betray: to deceive; to be disloyal.

commitment: a promise; an agreement; a pledge to do something.

ethical: having a system of standards for how to treat people.

faithful: to keep a commitment to someone; being loyal.

honest: truthful.

loyal: faithful to friends, a cause or country.

trustworthy: reliable; able to be trusted.

"innocent" lie: not telling the truth in order to avoid hurting someone's feelings, such as telling a relative who is ill that she looks fantastic. Sometimes a person's "innocent" lie can be viewed as a "big" lie by another.

Why Is Talking about Honesty and Trust Important?

Ask your child whether she thinks talking about honesty and trust is important. Here are some reasons you might want to offer:

- Talking about honesty and trust means learning to identify these traits in others.

- Talking about honesty and trust means setting a standard for all relationships—platonic or romantic.
- Talking about trust and honesty means clarifying family rules.

The Stories

In the next part of the talk, you'll be reading short stories to your child and discussing them together. You don't have to read all of the stories. Pick the ones that you think are appropriate for your child. The stories are very simple. Feel free to embellish them, adding details that you think might make the story more believable to your child.

The Story about "Innocent" Lies on the Phone

Read this story to your child. It is an opportunity to talk about telling "innocent" lies and the problems that can arise.

"The phone rings and the daughter asks her mom to tell the guy who is calling that she is not home. She doesn't like the guy who is calling."

Ask these questions of your child:

- What is the mom saying?
- What is the mom thinking?
- What is the daughter thinking?
- What is the daughter saying?

229

Now that your child has completed this scenario, ask the following questions:

- Will the mom make an "innocent" lie on the phone or have her daughter deal with the caller?
- How can an "innocent" lie like this one smooth over a potential confrontation or hurt feelings?
- How can an "innocent" lie like this one create more problems?
- What would happen if the girl took the call and told the guy she was not interested in seeing him?
- Have you ever been in a situation like this? If so, how did you feel? What did you do?

The Story about Kissing instead of Homework

Read this story to your child. This story gives you a chance to talk about keeping commitments and the consequences for breaking them.

"A mom is driving down the street when she spots her daughter, who was supposed to be doing homework, sitting on a park bench kissing her boyfriend. She pulls over to talk to her."

Ask these questions of your child:

- What is the mom thinking?
- What is the mom saying?
- What is the girl saying?
- What is the girl thinking?

230

- What is the boy thinking?
- What is the boy saying?

Now that your child has completed this scenario, ask the following questions:

- What kinds of excuses might the girl offer?
- What are the kinds of consequences the daughter might face?
- Does this completely break the trust between mother and daughter? What if this is the first time the daughter has been caught in a situation like this? The second time?
- Have you ever been in a situation like this? If so, how did you feel? What did you do?

The Story about a Boy Caught Cheating

This story gives you an opportunity to talk about how friends break commitments and face the consequences of betrayal.

"A boy and a girl have been going out for a year. One day the girl sees her boyfriend kissing another girl. She wonders what to do."

Ask these questions of your child:

- What is the girlfriend thinking?
- What is the boy thinking?

Now that your child has completed this scenario, ask the following questions:

- What is the girlfriend going to do?
- What might happen if she confronts her boyfriend?
- What might happen if she doesn't confront her boyfriend?
- What do people usually do in a situation like this?
- Have you ever been in a situation like this? If so, how did you feel? What did you do?

The Story about Online Truth

This story gives you a chance to talk about what kind of behaviors we accept and expect from people we meet on the Internet.

"A small, skinny, fifteen-year-old guy is online chatting with a person he does not know. The fifteen-year-old wants to seem attractive, so he says he is eighteen, tall, with big muscles."

Ask these questions of your child:

- What is the fifteen-year-old thinking?
- What do you think the person he is chatting with online is thinking?

Now that your child has completed this scenario, ask the following questions:

- Why would someone lie online when he wouldn't lie face-to-face with someone?

- Have you ever been in a situation like this? If so, how did you feel? What did you do?

Stories for Older Children

The following stories are about being honest in adult situations—situations in which the consequences of lying can be very serious. While some younger children may not be able to relate to them, you may find that to your older child these stories make perfect sense.

The Story about Marriage Commitments

This story gives you a chance to talk about what kind of ethics people have when it comes to keeping a commitment to a loved one.

"A man has been married for five years. The man is out of town on business staying at a hotel. At the bar he meets another person staying at the hotel on business. She is a very interesting, beautiful, married woman. The man and woman are clearly very attracted to one another. Hours pass, and the woman, after having a few drinks with the man, says she is tired and needs to go to bed. The man offers to walk her to her room."

Ask these questions of your child:

- What is the man thinking?
- What is the man saying?

- What is the woman thinking?
- What is the woman saying?

Now that your child has completed this scenario, ask the following questions:

- How does this situation bring up issues of trust and honesty?
- What should the man do?
- What should the woman do?

The Story about Truth and HIV

This story gives you a chance to talk about what kind of ethics people have when it comes to sharing information that would have long last-ing consequences.

"A college student is going out with a woman he has met in class. These two people have spent a few months forming a good friendship. They have not been sexual yet but they are clearly attracted to one another. The guy has not yet told the woman about his health situation. He has HIV. The guy is afraid that if he tells the woman about his situation there won't be any chance for a relationship. Since he feels great and shows no signs of HIV infection, the guy is wondering if he has to tell the woman about it before they have sex. He knows that even using a condom might not protect her from becoming infected with HIV. They are having dinner and the guy is wondering what to do."

Ask these questions of your child:

- What is the guy thinking?
- What is the guy saying?
- What is the woman thinking?
- What is the woman saying?

Now that your child has completed this scenario, ask the following questions:

- How does this situation bring up issues of trust and honesty?
- Why would someone be afraid to reveal that he has HIV or another sexually transmitted disease?
- Have you ever heard of a person being in a situation like this? If so, what happened? What would you do?

The Story about Truth and Health

This story gives you a chance to talk about what kind of ethics people have when it comes to sharing information that has long lasting consequences.

"A college student is going out with another guy he met on his rowing team. These two guys have spent a few months forming a good friendship. They are clearly attracted to one another, emotionally and physically. One of the guys has not yet told his friend about his health situation. He has herpes. He is afraid that if he tells his friend about his situation, then there won't be any chance for a romantic relationship. The guy is wondering, since he feels great and shows no signs of a herpes outbreak, if he has to tell about the herpes. He is talking to his friend on the phone and wondering what to do."

Ask these questions of your child:

- What is the guy thinking?
- What might he say over the phone?

Now that your child has completed this scenario, ask the following questions:

- How does this situation bring up issues of trust and honesty?
- Why would someone be afraid to reveal that he has herpes?
- What are common questions a person might ask if his friend said he had a health condition like herpes?
- Have you ever heard of a person being in a situation like this? If so, what happened? What would you do?

Clarify Your Family's Values

Discuss the following question with your child as a way of sharing your values about honesty and trust. We have included a number of potential responses from children to help you formulate your own responses.

Ask your child: "When a person has a friend who tells lies, what kind of a friend is that?"

Child response #1: A good one if they don't lie to me.

Parent: You think so? What makes you think that if a person lies to other people that he won't lie to you?

Child response #2: If you want me to give up every friend who ever lies, then I won't have any friends.

Parent: Finding friends who are trustworthy can take time. It might be better to have no friends at all than a friend who lies.

The Bare Minimum: A Quick Quiz for Kids

Ask your child the following questions to assess her knowledge and perceptions of honesty and trust.

1. Can you give me one example of how a person might show that she is trustworthy?
   Sample answers:
   - If a person makes a commitment to do something with you and shows up.
   - If you tell someone something private and that person doesn't share it with others.

2. How does a person know if someone is untrustworthy?
   Sample answers:
   - A number of people say that they have heard the person tell lies.
   - The person breaks commitments to do things and makes lousy excuses.

Talk about Your Family Rules

This is an opportunity to review your family rules. Ask your child the following question.

What are our family rules about being honest?
Sample answers:
- We are 100 percent honest (except when it means hurting others' feelings).
- There are consequences for lying. Betraying someone's trust is very serious.
- Being honest means keeping commitments. We take all our commitments, big and small, very seriously.

After the Talk

A Moment to Reflect

Some parents are surprised by how much kids pick up on "innocent" or "small" lies. And how much they'll put up with untrustworthy companions because they are so hungry for friends of any kind. Your goal is to help your child understand that she can make choices about the kind of friends she has and the kind of trustworthy friend she is.

Take a moment to reflect on the talk you just had with your child. How do you feel about it?

- What surprised you about your child's view of honesty?
- Do you think she has good and trustworthy friends? Can she be honest with them? Think about whether your child has the

ability to be candid with her feelings and express her thoughts and wishes.

- How much of the time were you listening to your child?
- Did your child view keeping commitments as important?

Warning Signs

The talks may reveal potential problems that your child is facing. Is your child feeling isolated and alienated from peers? Is he someone who has only superficial, somewhat untrustworthy relationships? Some potential warning signs include:

- He doesn't appear to care if he has trustworthy friends or not.
- She doesn't see anything wrong with breaking commitments to friends.
- He doesn't see anything wrong with his friends' lying to others.
- He thinks friends who talk about their feelings are weak.
- She shares some problems in the course of the talk that sound like they could be serious.

Trust your instincts on how your child is doing. When you meet your child's friends, do they appear well adjusted and trustworthy?

Finding Help

This talk may reveal a number of important issues. Your child may have hinted at having problems. Or he may have made up some serious problems for the characters in the stories. While presented as fantasy, the situations may indeed be based on real situations in your child's life. If needed, support and help for your child is available. Don't hesitate to contact your child's school to discuss your concerns with the school counselor. Some of your family members and friends may have resources to provide help.

Success Stories

You have made it through another important talk. This talk about trust and honesty has held a lot of surprises for parents. Some parents reported being surprised by their son's definition of "being faithful" (especially when the boys in relationships thought it was okay to kiss other girls). One boy in Flint, Michigan, had interesting ideas about being faithful; he told his mom that even though he was dating one girl, he could sleep with as many others as he wanted—as long as he slept with them no more than once. Rest assured, his mother used the opportunity to convey her own values about trust and faithfulness. We hope your talk, too, acts as a catalyst for longer discussions about your values and ethics.

Sample Talks

Between Parents and Children

If you are wondering how a talk based on this chapter might really sound, take a look at the following excerpts from real family talks.

Discussing the Story about Small Lies on the Phone

Participants: a father and his ten-year-old daughter.

Dad: I'm going to tell you a story. The phone rings and the mother answers it. The daughter asks her to tell the guy who is calling that she is not home. She doesn't like the person who is calling. You understand what I'm saying.

Daughter: Uh, huh.

Dad: It's like, if you answered the phone and Mommy says, "I don't want to talk to that person," and to tell them she's not home. What would she be doing?

Daughter: That she doesn't want to speak to them.

Dad: Is it the truth? Is she telling you to tell the truth?

Daughter: No.

Dad: Is she telling you to tell a lie?

Daughter: Sort of.

Dad: Is that something that bothers you to do? If Mommy asked you to do that?

Daughter: (Long pause.) Pretty much, yeah.

Dad: Do you sometimes tell little lies?

Daughter: (Whispers.) Little lies.

Dad: Because? (Pause.) When do you normally tell a lie?

Daughter: If you need to tell a lie, if it doesn't make them feel bad, it's okay.

Dad: What do you think the mom's thinking when she asks the daughter to do that?

Daughter: I don't know.

Dad: What is the daughter thinking?

Daughter: That it's not very nice to lie.

Dad: But she wants to please her mother?

Daughter: Right.

Dad: Do you think it's easier for someone to tell a little lie, or is it easier to get someone else to do it for them?

Daughter: Getting someone else would be easier.

Dad: Can lies sometimes make things easier for people?

Daughter: Sometimes.

Dad: Maybe stop a problem or solve a problem?

Daughter: Uh, huh.

Dad: Can a little lie sometimes hurt someone's feelings?

Daughter: Ah, ha.

Dad: Do you know of a case where that's ever happened? Did you ever lie and someone got hurt by it or someone lied to you and you were hurt by it?

Daughter: We just usually joke. We don't lie to friends.

Dad: Can a lie sometimes, like, lead to more problems?

Daughter: Yes.

Dad: Do you know of a time that that has ever happened?

Daughter: No.

Dad: Would it have been easier to have the mother get on the phone and talk to the person than to have the daughter lie?

Daughter: Ah, ha.

Dad: Have you ever been in a situation where someone has asked you to lie for them?

Daughter: Once.

Dad: Who?

Daughter: It was a little lie because Mom didn't want to talk to the salespeople.

Dad: How did that make you feel?

Daughter: Mom really doesn't like to talk to salespeople, so I think that one was okay.

Lessons Learned from This Sample Talk

Dad changes the situation to fit his daughter's age. In this talk, Dad shows his daughter how to think independently about lying—even if the situation involves a parent. This is a tough point to get across because "little lies" are common and often useful in everyday life. Still, talking about telling the truth and why you shouldn't lie for other people is an important discussion.

Discussing the Story about Kissing instead of Homework

Participants: a father and his ten-year-old daughter.

Dad: I'm going to tell you a little story here. A mom is driving down the street and spots her daughter, who is kissing her boyfriend instead of doing her homework like she is supposed to be doing. She pulls over to talk with her daughter. What do you think the mom is thinking?

Daughter: The mom thinks, "That was a very naughty thing to do."

Dad: What did the mom say, do you think?

Daughter: "Is your homework done?"

Dad: What would the girl say?

Daughter: "Uh-oh."

Dad: What do you think she is thinking?

Daughter: "I'm going to get in trouble."

Dad: Do you think there are any excuses the girl might say to her mother?

Daughter: (Pause.) "It was an accident?" which would be really weird.

Dad: What might happen to the daughter, in this case?

Daughter: She'd get in trouble.

Dad: What kind of trouble?

Daughter: Grounded?

Dad: Maybe the mom wouldn't let her see the boyfriend anymore?

Daughter: Right, yeah.

Dad: Do you think this would hurt the trust the mother has in the daughter?

Daughter: Yes. A lot.

Dad: Do you think it matters if this is the first time it happens, or second time, or tenth time?

Daughter: Yes.

Dad: Why would it make a difference?

Daughter: 'Cause if it happened a lot of times then the mom would be really mad, but if it was the first time that wouldn't be really bad.

Lessons Learned from This Sample Talk

This dad checks in on his daughter's sense of what's acceptable to a parent. He finds out that his daughter knows that when you tell your parents one thing and do another, you should expect consequences. The dad has used this story to make the point that trust between parent and child is important—and, incidentally, that parents do find out, sooner or later, if something sneaky is going on.

Discussing the Story about a Boy Caught Cheating

Participants: a father and his ten-year-old daughter.

Dad: This is a story about how friends break commitments and the consequences of betrayal. Do you know what "betrayal" means? It means to turn against someone close to you, someone who trusts you. A boy and a girl have been going out for almost a year. One day the girl sees her boyfriend kissing another girl. She wonders what to do. What do you think the girlfriend is thinking? She's the one watching her boyfriend kiss another girl.

Daughter: She thinks, "I don't trust him."

Dad: What is the boyfriend thinking, if he sees the first girlfriend while he's kissing the other girl?

Daughter: "Uh-oh."

Dad: He's gotten in trouble.

Daughter: Yep.

Dad: Yeah. What do you think the girlfriend will do?

Daughter: Dump him.

Dad: Dump him. Do you think she would confront him and come up and say something or ignore him and not talk to him anymore.

Daughter: I would go up to him and say, "What are you doing?"

Dad: You think it would be better to talk to him than not say anything anymore?

Daughter: Yeah.

Dad: How come?

Daughter: It's not right to let it go.

Dad: What would happen if she didn't do that?

Daughter: I think she'd ditch him.

Dad: What usually happens to people in situations like this?

Daughter: Go up to the person and say, "What are you doing?"

Dad: Have you ever been in a situation like that?
Daughter: No.

Lessons Learned from This Sample Talk

This dad has found out that his daughter has standards for how she wants to be treated. What a relief! She also is going to stand up for her rights and tell someone how she feels. He has the chance to support her so that if something like this happens, she knows "dumping the guy" is the right thing to do.

Discussing the Story about Online Truth

Participants: a father and his ten-year-old daughter.

Dad: I'll tell you another story. A skinny, short, fifteen-year-old boy is online chatting with a person he does not know. The boy wants to seem attractive to this person, so he describes himself as eighteen with lots of muscles and very tall. What do you think the fifteen-year-old is thinking?

Daughter: That it wasn't a very good idea (to lie about himself).

Dad: But he's the one who said it in the first place. He said he's tall and eighteen and has lots of muscles. This isn't exactly true.

Daughter: He is thinking, "She'll probably date me."

Dad: Aha. What do you think the other person online is thinking?

Daughter: "That I'd like to meet him."

Dad: Do you think it's easier for someone to lie on the computer than in person?

Daughter: Yes.

Dad: But why would someone lie?

Daughter: 'Cause they can't see them if they lie about themselves, except if they send them a picture.

Dad: What kinds of lies can people tell about themselves that they wouldn't normally lie about if you were looking at them?

Daughter: Their weight, their height, what they're wearing, their hair, how they look.

Dad: Do you think people online believe everything people tell them?

Daughter: I don't think so.

Dad: Have you ever been in a situation like this?

Daughter: No.

Dad: Anything else you want to add to this talk?

Daughter: No, not really.

Dad: How does it make you feel to answer these questions?

Daughter: Like I don't want to lie anymore.

Dad: Does it make you feel sad when you lie?

Daughter: Yeah.

Dad: Thanks for doing this.

Lessons Learned from This Sample Talk

This dad got to make an important point—that people lie about themselves on the Internet. This leads the parent and child to an even more important issue—lying about anything. Dad asked about feelings, too, and he found out that lying bothered his child. Near the end of this chat the daughter indirectly admitted she lied (as many children do) and said, after thinking about the topic, that she didn't want to lie anymore. Dad got to support his daughter's better instincts and his daughter got to talk about this difficult subject in a safe way.

Discussing the Story about Marriage Commitments

Participants: a mother and her fifteen-year-old daughter.

Mom: A man has been married for five years. The man is out of town on business staying at a hotel. At the bar he meets another person staying at the hotel on business. She is a very interesting, beautiful, married woman. The man and woman are clearly very attracted to one another. Hours pass, and the woman, after having a few drinks with the man, says she has to go to bed. The man offers to walk her to her room. What is the man thinking?

Daughter: Either he's trying to be nice or he's trying to sleep with her.

Mom: Imagine which it's likely to be in this scenario.

Daughter: They're both married. Hum. Under the influence of alcohol, I'd say he'd probably want to sleep with her.

Mom: What is the man saying?

Daughter: (Tries to find the right words.) He's kind of asking for her approval on what is about to happen.

Mom: What is the woman thinking?

Daughter: That she is drunk.

Mom: So what is the woman saying?

Daughter: That it's okay and she wants to sleep with him too.

Mom: How does this situation bring up issues of trust and honesty?

Daughter: They're both married and they're both away from their husband and wife, and they might have families, so this whole situation is really wrong. I think as mature adults they should, they could see something like this coming. On the other hand, he could be really nice and just want to walk her to her room, but I doubt that. With honesty and trust it's not cheating on your loved ones just because they aren't there.

Mom: What should the man do?

Daughter: The man should say, "Nice to meet you," and leave too. I don't think he should walk her back.

Mom: What should the woman do?

Daughter: She should just get up and leave.

Lessons Learned from This Sample Talk

Mom finds out her daughter not only has good values—she has good judgment. The child knows that alcohol fogs decision making and that certain situations are best solved by never beginning them. This mom will walk away knowing, trusting, and respecting her daughter more.

Discussing the Story about Truth and HIV

Participants: a mother and her thirteen-year-old son.

Mom: A college student is going out with a woman he met in class. These two people have spent a few months forming a good friendship. They have not been sexual yet, but they are clearly attracted to one another. The guy has not yet told the woman about his health situation. He has HIV. Do you know what HIV is?

Son: Yes.

Mom: The guy is afraid that if he tells the woman about his situation, there won't be any chance for a relationship. The guy is wondering, since he feels great and shows no signs of HIV infection, if he has to tell the woman about it before they have sex. He knows that even using a condom might not protect her from becoming infected with HIV. They are having dinner and the guy is thinking about telling the woman everything. What is the guy thinking?

Son: "Here it goes."

Mom: What is the guy saying?

Son: "I've got this problem."

Mom: That's how he is starting the conversation?

Son: Yeah.

Mom: What is the woman thinking?

Son: "Oh?"

Mom: What is she saying?

Son: (He shrugs.)

Mom: Well, is she interested? I mean the guy is saying, "I have a problem." Do you think she's going "Uh, oh, what's he going to say?"

Son: I don't know.

Mom: How does this situation bring up issues of trust and honesty?

Son: (Pause, then quietly answers.) If you have to tell them, you have to tell them to keep the trust up. I don't know.

Mom: Well, would you want to have sexual relations with someone who has HIV?

Son: No, 'cause I learned all about that in school.

Mom: And you've seen all the pictures. You would not want this disease. Right?

Son: No!

Mom: If you were very serious about a woman, wouldn't you want her to tell you if she had this disease?

Son: Yes.

Mom: Now, if you had this disease and you were emotionally attracted to someone but had not had sex yet, how would you feel about telling her? Do you think you might lose her?

Son: I guess.

Mom: Okay. And this would apply to other sexually transmitted diseases?

Son: Yes.

Mom: Have you ever heard of a person being in a situation like this?

Son: No.

Mom: Have you seen it on TV or anything?

Son: Probably, but I can't think of it right now.

Mom: Any other issues about this?

Son: I got a chain letter about this.

Mom: A chain letter?

Son: Yeah, about something like this.

Mom: On the Internet? What did it say?

Son: Something like this. The exact situation, except the girl had it.

Mom: The girl had HIV?

Son: I don't know, some disease.

Mom: Was it someone you knew?

Son: No. It was just that they were making it up.

Mom: They were making it up? How'd they get your name?

Son: I don't know. It was a chain letter.

Mom: People just send it to everybody?

Son: Yeah, it was, "It's never too late to tell somebody you love them." It was some large story. I deleted it.

Mom: Oh, it was a positive message?

Son: Yeah. It wasn't anything bad.

Mom: Do you think if one person has a disease and they can't have sexual relations they could still have a good relationship?

Son: Yes.

Mom: Are there other ways to have sex besides intercourse?

Son: (Agitated.) Yes.

Mom: The concerns are real that you might lose someone if you tell them. On the other hand, it might turn out she has HIV too.

Son: Is that it?

Mom: That's the end of the story.

Lessons Learned from This Sample Talk

This mom learned a lot! She learned that her son knows about HIV and is appropriately afraid of it. She also found out that he is getting messages about sex on the Internet and she could investigate whether or not the messages were harmful. Her son gave her enough time (before he lost patience) for her to give a cautionary tale and show how much incentive there might be to lie and how hard it is sometimes to tell the truth. Future talks can illustrate the importance of honesty in all relationships.

Discussing the Story about Truth and Health

Participants: a mother and her thirteen-year-old son.

Mom: This is a subject that might be difficult for you, but I want you to try and answer it. Okay?

Son: (Groans.)

Mom: Put yourself in other people's shoes. A college student is going out with another guy from his school. Two guys are going out. This is like someone we know—like Uncle Rick. These two guys have spent a few months forming a good friendship. They have not been sexual yet, but they are clearly attracted to one another. They are attracted to one another and having sex would be very important to their relationship. One of the guys has not yet told his friend about his health situation. He has herpes. He is afraid that if he tells his friend about his situation, then there won't be any chance for a romantic relationship.

Son: (Groans.)

Mom: The guy is wondering, since he feels great and shows no signs of herpes infection, if he has to tell about his situation. He is thinking about calling his friend and telling him everything. What is the guy with herpes thinking?

Son: "This could be bad."

Mom: What? Having to tell him? What might he say over the phone?

Son: (Pause.) "I've got herpes."

Mom: He's going to tell him? What might his friend be thinking?

Son: "Oh, man!"

Mom: What might a friend ask?

Son: "How d'you know you have herpes?"

Mom: Like, how could he be sure? That maybe there's a mistake or something?

Son: Yeah.

Mom: How does this situation bring up issues of trust and honesty?

Son: You have to tell people if you have a disease or not.

Mom: No matter what the consequences?

Son: Yeah.

Mom: It really wouldn't be right to have sex with someone and not tell the truth?

Son: Right.

Mom: You might hurt them.

Son: Yes.

Mom: Why would someone be afraid to reveal that he has herpes?

Son: For fear of losing them. (Pause.) I don't see the point of this talk.

Mom: It doesn't matter if it's between a man and a woman or two men or two women, trust and honesty should be the same for everybody.

Son: Yes.

Mom: Have you ever heard of a person being in a situation like this? Or watched a movie like this?

Son: *Philadelphia.* The guy has AIDS.

Mom: What happened?

Son: That was a tight movie.

Mom: It was a good movie.

Son: My PE teacher liked that movie.

Mom: Great. What happened when people found out the main character was HIV positive?

Son: He lost his friends.

Mom: He lost his job. That's what the whole movie was about. They fired him. What happened with his REAL friends?

Son: He lost some except the one guy.

Mom: His real true friends stood by him, but a lot of his acquaintances wouldn't have anything to do with him. You're right. And only one attorney would represent him. Do you have anything to add?

Son: No.

Mom: Thanks.

Lessons Learned from This Sample Talk

The son in the talk would really rather not participate in this talk. The topic of homosexuality is difficult for him, even though he has a gay relative. But the son does get engaged for a few minutes when talking about this situation in the movie *Philadelphia*. Mom gets to make her point about honesty, trust, and friendship. Her son gets to think about telling the truth—even when the stakes are high.

7

What's On?

Talking about TV, Movies, and Music

*My mom calls her daytime TV shows soap operas. I call them soft
porn.* —Alice, mother of three, Denver, Colorado

*If aliens viewed TV to understand humans, they would think that
most people have sex within one hour and two drinks after meeting
each other. This is what my thirteen-year-old daughter said.*
—Anna, mother of two, Portland, Oregon

*I lived a very wild life in the sixties. Decades later, I never thought I
would end up censoring my son's music. It's not so much the sexual
stuff as it is the degrading talk about girls and women that really
bothers me.* —Denise, mother of one, San Francisco

Sex sells. It's clear to anyone who's ever watched an hour of TV
that both shows and commercials are loaded with sexual talk,
images, and innuendo. The nature and degree of sexual imagery in
the media has been and will continue to be the subject of debate.
While researchers, industry representatives, and politicians debate
the impact of sexual programming, you, the parent, are forced
every day to decide which programs are reinforcing your values
about sexual relationships and which are promoting unrealistic and
downright unhealthy messages about sex.

The connection between viewing sexually themed programming on TV or in films and the actual expression of sexual activity continues to be debated and discussed by everyone—from parent organizations to the American Academy of Pediatrics. But the debate that may affect you most directly is the one between you and your child on a Friday night as you sit down to watch the movie of the week only to discover that it's filled with stereotypical roles with women as sex objects and men as faithless husbands. Even without definitive research establishing the direct link between watching irresponsible sexual activity and doing the real thing, you may decide that it's not the healthiest idea for your child to have a media diet of lying lovers, compulsive sex addicts, delusional women, and lecherous men. (And that's just one hour's worth of soap operas.) The media that surrounds you and your child conveys a set of values about how people should be treated, and these values may be very different from yours.

Believe it or not, a talk about media can actually engage a child. Talking about the latest TV show or movie is a topic young people can relate to. How you frame this talk may introduce a new way of talking about actors, scripts, plots, and special effects.

When it comes to the media, most Americans are bombarded from the day they are born. A very disturbing trend in TV programs and movies is the blending of violence with sexual behavior. As many children grow, popular music, electronic games, and films supplement a steady diet of TV—all with more messages about sexual attractiveness, sexual behavior, and violence. Entertainment blends with news programs and popular magazines, shaping our attitudes about sexual attractiveness, sexual activity, and sexual relationships. Of course, the mass media also contains programming that can enlighten, engage, and educate families about the world.

There are many clear, helpful messages, as well as mixed messages for your child to ponder.

Preparing for the Talk

This chapter will help you talk with your child about media messages and your family's values about the media's portrayal of sexual relationships and attractiveness.

In this talk you will help your child understand that

- all media, including TV, films, music, and electronic games, contains messages.
- messages about sexuality in the media may affect people's attitudes and behaviors.
- the media portrays sexual behavior and the consequences of being sexual in ways that often differ from real life.

What You Can Expect from This Talk

After the talk your child will

- have the ability to identify values and attitudes about sexuality in the media.
- understand how the media's messages can affect people's attitudes about sexual attractiveness and behavior—and how advertisers use sexual images to sell movies, clothes, and almost every other product of interest to young people.
- understand your values and beliefs about sexuality in the media.
- understand your family rules about viewing sexually themed programming in the media.

What Is Being Taught?

First, it's important to say that programming that shows meaningful relationships that include sex is not necessarily a bad thing. Quite the opposite can be true. Showing young people how healthy adults form and maintain relationships, weather problems, and cope with the consequences of being sexual is a very good thing. Unfortunately, these kinds of programs are very rare. When was the last time you saw a movie that told the story of people with values you respect and with the intelligence and emotional maturity to handle a sexual relationship? The norm is to show two people who, within five minutes, are suddenly "in love" and racing to the bedroom or the backseat of a car. What kind of message does that send to a young boy or girl?

In all fairness, many alternatives exist. You can monitor much of what your child views. You can also make sure that you are familiar with the values being communicated by your child's favorite TV shows, films, video games, and computer games. It just makes a parent's job more difficult when the highly effective Hollywood marketing machine hypes an action film, sending ripple effects into your child's world and yours.

What We Watch vs. How We Watch

Sexuality in the media is not going away. However, your family rules about TV and film viewing can help control both the flow and, perhaps more important, your child's interpretation of it. It's not realistic to ask every parent and child to stop watching all sexually themed programming on TV. Many parents feel that a small dose of talk show hysterics or overheated soap-opera romance is fun and harmless. The goal is to give your child the skills to watch sexually themed programming critically, and to be aware of the way people are portrayed and whether they understand the consequences of the characters' actions.

You can help teach your child to view television critically rather than passively. Try playing the role of movie critic with your child, pointing out plot holes, weak character development, stereotypical male and female roles, and less than subtle sexual imagery.

> *I can't stand the way most women are shown on TV. If you aren't super thin and young you must play an asexual grandma.*
>
> —Kathy, mother of two, Rockville, Maryland

> *I know how bad most TV shows are. And the sexual stuff on the talk shows and soaps are clearly sending negative messages about love and commitment. This is why I push reading over TV with my child.*
>
> —Cindy, mother of one, Seattle, Washington

> *What bothers me is the blending of sex and violence. Slasher films give me the creeps and my kids love 'em.*
>
> —Rae-Ann, mother of three, Memphis, Tennessee

When Violence and Sex Mix

Violence and sex mix constantly on TV and in films. Sexually attractive women are cast as victims of violence all the time. It's a horror-film tradition that the sexually active girl is the first to go. But before we look at sex and violence, let's look at what we know about violence on TV.

In general, violent programs on television appear to lead to aggressive behavior by children and teenagers who watch them, according to a 1982 report by the National Institute of Mental Health that confirmed and extended an earlier study done by the U.S. Surgeon General. As a result of these and other findings, the American Psychological Association passed a resolution in February 1985, informing broadcasters and the public of the potential dangers that viewing violence on television can have for children. What does the research show? In the many years that have passed since these events, researchers have continued to study the psychological effects of seeing violence on television. Three of the major effects that have been observed are that children may

- become less sensitive to the pain and suffering of others.
- be more fearful of the world around them.
- be more likely to behave in aggressive or harmful ways toward others. Researchers are concerned that children who watch a lot of TV are more desensitized by violent scenes than children who watch only a little TV.

In other words, children who watch more TV are less bothered by violence in general and less likely to see anything wrong with it. What does this mean when violence and sex mix?

In spite of the accumulated evidence, broadcasters, scientists, and politicians continue to debate the link between seeing violence on TV and actually committing it. Some broadcasters and political leaders believe that there is not enough evidence to prove that TV violence is harmful. But scientists who have studied this issue say that there is a link between TV violence and aggression, and in 1992 the American Psychological Association's Task Force on Television and Society published a report confirming this view. The report, "Big World, Small Screen: The Role of Television in

American Society," concludes that the harmful effects of TV violence on young viewers clearly exist.

What's Your View?

Parents differ greatly in their views about the media's portrayal of sex. Do TV shows and films, which often show people having sex, really affect our own sexual attitudes—even how we think about birth control, having a baby, sexually transmitted diseases, or our own sexuality?

When you were growing up, did you have a parent who talked with you about the TV shows and films you watched? Did they point out sexual relationships on TV that appear healthy and strong? Did they ever comment on relationships that seemed healthy and worth modeling? Consider the reflections of the following parents as they look back on their childhood talks about sexual relationships in the media.

It's funny. When I was a kid I was thinking that I never saw sex on TV. But I actually saw it all the time and somehow sex under the covers didn't seem like sex. It wasn't until I was in college and saw porno films on a sixteen-millimeter projector at a bachelor party that I saw real, buck-naked sex. Of course with video and the Internet, kids can see this stuff all the time.

—Ernie, father of two, Jamestown, New York

I've got to admit that I liked the romance on TV and movies. As a girl it was really nice to see two sexy people fall in love. Looking back, I realize that all those actresses were playing helpless, naïve girls and the guys were total stereotypes of macho. But when I was young, it didn't occur to me to scrutinize the characters.

—Heidi, mother of two, Portland, Oregon

How Healthy Is Your Child's TV Diet?

The American Academy of Pediatrics has come out in favor of parents' managing their children's TV viewing. Groups of health educators, sex educators, and health care professionals see the influence of the media as a public health concern. Consider responding to the following questions from the American Academy of Pediatrics about your children's exposure to television, movies, video games, the Internet, and other media. As you read these questions, remember how common it is for TV shows and films to combine sexual themes with violence.

- Does your child watch more than one or two hours of television a day?
- Do you watch television with your child, or know what your child is watching?
- Do you discuss television shows with your child?
- Does your child have a television in his or her room?
- Do you limit your child's watching of television shows that often contain violence, sex, foul or explicit language, or images of tobacco or alcohol use?
- Does your child have nightmares or trouble sleeping after watching movies?
- Do you allow your child to own or rent videos or computer games with violent content?

How do you feel about these questions? In the real world of over-worked parents, how much media can you realistically monitor?

Peer Pressure to Watch

All of us feel peer pressure to dress, act, or talk a certain way. The pressure is especially intense for school-age children—some kids say that pressure from friends and schoolmates is the single biggest influence in their daily lives. Is your child under pressure to consume sexually themed programming? Do you have a child who obsesses over sexually themed TV shows, films, or songs? Does your child have peers who favor a particular kind of sexual media or one in which particular types of people are sexually active with no mention of consequences?

> My sons and their friends like "Baywatch" and "VIP"—anything with big-breasted women. It's pretty close to soft porn sometimes, even though it's shown during the day.
>
> —Donna, mother of two, Orlando, Florida

> I don't know that there is any special pressure to watch sexual stuff on TV. It's just that almost everything on TV, especially the commercials, are outright sexual. I guess the networks think that getting people aroused will get big ratings.
>
> —Dan, father of one, Memphis, Tennessee

Giving Your Child the Big Picture

Number of hours the average American spends watching TV per day: 4

Amount of time the average American has spent watching TV by age 65: 9 years

(Source: Teenage Research Unlimited/Mediascope, 1998)

There are many ways to frame a talk about media and how it portrays sexual relationships. One angle is to focus on the kind of relationships the characters have *before* they become sexual. How long did they know each other? What kind of commitment, if any, did they make to one another before becoming sexual? How honest do they appear? Are they breaking any commitments to others by being sexual with someone else? Is there a double standard presented in the program, with males being allowed to do things females can't?

Children today grow up perceiving themselves as media-savvy in a media-saturated world. Many can discuss what is on the screen and who works behind the camera. You can ask your child why she thinks the show was scripted the way it was. Were the actors given smart lines or did they seem dumb? If your child had been writing the script or directing the show, what might she have done differently?

My daughter says that TV shows involving sex and violence are "no big deal" and that she and her friends laugh because the characters are so predictable. Even so, I think these shows are influencing her in subtle ways to be callous about some very serious things.

—Arliss, mother of three, Denver, Colorado

My son won't talk about anything having to do with his personal life unless I introduce the topic by using a situation that he has seen in a TV program.

—Kerry, mother of two, Rockville, Maryland

Different Families: Different Values

Everyone defines acceptable levels of sexuality in the media in his or her own way. Here are some examples of media content that may be experienced differently depending on a person's background:

A soap opera repeatedly shows married characters having affairs. These people lie, cheat, and act like spoiled children as their spouses and children suffer.

Some parents see these soap operas as harmless fun. They don't think anyone takes these stories seriously. Other parents feel that this kind of programming gives the picture that relationships and commitments should not be taken seriously.

■

A TV drama portrays an unhappy man who stalks pretty women, kidnaps them, and kills them.

Some parents view this as a typical night of TV. Others see this as a guide to sociopathic behavior, full of messages about hating women and punishing females who are sexually attractive.

■

A movie tells the story of two people who meet for the first time on a plane and are "in love" by the time they reach their destination. The rest of the movie follows their exploits in trying to get together.

Some view this as harmless, light comedy, while others would say that the movie offers confusing messages about the difference between love and sexual attraction.

Last-Minute Checkups before the Talk

Before you talk with your child, think back to your own childhood feelings about sex on TV.

- When you were a child, were there clear rules on what kind of sexually themed shows you could watch?
- Did a parent talk with you when topics like herpes, venereal disease, and teen pregnancy were in the news?
- Did you ever have bad dreams after seeing sexually themed shows with violent images?

How different is life for your child?

- Do you have clear family rules about what kinds of shows, films, or videos she can watch?
- Have you talked with him about sexually themed messages in the media?
- Does she ever have bad dreams as a result of seeing sexually themed shows with violent images?

This is a good time to think about your childhood experiences with sexual images or themes in the media. Do you have any stories that you could share with your child? For example,

- an experience watching a sexual relationship on a TV show and how it made you feel.
- a movie you saw that changed your views on sexual relationships.
- a time you listened closely to the lyrics of a song you thought

you liked and realized it contained statements you found offensive and hurtful.

Consider telling your child about the TV shows or movies you grew up watching and how they shaped your view of the world and relationships.

What Are Your Family Rules?

Do you have family rules about what kind of TV, films, and videos your child can watch? If not, this is a good time to think about them. The talk outlined in this chapter highlights the following situations.

- A family talks about a TV show where young people have sex.
- A boy and girl watch a movie in which a man kills lots of teenagers who are having sex.
- A family watches a TV talk show about being unfaithful.
- A boy and girl watch a TV talk show focused on all kinds of sexual issues.

Talking about each of these situations will raise issues about sexuality in the media. What rules have you discussed with your child about TV, films, or computer games? Do you allow your child to have a TV in his own room? Do you ask what kind of movies she is going to see? Do you preview electronic games he wants to buy? Do you know what videos she is renting? Do you know what ratings his music has? These are the kinds of questions that can help you form family rules about violence in the media. At the end of the talk you will have a chance to review your family rules with your child.

The Talk

Introduce the Talk

With *Ten Talks* nearby, you could tell your child you need him for a few minutes and ask, "Can I get your views about TV?" A good time for this talk might be just after the TV has been turned off, or just before it's turned on. You can begin your talk by asking, "What does media mean?"

After identifying some examples such as TV, cable news, film, video, radio, billboards, and the Internet, you may proceed with the next section. Note that Chapter 8 will focus on the Internet.

Review These Words

Please review the terms in this section. Discussing all of them with your child is optional. You know what's appropriate for your child's age and maturity level. More than likely, even the youngest children have heard some of these words on TV.

critic: a judge of media. For example, "The movie critic said the movie was worth seeing because it had an interesting message, and was well scripted and well acted."

media: TV, films, video, cable, newspapers, radio, billboards, magazines.

media literacy: the ability to analyze and judge media and to see what kinds of messages are being sent and why.

news: reports of recent events, in print, on radio, TV, or the Internet. Each news show has its own perspective on the day's events.

pornography: images and words that are erotic and sexual.

propaganda: systematic spreading of unquestioned ideas and beliefs.

ratings: rankings or classification by content. For example, TV programs have ratings based on how much violence, nudity, and sexual activity they include.

Why Is Talking about Sex in the Media Important?

Let your child tell you why talking about sex in the media is important. Some responses might be:

- Some TV shows and films present good models for real-life relationships.
- Some TV shows and films can show us how unhealthy some relationships are and what the consequences are for staying in them.
- Talking about sexual relationships on TV can help us become better critics of TV, film, and music.
- Talking about sexual themes and the blending of sex and violence in the media means clarifying family rules about ratings, TV and film viewing, music, and electronic games.

The Stories

In the next part of the talk, you'll be reading short stories to your child and discussing them together. You don't have to read all of the stories. Pick the ones that you think are appropriate for your child. The stories are very simple. Feel free to embellish them, adding details that you think might make the story more believable and inviting to your child.

The Story about TV Night

Read this story to your child. It gives you an opportunity to discuss sexual relationships on TV.

"Dad, Mom, and their son and daughter have just finished watching a TV show about a big group of friends, all of them young adults. It's a nighttime soap opera filled with attractive, sexually compulsive people, affairs, and betrayals. The family is talking about the TV show."

Ask these questions of your child:

- What is the dad saying?
- What is the mom saying?
- What is the son saying?
- What is the daughter saying?

Now that your child has completed this scenario, ask the following questions:

- Were there any sexual stories on the TV show? If so, what kind?
- What might be entertaining about the TV show?
- Why do companies make TV shows like this?
- What were the commercials for? Why would those advertisers want to sponsor a show like this?
- How often should families talk about the TV shows they watch?
- How often should families watch TV together?
- What could a family talk about after a TV show?

Follow up with any questions you feel are appropriate given your child's responses.

Clarify Your Family's Values

Discuss the following question with your child as a way of sharing your values about sexual themes in the media. A number of potential responses from children are included to help you formulate your own responses.

Ask your child: "If children watch hundreds of programs that show people using sex to solve their problems, can it affect their attitudes about how to solve problems?"

Child response #1: I don't know.
Parent: We learn from role modeling. Kids learn things by watching their parents. Kids also learn things from watching TV. If kids only see people using sex to solve problems (like being lonely or fitting in) then they might think that being sexual is the only way to solve those problems.

Child response #2: It's only TV, not reality.
Parent: That's right. But sometimes media messages are powerful. They tell us what to think. I want to see messages in the media that support positive values and healthy attitudes.

The Story about Sex and Slasher Films

Read this story to your child. It gives you a chance to discuss how sex and violent programming are blended together to create "entertainment."

"A boy and girl have gone to see a movie about a man who kills lots of teenagers. The kids are always killed once they start kissing. On the screen the man attacks a couple who have just started to kiss."

Ask these questions of your child:

- What is the boy thinking?
- What is the girl thinking?

Now that your child has completed this scenario, ask the following questions:

- What might the boy and girl talk about after the movie?
- How old should people be before they're allowed to see movies like this?
- What might be entertaining about this movie?
- Have you ever seen a movie like this? If so, how did you feel about it?
- Why do companies make movies like this?
- What are our family rules about watching movies like this?

Follow up with any questions that you feel are appropriate given your child's responses.

Clarify Your Family's Values

Discuss the following question with your child as a way of sharing your values about violence in the media.

Ask your child: "If people watch thousands of TV shows where sex and violence are combined, can it affect their attitudes about men and women in real life?"

Child response #1: I don't know.

Parent: We know lots of TV shows and films show men being violent toward women. The message in these kinds of shows upsets me. I don't like seeing females as victims. I don't like seeing females made to look defenseless. I don't think that it helps boys or girls to see anyone, male or female, tortured or killed.

Child response #2: There are TV shows with women who kill, too.

Parent: I don't want to see women being violent any more than I want to see men being violent. It's good to see strong women who are not victims, but I'd rather they be both strong and respectful of human life.

Stories for Older Children

The following stories are about media portraying adults discussing explicit sexual themes and situations. While some younger children may not be able to relate to the situations, you may find that to your child, these stories make perfect sense.

The Story about the TV Talk Show

Read this story to your child. This story gives you an opportunity to discuss how unhealthy sexual relationships are used on TV as entertainment.

"A mom and her son and daughter are watching a TV talk show. The guests include women who are about to marry men—who have a secret to tell first. The secret is that these men have been having sexual relationships with lots of other women. When the secrets are revealed, the men and women curse, cry, and throw chairs at each other. Some of the women still want to marry their guy."

Ask these questions of your child:

- What is the son thinking?
- What is the daughter thinking?
- What is the mom thinking?
- What is the mom saying?

Now that your child has completed this scenario, ask the following questions:

- What kind of messages does a show like this give young people?
- What might be entertaining about the show?
- What should parents and kids talk about if their kids are watching talk shows like this?

The Story about Channel Surfing

This story gives you an opportunity to discuss how dysfunctional and unhealthy sexual relationships and distressed individuals are viewed as entertaining on TV talk shows.

"A daughter and son are watching an afternoon of TV talk shows. In the course of two hours they have been channel surfing and catching parts of four different shows. The guests on the shows included teenagers who want to get pregnant against their moms' wishes, married men who want to tell their wives that they are having affairs, mothers who hate their sons' wives, and married men who are addicted to visiting strip clubs."

Ask these questions of your child:

- What is the son thinking?
- What is the daughter thinking?

Now that your child has completed this scenario, ask the following questions:

- What kind of messages do everyday talk shows like these give young people?
- What might be entertaining about these shows?
- What should parents and kids talk about if their kids are watching shows like these?

- Why is it best for teenagers not to become parents?
- What kinds of men would have affairs? What can a wife do when she gets this kind of information?
- When parents try to break up the marriage of their grown child, what are the possible consequences? How can a healthy person respond to such behavior?
- What is a healthy response to a husband who says he is addicted to visiting strip clubs?
- What could a family talk about after watching shows like these?

Follow up with any questions you feel are appropriate given your child's responses.

Clarify Your Family's Values

Discuss the following question with your child as a way of sharing your values about behavior.

Ask your child: "What do these TV shows teach people about sexual relationships?"

Child response #1: Nothing. It's not real.
Parent: Well, some of it is real and some of it is scripted. But some of the situations are real. And lots of very emotionally abused and confused people are often put on these shows to provide entertainment. Watching talk shows means viewing a wide variety of unhealthy relationships. In the course of watching a few TV talks shows you could be introduced to more topics than a person is introduced to in a college class on human sexuality.

Child response #2: I don't know.

Parent: Let's talk about our family rules on watching these kinds of shows. I know that some of these shows just appear funny and the people seem lost and crazy. But I'm concerned that some of the messages that come through are unhealthy. It appears that so many of the people on the shows don't know how to tell the truth, how to keep commitments or marriage vows, or learn how to respect themselves or anyone else.

The Bare Minimum: A Quick Quiz for Kids

Ask your child the following questions to assess her knowledge of sexual themes in the media.

1. Can you give me one reason why so many companies make movies and TV shows that have a lot of sex?
   Sample answers:
   - To get good ratings, which lets them charge more for advertising.
   - To attract lots of young male viewers, who have more money to spend than young women.

2. Why do TV shows like to use stories that contain both sex and violence?
   Sample answer:
   - To attract viewers, which means better ratings, which means more advertising dollars

3. Why do people like to watch TV talk shows that show unhealthy sexual relationships and emotionally disturbed people?

Sample answers:
- It's an escape from reality.
- It makes a regular person seem normal and pretty well off compared to the average talk show guest.

Talk about Your Family Rules

This talk is an opportunity to review your family rules. Ask your child the following question.

What are our family rules about watching sexual themes in the media?

Sample answers:
- TV viewing is limited to two hours on a school night.
- Video and movies are approved by a parent in advance.
- Electronic games that show excessive sex and violence are not appropriate for young people. A parent will review purchases to see how much sex and violence they contain.
- Publications that glorify sexual activities that demean people in any way are not welcome in this house.

After the Talk

After the talk about sexual themes in the media, many parents report learning more about their child's viewing habits. Some parents were surprised to hear about their children viewing adult movies at their friends' homes. Others found that even the smallest child had been exposed to programs with adult themes and sexual imagery.

A Moment to Reflect

Take a moment to reflect on the talk you just had with your child.

- Do you feel comfortable with your child's ability to analyze media?
- Are you comfortable enforcing the rules about TV viewing?
- How much of the time were you listening to your child?
- Did you feel that you needed to read between the lines of his comments?

Warning Signs

The talks also may reveal potential problems your child might have. There may be cause for concern if you see that your child

- would spend most of his day watching sexually themed programs on TV if you let him.
- finds extreme violence in sexual situations in films and TV shows funny.
- is modeling his behavior after TV characters you find less than ethical.

As with all the talks, use your intuition. If your child seems obsessed with sexually themed media to the point where he is neglecting his schoolwork and household chores, you may want to consider getting help from a counselor. If this talk revealed what you consider to be a serious problem—for example, compulsive watching of sexually themed TV shows, or a near-addiction to electronic games—there may be cause for concern.

Finding Help

Your child's behavior may be perfectly normal for his age. (People of all ages use TV as an escape.) But if you still feel unsettled by something you heard, consider talking with a trained counselor or a therapist, or checking in with your child's teacher on your child's behavior and academic progress.

Success Stories

Talk number seven is done! Many parents use this talk as a way to introduce their reasons for limiting the amount of TV viewing, and for screening video and computer games. Many parents report very animated talks about the mixing of violence and sexual themes in TV shows and movies. One dad in Fairfax, Virginia, was shocked when he discovered what his kids' viewing habits really were, and how much sex and violence they were being exposed to. He ended up giving his kids a choice: two hours of TV a day, after homework, or no TV at all. A mom in Maryland decided to screen all her kids' CD purchases before handing them over. These parents didn't just impose new rules without reason; the new family guidelines came about through a series of family talks. No matter what your values, we hope your talks will give you a chance to get them across to your kids and to follow up with family rules accordingly.

Sample Talks

Between Parents and Children

Before you begin your first talk, you might want to read this sample conversation. The following are excerpts of actual talks between parents and children.

Discussing the Story about TV Night

Participants: a mother and her fourteen-year-old son.

Mom: Dad, mom, and their son and daughter have just finished watching a TV show about a big group of young adult friends and all their relationships. It's a nighttime soap opera filled with lots of attractive, sexually compulsive people, affairs, and betrayals. The family is now talking about the TV show. First off, do you understand what they mean by "sexually compulsive?"

Son: Well, pretty much.

Mom: People just dating and going to bed with whoever.

Son: Right.

Mom: What do you think the dad is saying to the family about this show?

Son: That he doesn't like it.

Mom: Why?

Son: Because moms and dads normally like to see their kids watch good stuff. They don't want them to see bad stuff at the movies.

Mom: "Bad stuff" meaning "stuff with sex"?

Son: Like sex and everything.

Mom: And violence?

Son: Yeah.

Mom: So (in the story) what is something the mom might be saying? Like, what would *I* say? (She laughs.)

Son: You'd be like, "That was really bad," "That's bad language," and all that stuff. You'd probably say that throughout the show, though.

Mom: What do you think the son would be saying? Let's say the son is your age. What do you think?

Son: (Sighs.) I don't know.

Mom: Well, what would you be saying?

Son: I'd be like, "I have no respect for those people." I'd like people to be married before they do that kind of stuff.

Mom: What do you think the daughter is saying?

Son: She'd be all grossed out, I think. She'd say, "Oh, that's so gross."

Mom: Meaning what parts? Like the sex?

Son: Yeah. She'd say, "That's gross when they're kissing."

Mom: Okay.

Son: I think she wouldn't understand some of the parts about affairs and betrayal and stuff.

Mom: What might be entertaining about the show?

Son: Maybe like some of the story line, not the sex or anything. But the story line might have an interesting twist to it.

Mom: Okay. Why do companies make TV shows like this?

Son: I don't know.

Mom: Think about it.

Son: 'Cause it turns people on.

Mom: And when it turns people on, what happens between the shows? (Pause.) You watch what?

Son: I don't know.

Mom: The commercials! What are the commercials for?

Son: Different stuff. Like makeup and stuff.

Mom: Ah, makeup. What are the types of companies that might advertise during this type of show? (Pause.) Makeup was a good one.

Son: Condoms and stuff like that.

Mom: But I'm not sure I've ever seen an ad for a condom.

Son: I have.

Mom: (Surprised.) Have you? What television have you been watching? Okay. How often should families talk about the TV shows they watch?

Son: What I think, as long as they know what their kids are watching or as long as they have seen the show or previewed it first, then I think they should have talks with their kids every once in a while to see what they are watching. Then if they're okay, then I don't think there's any need to have talks all the time.

Mom: By "okay" do you mean no sex or violence in it?

Son: Right. There's stuff that the parents don't mind them seeing.

Mom: How often should families watch TV shows together?

Son: I don't know.

Mom: Do you enjoy our family watching a TV show together?

Son: Yeah. I don't really care.

Mom: Well, how often do you think families should watch?

Son: Well, like we do, every night, well, not EVERY night, but every once in a while. Like on the weekends.

Mom: That's right, we watch shows on weekends. We don't watch during the week too much.

What could a family talk about after a TV show?

Son: What it's about.

Mom: Whether you like it or not?

Son: Right. All that sort of stuff.

Lessons Learned from This Sample Talk

This talk brought out lots of interesting topics: the definition of "bad stuff" on TV (sex and violence), the role of advertising (Advertisers like sex on TV), and condoms (a topic that could take another entire talk to fully explain). This mom and son have good communication skills, and further talks could take any element of this talk and expand it. It might be good for the mom to fully explain why she does not approve of sex and violence on TV, with more complete definitions of the terms.

Discussing the Story about TV Night

Participants: a mother and her ten-year-old daughter.

Mom: In this story a dad, mom, and their son and daughter have just finished watching a TV show about a big group of young adult friends and all their relationships. It's a nighttime soap opera filled with lots of attractive, sexually compulsive people, affairs, and betraying one another. The family is talking about the TV show. Do you know what sexually compulsive is?

Daughter: No.

Mom: When someone is sexually compulsive it means they want to have sex whenever they want to. A lot of those people on TV who are sexually compulsive don't care about being married. Now, what do you think the dad is saying about this show?

Daughter: He says, "Never do this."

Mom: What is the mom saying?

Daughter: "This is the reason why people might get divorced."

Mom: What might be entertaining about the TV show with sex and affairs and people who are pretty to look at?

Daughter: They might be pretty to look at, but if they have something disgusting on I don't find anything entertaining.

Mom: What do you mean by "having something disgusting on?" You mean what they're wearing?

Daughter: Something that barely covers their breasts.

Mom: Why is that disgusting?

Daughter: Why should all the world be seeing all of your breasts?

Mom: Okay. So that's something private.

Daughter: Yes.

Lessons Learned from This Sample Talk

This talk led to the subject of appearance and how the daughter views some attire on TV as "disgusting." Since TV is filled with images of provocatively dressed women, it is helpful for parents to explain why actresses are dressed in such a way (advertisers say, "Sex sells") and how it might make girls feel to see such attire. Future talks could explore the daughter's views on attractiveness and her feeling of self-esteem. Mom has learned something new about what her daughter sees, and the strength of her daughter's reactions indicated that further talks about boys, girls, bodies, dating, and sexuality would be a good idea.

Discussing the Story about Sex and Slasher Films

Participants: a mother and her fourteen-year-old son.

Mom: This is a story about sex and slasher films. Have you ever heard of those kinds of films?

Son: No.

Mom: Usually what happens is somebody is having sex and they are getting killed. *Friday the 13th* is a slasher film.

Son: I never saw it.

Mom: I know you've never seen them, but that's what the deal is, okay? A boy and girl have gone to see a movie. This could really be you in the next year or two. They are watching a movie about a man who kills lots of teenagers. The kids are always killed once they start kissing. On the screen the man attacks a couple who have just started to kiss. What is the boy thinking?

Son: "Cool."

Mom: I knew you'd say that. (She laughs.) Why do you think it's cool?

Son: 'Cause it's like blood and guts.

Mom: Okay. And you enjoy watching blood and guts.

Son: Well, sometimes. You have to be in the mood for it. I wouldn't just go out and randomly see just people killing each other and stuff. If it was a good action flick, like *Air Force One*, like that was a cool movie.

Mom: What is the girl (in the story) thinking?

Son: She'd be thinking, "Oh that's such a shame."

Mom: Do you think she'd be hiding her eyes or screaming?

Son: Yeah, something.

Mom: Do you think she'd be laughing like you?

Son: Maybe.

Mom: (Laughs.) Depends on what kind of girl?

Son: It depends on who you're talking about. If it's like Marie, she'd be cool. But some of the other girls would be screaming their heads off.

Mom: What might the boy and girl talk about after the movie?

Son: They'd probably get in an argument. The boy would be like, "That was a cool movie," and the girl would be, (In a high voice) "Oh, that was sooo sad."

Mom: How old should people be to see movies like this?

Son: I think it all depends. I'm not going to say how old. It all depends on how old the parents think their kids should be.

Mom: I'd like to get your opinion on it. These sex and slasher films are pretty violent films. They aren't like *Air Force One*.

Son: Yeah. I know. It's like *Scream*.

Mom: Have you seen *Scream*?

Son: No.

Mom: I'm glad you haven't. *Scream* is filled with random violence and sex. These are acts of violence just to have acts of violence. How old do you think kids should be to see that?

Son: I think (Pause) sixteen, seventeen, eighteen, between the ages of sixteen to eighteen.

Lessons Learned from This Sample Talk

A productive talk with a communicative child. The son viewed a boy's and girl's reactions to a movie as different—along the lines of sex role stereotypes—noting that the male likes the violence and the female finds it sad or disturbing. Further talks could explore why he feels that way. The mom seemed to think that a movie like *Air Force One* portrayed violence against people differently from *Scream*. In both movies, sociopaths kill lots of innocent people. It might be good for the mom to more fully explain why she sees those movies as different. Other talks could also illustrate the disturbing trend in TV and films—especially in slasher films and TV cop shows—of the vast amount of male violence directed toward women.

Discussing the Story about the TV Talk Show

Participants: a mom and her fourteen-year-old son.

Mom: A mom and her son and daughter are watching a TV talk show. The show's guests include women who are about to marry men, but the men have a secret to tell first. The secret is that these men have been having sexual relationships with lots of other women. When the secrets are revealed, the men and women curse each other, cry, and throw chairs at each other. Some of the women still want to marry their guy. Okay, what is the son thinking? Okay, what do you think of this show?

Son: Stupid.

Mom: You think it's stupid?

Son: Oh, yeah.

Mom: Do you think the daughter (in the story) is thinking the same thing?

Son: Probably, she might have a different reaction, like, "That's gross. I wouldn't want to marry that guy."

Mom: I agree with you. What is the mom thinking?

Son: Probably the same thing as the son. She thinks, "This is just stupid."

Mom: What is the mom saying? If it was your mother, what would have happened?

Son: You would have changed channels.

Mom: Immediately, yeah! But since we didn't, we are going to talk a little bit about it. What kind of messages does a talk show like this give to young people? What's it saying?

Son: Don't have sexual relationships with other people before you are going to get married.

Mom: You think that's what it says? If that's what it says to you, I'm glad.

Son: That's what it says to me.

Mom: But what do you think it's saying to a lot of young people?

Son: For some people it's, like, you want to stick with your guy no matter what happens.

Mom: Do you think it's showing young people a side of life that is not appropriate?

Son: Probably. Yeah. What do you mean when you say young people? How young?

Mom: Say, your age, fourteen, fifteen, sixteen. That's what I think of when I think of young people.

Son: My friends, people I know, they don't watch that kind of stuff and, if they do, they just laugh out loud about it. It's stupid. They know it would never happen to them.

Mom: What might be entertaining about this TV talk show?

Son: Throwing chairs. (He laughs.)

Mom: You think it would be entertaining to watch people throwing chairs at one another?

Son: Yeah, I think so.

Mom: What should parents and kids talk about if their kids are watching TV talk shows like this?

Son: They shouldn't be watching it. It's stupid.

Mom: Would this be a good time for a parent to talk about their morals?

Son: Yes.

Lessons Learned from This Sample Talk

This talk shows how a parent and child can discuss with their child the topic of affairs, distrust and non-monogamy. The son viewed such behavior as something most kids think "would never happen to them." Since affairs and deceit are an unfortunate fact of life, and a very common program theme on daytime and nighttime TV programs, it's important for a child to hear how their parents view such behavior. A future talk about mom's moral position could be very enlightening. Also, this might be a good time to talk about jealousy and why violence is never the right answer—and should never be tolerated.

Discussing the Story about Channel Surfing

Participants: a mother and her thirteen-year-old son.

Mom: A daughter and son are watching an afternoon of TV talk shows. Now we don't do this too often, but think about it as if you did.

Son: Like *Ricki*?

Mom: We don't watch that kind of stuff, but in the course of the story, in two hours they (the son and daughter in the story) have been channel surfing and catching parts of four talk shows.

Son: Two hours?

Mom: The guests on the shows included fifteen-year-olds who want to get pregnant against their mom's wishes, married men who might tell their wives that they are having affairs with other women and men, mothers who hate their sons' wives and want to destroy the marriages (Mom starts to laugh), and married men who are addicted to visiting strip clubs. First off, do you know what a strip club is?

Son: Yeah.

Mom: Okay. What is the son thinking?

Son: Is he my age?

Mom: Yeah, let's go with your age.

Son: I don't know. (Long pause and starts and stops.) That some of the people in these shows are just stupid.

Mom: Yeah.

Son: Some might be interesting just to watch.

Mom: Because they argue?

Son: Yeah. And the fighting.

Mom: Do you find those funny? Disgusting?

Son: I find them funny 'cause it's all playacting.

Mom: Oh, so you don't think it's real?

Son: Right.

Mom: What do you think the daughter (in the story) is thinking?

Son: She'd be thinking, "This is gross. Just get rid of this. This is stupid."

Mom: Do you think this would embarrass her?

Son: Maybe. Yeah.

Mom: Would you be embarrassed at all?

Son: Not really. Because it's not real.

Mom: What about the married men who are addicted to visiting strip clubs? Would that be a little embarrassing?

Son: Maybe a little. But I don't watch those shows anyway.

Mom: What kinds of messages do everyday talk shows like these give young people?

Son: I think to different people it conveys a different message.

Mom: But what about to people your age?

Son: Like try and work things out.

Mom: So that you don't end up on one of these talk shows?

Son: Right!

Lessons Learned from This Sample Talk

A good talk. Mom was able to ask her son about men's interest in strip clubs and he seemed a little embarrassed about the topic. Another talk might further explore the source of the embarrassment. The son came up with a very interesting "message" that young people may get from talk shows about "trying to work things out." The mom could also point out that some people see these folks as role models, and such talk shows plant all sorts of ideas in young viewers' minds about morals, values, and relationships.

8

Cyberspace and Sexuality

Talking about What's Online

I found that my son had downloaded pictures of women doing sexual acts that froze me in my tracks. I didn't know what to do. Obviously, I wasn't supposed to find these pictures.
—Anita, mother of two, Jamestown, New York

My daughter confided in me that she had corresponded with adult men in chat rooms and had even posed as a twenty-six-year-old several times. She is fourteen years old!
—Bess, mother of two, Portland, Oregon

I had a program on my son's computer that was supposed to keep out the particularly vile sexual sites. But it seems to be impossible. I worry about letting him use the computer at all except when I am right there. —Marta, mother of two, Seattle, Washington

A lot of parents are just now timidly getting on the Internet, learning how to order groceries or books online. People are also going to the Internet for sexually explicit pictures, movies, and live video and chat rooms, where people trade personal desires, secret fantasies, raw language, and phone numbers. This is the territory that terrifies parents—and often, rightly so.

Millions of kids are going to the Internet for their sex education. While they may not be able to access the most sophisticated porn sites, which require credit cards to join, the tens of thousands of smaller, free sites will more than satisfy their curiosity.

Don't have a computer at home? You're not out of the woods yet. Think of all the other computers your child has access to—at school, at the library, or at friends' houses

Raising Internet-safe children is a challenge. It is hard enough to teach kids how to deal with strangers at the mall. But now the Internet can bring millions of strangers into a child's own bedroom. Obviously, there's plenty to worry about. But there is also some good news about the Internet. When used appropriately, it's an exciting educational tool: there are resources and virtual libraries on almost every subject. Virtual communities link people interested in everything from global peace to animal rights. Kids can find pen pals or get their questions answered by experts on a variety of subjects. And some new sites for young people have great content.

But the dangers are real. Parents need to know that there are sexual predators on the net, just looking for children. They also have to be aware of their own child's Internet-surfing habits and what their child might be looking for, and why. Your child could be chatting with adults, sending her picture or home address to strangers, or giving out personal information. The goal is to help your kids make healthy choices on the net and stay out of harm's way.

Preparing for the Talk

This talk about the Internet touches on many controversial topics, including personal boundaries; private versus public information;

your family's values about sexually explicit images, videos, and web sites; and the risk of sexual predators. In this talk you will let your child know that

- the Internet can be a great tool for learning and socializing, but it has to be used thoughtfully and carefully.
- not everything on the Internet is what it seems to be. People can lie and information can be false.
- it is dangerous to give out personal information online.

What You Can Expect from This Talk

After the talk your child will

- understand that the Internet can be a confusing place and it's good to talk about any problems the Internet presents.
- understand that ethics about honesty and trust will be extended to the world of Internet chat rooms.
- understand family rules about using the Internet.

The Internet's Impact on Your Child

Some web sites are great for kids. Others are a parent's worst nightmare. The net is a complex, largely unregulated environment that kids need help in navigating. Developing rules on Internet use doesn't have to be complicated; they might be the same rules you have for watching TV. Your rules about talking with strangers, using the phone, and visiting adult bookstores will also apply. If you have rules about what kinds of personal information your child can share with a stranger on the street, the same rules can apply to "friends" she meets in a chat room. If you have rules about buying sexual magazines, the same rules can also apply to X-rated web sites.

Influence of the Media

The Internet is being hyped in TV and films as an indispensable tool. Mass media also offers few guidelines for young people about its pitfalls if abused. The Internet is now an integral part of most advertising campaigns on TV and in print—extending the reach of advertising agencies with the goal of getting your child to be consumers of CDs, movies, jeans, makeup, cologne, and cola.

A Rapidly Changing Media

The web is changing daily. And laws about web content are sure to come. One thing is certain: sex on the net is here to stay. Whatever your child's particular experience with the net, you have to assume she'll someday be exposed to this highly sexualized environment. Parents need to realize that this new medium could change the way kids learn about sexuality and relationships.

Addiction to the Internet

On the net, the chat rooms are where the action is. Young people in increasing numbers are joining peers in chat rooms and getting attached to meeting people there. But chat rooms can become addictive. If you have visited chat rooms, you can see why they are so engaging. If you have not been in a chat room yet, get your child

to help you navigate through one or go to your local library to give
it a try.

*When my son would come home from high school and go straight up
to his room, I thought it was great because I thought he was doing his
homework. Until his sister told me, I didn't realize that he was spending most of his time having chats with girls in their twenties!*

—Max, father of two, Great Neck, New York

*My daughter is a loner in real life. But not on the Internet. She is in
several chat rooms with other girls who like horses and dogs, and now
she has made friends with kids who do photography as a serious
hobby. I encourage all of this. It's good for her. But I do worry if she
is looking at sites that I would not be so happy about.*

—Sally, mother of three, Great Falls, Idaho

Giving Your Child the Big Picture

Proportion of 18- to 24-year-olds who are online: 49%

Proportion of 50- to 64-year-olds who are online: 21%

Proportion of U.S. households that are online: 30%

**Numbers of people who go to Playboy.com a month:
50 million**

**Numbers of people who belong to a typical match-
making site: 9 million**

Proportion of the web-using population that has been online for 30 months or less: 80%

(Source: Harris Survey Unit, Baruch College, in The Public Perspective, *April/May 1998)*

Percentage of American schools with Internet access in 1999: 90%

(Source: "Technology in Education 1999," Market Data Retrieval)

In some ways, web surfers mirror U.S. society almost perfectly; women and men are represented in just about equal numbers, and the racial breakdown is a near-perfect reflection of society at large.

When the web first started, its audience was mostly male users. While that's obviously changed, there's still one part of the web that is visited almost exclusively by males: the sex sites. And if your son is not already searching for them, they're on the lookout for him. Anyone who has ever opened an e-mail account has found it quickly filled with junk mail promoting sex sites. That's why a chat about the Internet is so important. Like it or not, it's part of your child's world—or will be.

I don't like the idea of my son having such free access to porno shop merchandise. At sixteen he can't be expected to show total restraint while his testosterone overflows. But I draw the line on him downloading porno and putting it up on his walls.

—Rosa, mother of two, Atlanta, Georgia

My fourth-grade son has been exposed to tons of porno on the Internet. Stuff he really doesn't like to see. I didn't see those kinds of raw sex pictures until I was almost seventeen and in high school.

—Tim, father of three, Seattle

Different Families: Different Values

The web presents a staggering variety of sexual information. Some young people may be getting a distorted view of what "average" sexuality is and what commonly happens in relationships. The following scenarios illustrate the kinds of messages your child may be receiving. Consider the following:

A teenage boy goes to an adult site, where writing about sexuality is supposed to have "an edge." He reads about topics that vary from what makes a good lover to gay rights.

Some parents might see this web site as acceptable—after all, this isn't a porno site and the writing is generally of high quality. Other parents would be appalled to know their child was looking at material meant for sexually experienced adults.

■

A parent comes in to his thirteen-year-old son's room and sees that he has downloaded lots of nude pictures from the Internet.

One parent may take the "boys will be boys" approach. Another parent may feel that the child's moral fiber is being degraded and may monitor his Internet use more closely.

■

An eighth-grade girl has met a ninth-grade boy in a chat room, who is, like her, a serious chess player. He wants to meet her.

Some parents, after talking with the boy and his parents over the phone, might arrange for the two to meet at a local restaurant while a parent was present. Other parents would feel that any relationship begun over the net was suspect and would try to end the online relationship altogether.

■

A high school girl likes to spend her time in chat rooms, sending her picture to guys who seem nice.

Some parents let their children go into teen chat rooms and don't mind their trading pictures or names. Other parents know that teen chat rooms often have predatory adults in them pretending to be teens, as well as the occasional emotionally disturbed young person. Some parents don't want their child giving out pictures or any personal information online and have clear rules about such behavior.

■

A boy goes into an adults-only web site where there are sexually explicit pictures of women in scenes that include oral and group sex.

Some parents might see this as normal curiosity, comparing it to sneaking a peak at a Playboy centerfold when they were young. Other parents might find this material objectionable, block all such sites from their computer, and perhaps take their child to see a trusted professional or religious counselor.

Last-Minute Checkups before the Talk

You didn't have the Internet when you were a child. But there were still rules about access to sexual materials. Before you talk to your child, it might be helpful to think about the kinds of cautions your family gave you about sexually explicit materials when you were young. Think about the following questions:

- When you were a child, did a parent ever tell you not to give your name, address, or phone number to strangers?
- Were you allowed to go into adult bookstores or to read X-rated magazines?
- Whether or not you were allowed to see sexually explicit materials, did you ever look at them anyway?
- Have you talked with your child about how he uses the Internet?
- Does she ever surf the Internet at home, at school, or at a friend's home?
- Does he know what a chat room is? And if he entered one, would he know not to reveal his last name, address, or phone number?
- Does your child send pictures of herself to others across the Internet?
- Have you set limits on the amount of time he can spend online?
- Have you kept up-to-date on the latest screening software?
- Have you screened out X-rated web sites with the appropriate screening software?
- If your child were to find a predatory adult on the net, would he tell you about it?

What Are Your Family Rules?

Your child may not have computer access at home, but you can bet she will have a friend who does. That means you need family rules about the Internet whether you have a home computer or not. This is a good time to think about what rules would suit your family values. The talk outlined in this chapter highlights the following situations:

- A girl who is not allowed to use the Internet chat rooms is using those chat rooms regularly at her friend's house.
- A mom walks in on her son to find him downloading pornographic pictures.
- A boy is spending many hours a day surfing the net trying to "hook up."

Discussing these situations will give you an opportunity to discuss your family rules. Before the talk, think about what rules you want to communicate to your child. What would you want your child to do in each situation? What are your expectations? At the end of the talk, you will have the chance to review the rules with your child.

The Talk

Introduce the Talk

With five minutes of free time and your book in hand, tell your child, "I want to have a talk with you about the Internet." Ask your child, "What do you know about the Internet?"

The response may range from, "I don't know" or "I haven't used it yet" to "Do you want me to show you the best sites?"

If your child doesn't know much about the web, you might talk about the variety of sites and images that are available for research, hobbies, shopping, and chatting. You should explain however, that there are also sites on the web that you don't approve of and tell your child why. If your child is quite young she is going to be very interested in your opinion about what is good for her and what is dangerous. This can be an important orienting talk about exploration and safety. If it isn't relevant to her interests right now, it soon will be.

If your child has been on the web, however, she will have her own knowledge about what is out there. You tell her this chat is going to be about situations that could arise on the net and what she might do in each case. It should be noted that some Internet-savvy young people are very protective of anything they do on their computer—especially what they talk about in chat rooms (which they equate to writing in a personal journal.)

Review These Words

You may want to review these terms with your child. Reading them aloud is optional, depending on your child's age. If your child has been online, she is most likely familiar with the most of them. The term "First Amendment rights" may be new, but it is a very important one.

chat room: an area on the Internet where people type messages back and forth.

compulsive Internet behavior: when a person starts to organize the day around getting on the Internet and spends many hours there.

First Amendment rights: the right to free speech, enshrined in the First Amendment of the U.S. Constitution, means that we can say almost anything we want about anything, even if it is hurtful or disrespectful. This applies to what people say and write on the Internet.

hook up: to meet someone in person, usually with the intention of having sex.

IM: abbreviation for instant messages, an Internet feature that allows any two people to have a private real-time "chat."

Internet: a worldwide network of hundreds of thousands of computers, allowing people access to millions of images and words.

LOL: abbreviation used in Internet chat rooms, meaning "laughing out loud"—one of many abbreviations in common use on the web.

network gaming: computer games on the Internet played simultaneously by many people, often from all over the world. Some of the games are very violent.

parental controls: software that lets you block users of your computer from accessing certain kinds of web sites, or sites containing certain words.

pic: stands for "picture." It's common for people to scan a picture of themselves into the computer and then send it to people they talk to online.

private chat room: a place on the Internet where two people go to talk privately; no one else can join in and/or watch.

profile: people using chat rooms usually have a profile of themselves that other visitors can access at the touch of a button. This profile can contain any kind of personal information that the person wants to share with the world (age, marital status, height, weight, interests, etc.).

screen name: the name you give yourself for your e-mail address; also called a "handle."

trading pics: sending a picture of yourself to someone in return for someone else's.

X-rated sites: web sites with sexually explicit content.

Why Is Talking about Content on the Internet Important?

Let your child tell you why talking about the Internet—and having rules about using it—might be important. Here are some reasons to consider. Talking about the Internet helps people

- identify potentially dangerous situations that may occur online.
- understand that the chat rooms are filled with all kinds of people, some good and others who are not who they appear to be.
- know what to do if they are asked to visit sites that are sexually explicit or why certain sexual images might be disturbing and should be avoided.

The Stories

In the next part of the talk, you'll be reading short stories to your child and discussing them together. You don't have to read all of them. Pick the ones that you think are appropriate for your child. The stories are very simple. Feel free to embellish them, adding details that you think might make them more believable to your child.

The Story about the Girls in the Chat Room

This story offers a chance to discuss rules about Internet use, the consequences of not following family rules about using chat rooms, and potential problems that can arise from meeting people on the Internet.

"A girl is visiting her friend's home.

They are online and in a chat room, writing messages back and forth to a boy. The girl's parents have told her that she is not to use chat rooms. The boy asks the two girls if they would like to trade pictures."

Ask these questions of your child:

- What is the girl thinking?
- Will the girl or her friend send a picture to the boy?

Now that your child has completed this scenario, ask the following questions:

- Can the girls be certain that the boy is really who he says he is? Who else could the boy be?
- 'Why would anyone lie about himself in a chat room?
- The person has sent a picture and it looks like a boy near the girls' age. Does that mean it really is a picture of the person the girls are chatting with?
- Should the girls send pictures of themselves?
- Should the girls give out their phone numbers? Addresses? The name of the school they attend?
- Should the girls agree to talk with the boy on the phone?
- Should the girls agree to meet the boy? How might the girls feel about the idea of meeting a guy their age who seems to be kind and attractive?

Clarify Your Family's Values

Discuss the following question with your child as a way of sharing your values about the Internet. A number of potential responses from children are included to help you formulate your own responses.

Ask your child: "How does someone know if the person she is talking with in a chat room is really who he says he is?"

> *Child:* If he sends a picture of himself.
> *Parent:* How do you know that the picture he sends is really him?
> *Child:* Why would he send a fake one?
> *Parent:* He might think that he is not the right age or attractive enough to be of interest to you. He might think that if he sends a picture you find attractive, you might want to meet him.

The Story about the Boy and Online Erotica

Read this story to your child. It provides an opportunity to discuss sexually explicit material. The discussion questions that follow will allow you to find out how your child feels about viewing sexually explicit images.

"A boy is online at a porn site, downloading some images of people having sex. His mom walks into his room."

Ask these questions of your child:

- What does the boy say?
- What does the mom say?
- What is the boy thinking?
- What is the mom thinking?

Now that your child has completed this scenario, ask the following questions:

- What can be interesting to children about viewing sexually explicit images?
- What problems can occur when young children visit porn web sites?
- What messages does a porn web site give to children?
- How often do people visit sites like that?
- Have you ever seen or been in a situation like this? If so, how did you feel? What did you do?
- What would be the best thing to do if you were in a situation like this?

Clarify Your Family's Values

Discuss these questions with your child as a way of sharing your values about viewing sexually explicit images. A number of potential responses from children are included to help you formulate your own responses.

Ask your child: "Why would moms and dads not want their kids collecting images that are sexually explicit?"

Child response #1: I don't know.

Parent: There are different kinds of sexual images. Some paintings of nude people in a museum can be very beautiful. Sometimes there are lovely photographs of people embracing. There are other images of naked people having sex that can be very disturbing. The images can show situations that are very disrespectful.

Child response #2: Dad has some magazines with nude pictures, so it can't be all bad.

Parent: Collecting erotic images is something that some adults do. When you are eighteen you can do it if you like. Until then, let's abide by our family rules and not download such images.

Clarify Your Family's Values

Erotic and sexually explicit images have been around for thousands of years. Many people—mostly males—enjoy them. Parents should have family rules about buying such materials and having them in the home. A discussion of the rules might include reasons why such images are not welcome in the house, how they represent males and females, and how respectful or disrespectful they are.

Discuss these issues with your child as a way of sharing your values about viewing sexually explicit images. A number of potential responses from children are included to help you formulate your own responses.

Parent: What are our family rules about sexually explicit images in this house?

Child: I don't know.

Parent: Well, let's talk about the rules we have for young people viewing sexually explicit material. It's the same whether it's a magazine, video, or a web site.

The Story about the Boy and the Chat Rooms

This story provides an opportunity to discuss your rules about Internet use and spending time online looking to meet people.

"A boy has just come home from school and rushes to his room. He has been thinking about chat rooms all day and can't wait to get online. He sits down at his computer and logs on, going directly to his favorite chat room in hopes of meeting someone. He spends hours there trying to meet people. He signs off only when his mom calls for dinner. He rushes through dinner and goes back online, spending the next few hours in chat rooms trying to meet someone. He finds himself happiest during the day when he is in a chat room."

Ask these questions of your child:

- What is the boy thinking as he writes to people in the chat rooms?
- What does he think his parents would think of him visiting the chat rooms this often? Would most parents be aware of how often their child was in a chat room?

Now that your child has completed this scenario, ask the following questions:

- Why would someone become so addicted to using chat rooms?
- What could the person be doing to meet people besides using chat rooms?
- How much time is healthy to spend in a chat room per day?

The Bare Minimum: A Quick Quiz for Kids

Ask your child the following questions to assess her perception and knowledge of the Internet.

1. What is the best thing about the Internet?
   Sample answers:
- It's a great to way to learn.
- It's fun.
- It's a great way to meet new people.

2. What is the worst thing about the Internet?
   Sample answers:
- There is lots of advertising and junk online.
- Some people in chat rooms lie about who they really are.
- You can waste time and not see your friends.

3. What is an example of how someone could get into a potentially dangerous situation by using the Internet?
   Sample answers:
- After giving out your phone number to someone in a chat room, you start getting frightening phone calls.
- After giving out your address to someone in a chat room, you get a visitor you don't want.

- After giving out your picture and school name to someone in a chat room, you are visited by someone you don't want to meet.
- You get unwanted or threatening messages from someone you met in a chat room until you block the unwanted e-mails.

Talk about Your Family Rules

What are our family rules about using the Internet?

Sample answers:

- If you find out someone you are talking to is an adult, or significantly older than you, please stop chatting right away. If this person bothers you, let us know immediately.
- Never give out your password, last name, phone number, address, the name of your school, or our family income when talking with people in chat rooms.
- Always tell me if you get invitations to visit sexually explicit sites. And please don't download pictures that are sexually explicit.
- Don't ever give out a credit card number or your photo online without my permission.

After the Talk

A Moment to Reflect

Take a moment to reflect on the talk you just had with your child. You have many options when it comes to helping your child navigate the Internet safely. How do you feel about your computer now?

- Did your child share any information that surprised you?
- Do you have a new interest in blocking certain adult sites? The computer is like the TV. It contains programming that needs screening and that can come only from the parent.
- Does your child understand the serious consequences of sharing personal information over the Internet?
- Do you feel that you can trust your child to refrain from using Internet chat rooms to meet people you might not approve of? Are you satisfied that everything is under control?
- Is your child looking at any material that worries you and needs further discussion?
- Is your child using the net too much?
- How much of the time were you listening to your child?

Warning Signs

If your child is spending hours online in chat rooms, this may indicate a problem. It's normal to find the novelty of chat rooms pleasurable. But cyberspace chat rooms are best visited in moderation. Staring at a computer screen for hours on end is physically unhealthy. Compulsively visiting chat rooms to meet people is not a substitute for learning how to be social in the real world. Chat rooms can become addictive. This is true for adults and youth alike. If your child refuses to limit his time online you may want to consider getting outside help or restricting the use of the computer.

Finding Help

The best place to look for help is often with family and friends, especially those who have computers and kids. If they have been through this and have set up their own family rules about Internet use, they may be able to provide valuable insights. If your child is obsessed with using the Internet for chatting and visiting adults-only sites, you might ask the school counselor for advice and referrals.

Success Stories

How did it go? Many parents report that young people have strong feelings about the Internet, and discussing rules about its use can be stressful. Parents realize that the Internet is both a great resource and a tool that can be abused. A mom in Maryland reported that the best way to control her son's net use was to put the computer in the kitchen (where she spends a lot of time). One mom reported that it was not the Internet that was difficult to talk about with her twelve-year-old son, but the topic of pornography that was a challenge. When it comes to the Internet, your family rules may have to evolve as the technology changes (which is happening at lightning speed).

Sample Talks

Between Parents and Children

If you are wondering how a talk based on this chapter might really sound, take a look at the following excerpts from real family talks.

Discussing the Story about the Girls in the Chat Room

Participants: a mother and her twelve-year-old daughter.

Mom: Here is a story. A girl is visiting her friend. They are on-line and in a chat room, writing messages back and forth to a boy. The girl's parents have told her that she is not to use chat rooms. The boy in the chat room wants to trade pictures with the girls. What is the girl thinking?

Daughter: Maybe if he lives nearby they could meet, maybe, some day. Like in (the movie) *You've Got Mail*. Or maybe she's thinking, if he wants my picture, maybe a school picture or something. Maybe she could send it to him.

Mom: Will the girl or her friend send a picture to the boy?

Daughter: Probably not.

Mom: Why?

Daughter: A lot of people ask for pictures.

Mom: Can the girls be certain that the boy is really who he says he is?

Daughter: No, because if he's the same age as the girls, his parents have probably already told him to not give away his identity to anyone online 'cause you don't know who they really are.

Mom: Who else could the boy be?

Daughter: He could be a rapist.

Mom: Why would a boy lie about himself?

Daughter: Maybe so he could get friendly with the girls. Maybe he said he was their age so he could find out where they lived and stuff.

Mom: The boy online has sent a picture to the girl and it looks like a boy her age. Does that mean it really is a picture of the person she is chatting with?

Daughter: No. It could be his brother or something or cut out of a magazine.

Mom: Or a friend or something like that. Should the girls send pictures of themselves?

Daughter: No.

Mom: Why?

Daughter: Because.

Mom: Should the girls give out their phone numbers? Addresses? The name of the school they attend?

Daughter: Definitely not. A picture would be okay if there's nothing on the picture to show their identity.

Mom: There might be something in the picture that would show their school or address or identity. Should the girls agree to talk with the boy on the phone?

Daughter: No. 'Cause he could push "star 69" when she called him.

Mom: Should the girls agree to meet the boy?

Daughter: No way.

Mom: How might the girls feel about the idea of meeting a guy their age who seems to be kind and attractive?

Daughter: She might feel a little nervous, but she'd be stupid to want to meet him.

Mom: So what do you know about using the Internet?

Daughter: I usually just use it for homework, but I e-mail my friends too. And sometimes I chat with Grandma in a private chat room.

Mom: But you don't go to regular chat rooms?

Daughter: I don't go just anywhere where anybody chats, I only go to my "buddy" chats of people I know.

Lessons Learned from This Sample Talk

This talk sounds like a dream conversation. The child appears to know and respect all the sensible rules about Internet use and chat rooms. The mom finds reassurances in her child's every response. This does not mean there aren't potential problems. Many kids know what their parents want to hear. This daughter clearly uses chat rooms, and she may be visiting the private rooms (the one-on-one areas for private chat) with someone in addition to "Grandma." We are not saying that parents should distrust their children's responses, but when it comes to the Internet, it's important not to confuse perfect responses about following family rules with 100 percent compliance. The Internet is a seductive environment, especially to curious young people seeking to experiment with their identity and independence.

Discussing the Story about Online Erotica

Participants: a father and his thirteen-year-old son.

Dad: This is the story about the boy and online erotica. Do you know what erotica is?

Son: No.

Dad: It's pictures of sex and women.

Son: Porno.

Dad: Well, yes, but it's not quite that gross.

Son: Oh. I've seen those.

Dad: (Pause.) Here is the story. A boy is online in some porn site, downloading some images of people having sex. His mom walks into the room. What does the boy say when his mom walks into the room? Now be serious.

Son: Yeah, right. He says, (Pause) "It's for a project."

Dad: It's for a project?

Son: Yeah. He's going, " I, er, ah . . ."

Dad: What does the mom say?

Son: "You're dead—you're grounded—you're in trouble—you get the point."

Dad: What is the boy thinking?

Son: Sorta like "Oh, darn."

Dad: What is the mom thinking?

Son: She thinks, "I'm glad I didn't knock. It's terrible! I can't believe he's doing this."

Dad: What can be interesting to children about viewing sexually explicit images?

Son: They're perverts.

Dad: It could also be normal curiosity, right?

Son: No, they are desperate.

Dad: Some people might be desperate or just interested to see what people do. How they have sex.

Son: Dad, okay. (He gets fidgety and does not want Dad to say anymore.)

Dad: What problems can occur when young children visit porn web sites?

Son: They can get the wrong impression (Pause), misleading information.

Dad: Yes, very good. What message does a porn web site give to children?

Son: Not good.

Dad: What's not good?

Son: It's not a good thing for children.

Dad: Well it's giving them a misleading impression about sex, isn't it?

Son: Yeah.

Dad: How often do people visit porn sites?

Son: I don't know.

Dad: It kind of depends on the person. Some people never do. Have you ever seen or been in a situation like this?

Son: Yeah, I was looking for a download on the Internet and I came across it.

Dad: A porno site?

Son: Yeah. It was disgusting.

Dad: But your parents didn't walk into the room.

Son: No.

Dad: What did you do when you saw the site?

Son: Not much.

Dad: Did you look at it?

Son: Yeah.

Dad: Just to see how disgusting it was?

Son: Yeah. Ah, I didn't want to see anymore.

Dad: You clipped that site?

Son: Oh, yuck.

Dad: What would be the best thing to do if you were in a situation like this where your mom or dad walked into the room?

Son: I think I'd pretend I was deathly ill so they wouldn't take away my computer.

Dad: Or you might say it was an actual mistake. You could say just what you told me, "I was trying to look for a download and I got this by mistake." But if it wasn't a mistake, you could say, "I just wanted to see what this kind of thing was."

Son: Oh, I don't know if I'd say that.

Dad: Oh?

Son: I'm not trying to get myself in trouble.

Lessons Learned from This Sample Talk

This talk revealed some interesting perceptions on the part of the parent and son. The son described people who look at porno as "perverts." The dad calmly suggested such people could have "normal curiosity." The son's many declarations of lack of interest in and disgust toward sexually explicit materials might have been a way to test his dad—and look for reactions. Or, the pictures could really have upset him. The dad's reactions were very laid back, and, for the most part, his responses to his son were non-judgmental. In future talks, the dad can check in on the son's attitudes about sexual imagery and normal curiosity about sexuality. He can also share family rules about looking at and collecting such images. If his son has possibly gotten a distorted view of sex from the time he downloaded pictures, Dad could find out more about what his son saw and may be able to explain images his son found disgusting.

9

How Are You Feeling?

Talking about Alcohol and Other Drugs

I don't want to sound like a hypocrite when I talk to my kids about drugs and sex. When I was in college I experimented with both—it seemed like almost everybody did. And my kids know that. This makes the discussion complex.
—Edward, father of two, New York City

Being sexual can make people feel nervous. I had a boyfriend who always seemed to be drinking when we went out. A healthy person should be able to be intimate without drinking.
—Linda, mother of three, Charlotte, North Carolina

The craving for alcohol and drugs originally arose from an emotional context. Someone may have felt anxious, experienced relief from the use of alcohol or drugs and over time the behavior became a habit.
—April Roseman, psychotherapist, Seattle, Washington

Looking back, I don't think I ever had sex without first drinking until I was into my thirties. —Vanessa, mother of two, Memphis, Tennessee

Drugs are a common part of our lives. Where would we be without aspirin, caffeine, antihistamines and a cabinet full of prescription medicine? Many of us use a cup of coffee to give us a boost in the morning. We look forward to a glass of wine to calm us down after a stressful day. Anti-depressants have become accepted by many as a normal way to deal with anxiety or blue moods. Using drugs to change our feelings is commonplace for most of us.

It's not easy to talk about all drugs at once. The legal ones can save lives or ruin them if used improperly. Talking about illegal drug use is even more complicated still, especially when we talk about drugs in connection to sex. These are tough topics of conversation. But as parents, we cannot avoid these conversations. What's more, we have to start them early in our children's lives. This chapter is not meant to cover all the aspects of drug use and abuse (that could easily fill another book), but it will give you the tools you need to begin talking about how drug use and sexual activity relate to one another.

Preparing for the Talk

This talk will give you the chance to talk to your children about alcohol and other drugs and how these substances affect all our relationships as well as our decisions about sex.

In this talk you will help your child understand that

- alcohol and other drugs are a part of the culture.
- there is a difference between drug use and drug abuse.
- alcohol and other drugs change our feelings and it's important to know which feelings are changed and in what way.
- use and abuse of alcohol and other drugs does not excuse harmful behavior.
- there are family rules about alcohol and drug use.

What You Can Expect from This Talk

After the talk your child will be able to

- define alcohol and drug use and abuse.
- understand how all relationships suffer when a person is abusing drugs.
- understand how peer pressure can lead to drug use and abuse.
- know what to do when someone they know is abusing alcohol or other drugs.

How Do You Define Drug Use?

"Drugs" is a provocative word. When most parents of a young child hear that word, they think of crack, heroin, or other street drugs. Many parents can't imagine that drugs will impact their child's life. Of course, if a parent is living in a neighborhood afflicted with open drug use, he or she is probably savvy about the potential threat to their child. But middle- and upper-middle-class parents may assume that because they are anti-drug and vigilant parents, their child is protected. Sadly, some of households are headed by untreated alcoholics who don't define alcohol as a drug. Or parents may be abusing prescription anti-depressants, yet not think of themselves as drug addicts. It's all a matter of perspective, and in some cases denial. As a parent, the first thing you need to do is to define the term "drug" and compare your definition with your child's. Do both of you view wine, beer, cigarettes, coffee, and pot the same way?

Influence of the Media

In movies or on TV programs, alcohol is a common prelude to sex. Many scenes are set in bars, parties always include alcohol, some characters smoke (sometimes after sex), and sly "in" jokes are made about whatever illegal drug is sweeping the country at the time. Beer ads are all over TV: the ads' themes are partying, sexuality, macho sports, and glamour. Beer commercials also use talking animals that children find amusing and engaging. If you read a magazine, you'll see slick ads for alcohol indicating that if you want to enjoy life, you have to drink.

Illegal drugs are portrayed differently. The stories usually have unhappy endings and the drug use isn't usually glorified. Still, there are movie scenes of people using marijuana that suggest that hip people use it recreationally. If your kids watch MTV, most of the rockers they idolize act like they are on drugs and your kids assume they are. Many kids who are interested in a career in music assume that drugs are part of the glamorous lifestyle and creative process. Parents can get discouraged when they see how drugs, sex, and rock and roll are deeply intertwined. Thank goodness they have you to point out the difference between fantasy and reality!

Different Families: Different Values

Everyone interprets behavior in his or her own way. Here are some behaviors that may be experienced differently depending on a person's background.

A bunch of middle school and high school kids are hanging out at a kid's home without any parents around. Some older kids have brought over some beer. One of the middle school girls is alone in a room with some older guys, who start making sexual advances toward her.

Some parents would say that a sensible girl wouldn't be alone in a room with a bunch of older guys who are drinking. Others feel that if you give kids half a chance, just this kind of thing will happen and abuses can occur when children gather without adult supervision.

■

A teenage girl is looking forward to going out with her new boyfriend. She is nervous and drinks a few glasses of wine to relax before he picks her up.

Some parents would see nothing to worry about, since they also use wine to relax. Others might see the start of a serious problem.

■

A fifth-grader comes home from school after smoking some cigarettes. The girl he likes smokes, so he does too, hoping to impress her. His mom asks, "Have you been smoking?" He says, "No."

Some parents would say that it's normal for kids to experiment with cigarettes; it's a personal choice that the kid can make for himself. Other parents might confront their son and let him know about the consequences of smoking—both on his health and on their family life. Others might be alarmed by the son's denial.

■

A teen is at a dance club and offered "some fun stuff" by a friend of a friend. All her friends take these pills. So she does and pretty soon she feels great and very drawn to one of her friends sexually. She loses her inhibitions and considers having sex with one of her friends.

Some parents would be happy to hear that their daughter has a full social life, and they would trust her to make healthy decisions. Others would have had talks with their daughter early on and created a contract about not using drugs. Still other parents would be ever watchful for any sign of drug use or availability of drugs at parties. Some parents may also talk with her about her self-esteem in social situations.

■

A guy is mad at his girlfriend. He goes out to a club and gets drunk. He ends up in the backseat of a car having sex with someone he met that night. Later he feels bad and regrets the whole episode.

Some parents might say that it's not such a big deal if their son has sex with someone he doesn't really like; maybe a hangover is the best teacher of all. Some parents would feel very disappointed that their son deals with difficult feelings (like anger) by sedating himself. Other parents would be frightened that their son might have exposed himself to a serious disease.

■

A senior in high school tells his mom that she can't lecture him about pot smoking because she drinks a bottle of wine every night. The son knows that his mom has a drinking problem but does not think he has a problem with marijuana.

Some parents would sympathize with the son. They say the mom is giving her son a mixed message and modeling unhealthy behavior—leading him to smoke pot. Other parents would side with the mom and think that she has every right to say, "Do as I say, not as I do."

Last-Minute Checkups before the Talk

Before you talk with your child, try to remember what your parents taught you about drugs and alcohol when you were growing up.

- Did a parent ever talk to you about alcohol and drug abuse?
- Did they tell you how to identify alcohol and drug abuse?
- Did they role-model healthy coping skills to deal with stress without using alcohol or other drugs?

As a parent, what are you teaching your child about drugs and alcohol?

- Do you encourage her to talk about the drug use she sees?
- How do you let your child know that you welcome any concerns she has about alcohol or other drugs?
- Do you talk to your child about finding friends who don't abuse drugs?
- Do you role-model the ability to deal with stress without alcohol or other drugs?

Do you have any stories you can share with your child about alcohol or other drug use, or how you confronted someone who was abusing alcohol or other drugs? For example:

- The time a friend tried to get you high or drunk
- The time you used alcohol to deal with sadness or anger and why that turned out badly
- The time you felt scared by a family member's alcohol or drug use

Sharing your stories lets your child know how you feel about alcohol and drug use and what impact it had on you when you were growing up.

What Are Your Family Rules?

Do you have family rules about alcohol and drug use, along with clear consequences for breaking the rules? If not, this is a good time to think about them. This talk highlights the following situations:

- Two kids watch their parents drink beer and smoke cigarettes.
- A girl is at a party where everyone is drinking.
- A boy and girl are on the couch drinking.

The stories in the next section are meant to give you a chance to discuss how alcohol and other drugs are abused and how there is pressure to use drugs of all kinds. But the stories and questions are open-ended, allowing your child to reflect on a range of topics, including the things friends do to protect one another, peer pressure, and any other problems or concerns. Depending on your child, the talk could even include issues of date rape, mixed messages from parents, and sexual relationships. Discussing these situations will give you an opportunity to share your family rules about alcohol and drug use and your views on acceptable behavior.

The Talk

Introduce the Talk

To start this talk you could say, "I've got some questions for you about drugs!"

Your child may offer the following: "We've already gone over that in school." Or, "You are always getting into my business." As we have mentioned before, this talk is much easier with a fourth-grader than with a high-schooler on the road to independence. Our advice is to persevere.

You can add, "Which drugs can change a person's feelings?" He might respond with, "Your coffee gets you up in the morning," or, "Your wine calms you down at night." If he is both older and candid he might try to press your buttons with, "I hear that pot makes people want to have sex."

Review These Words

Please review the terms in this section. Discussing all of them with your child is optional. You know which are appropriate for your child's age and maturity level. More than likely, even the youngest children have heard these words on TV.

addiction: habitual use of alcohol or other drugs.

alcoholism: the habitual use and need of alcohol.

enabling: misguided attempt to help alcohol or drug addicts. Protecting someone from the consequences of his or her addiction is an example of enabling.

euphoria: a temporary sensation of extreme happiness and inhibition.

recovery: the healing and treatment process of becoming sober.

sedative: a drug prescribed to treat pain or anxiety.

anti-depressant: a drug prescribed to treat depression.

drug rehab center: a recovery health facility staffed by addiction counselors who provide inpatient and outpatient treatment.

self-medicating: using alcohol or other drugs to alter one's feelings.

Why Is Talking about Alcohol and Drugs Important?

Ask your child whether she thinks talking about alcohol and drug use is important. Here are some reasons you might want to offer. Talking about alcohol and drugs means

- learning to identify alcohol and drug abuse in others or oneself.
- seeing how alcohol and drugs can change all relationships, platonic or romantic.
- clarifying family rules about legal and illegal drug use.

The Stories

In the next part of the talk, you'll be reading short stories to your child and discussing them together. You don't have to read all of them. Pick the ones that you think are appropriate for your child. The stories are very simple. Feel free to embellish them, adding details that you think might make them more believable to your child.

The Story about Mom, Dad, and Mixed Messages

This story is an opportunity to talk about the mixed messages adults give kids about alcohol and other drugs.

"A brother and sister are home watching

their dad drink several beers while mom has a few glasses of wine and smokes some cigarettes."

Ask these questions of your child:

- What is the mom thinking?
- What is the dad thinking?
- What is the daughter thinking?
- What is the son thinking?

Now that your child has completed this scenario, ask the following questions:

- Do the kids think their parents are "doing drugs"?
- Do the parents think they are "doing drugs"?
- Would the parents be sending a mixed message to their kids if they told them not to drink and smoke?
- Have you ever been in a situation like this? If so, how did you feel? What did you do?

The Story about the Party

This story gives you a chance to talk about keeping commitments to parents and feeling pressure from peers.

"A girl is at a party with some friends. Everyone seems to be drinking and smoking. The girl is offered a drink by some popular kids at school whom she likes."

Ask these questions of your child:

- What is the girl thinking?
- What is the girl saying?

Now that your child has completed this scenario, ask the following questions:

- What kinds of excuses might the girl offer?
- What are the kinds of consequences the daughter might face if she starts drinking, something that's against her family's rules?
- Has the daughter completely betrayed her parents' trust? What if this is the first time the daughter has been caught in a situation like this?
- Have you ever been in a situation like this? If so, how did you feel? What did you do?

The Story about Two Friends and Too Many Beers

This story gives you an opportunity to talk about how friends can find themselves drunk and in a sexual situation that they might not be ready for.

"A high school senior and a high school freshman have been going out for almost a year. They have not been sexual. One night at a party they both get drunk and end up in a dark bedroom having sex. Hours later they wonder what they have done."

Ask these questions of your child:

- What is the senior thinking?
- What is the freshman thinking?

Now that your child has completed this scenario, ask the following questions:

- Was this a good experience for both of these people?
- How could this situation have been prevented?
- What do people usually do in a situation like this?
- Have you ever been in a situation like this? If so, how did you feel? What did you do?

Clarify Your Family's Values

Discuss the following question with your child as a way of sharing your values about alcohol and drug use. We have included a number of potential responses from children to help you formulate your own responses.

Ask your child: "When people have painful feelings and want to stop feeling sad, what can they do to feel better, outside of drinking alcohol or taking other drugs?"

Child response #1: Talk to a friend.
Parent: Right. Sometimes talking about problems with a trusted friend, or even a new acquaintance, can help someone feel better.

Child response #2: See a school counselor to help with the problem.

Parent: Finding some help is a good idea. There are all kinds of people who can help, including relatives (name some that you trust), people from our religious group, and people at school.

Child response #3: Well, one beer couldn't hurt.

Parent: That may be true sometimes. A beer or a glass of wine might not hurt at all. It all depends on the situation and the age and emotional maturity of the person who wants to drink. If the person used alcohol moderately that might be fine. But some people become addicted to alcohol, or sedate themselves in order to mask difficult feelings. For these people, even one glass of alcohol can hurt.

Child response #4: I don't know.

Parent: Well, when you feel really bad, what do you do to feel better? Take a long walk, talk on the phone with a friend, write in a journal, play a game, go for a run, watch TV, or just sleep?

The Bare Minimum: A Quick Quiz for Kids

Ask your child the following questions to assess her knowledge and perceptions of alcohol and drug use.

1. Can you give me one example of what might happen to make a person want to change her feelings by using alcohol or other drugs?

   Sample answers:

   • If a person was nervous about meeting someone
   • If a person has a friend who died
   • If a person was hurt by someone

- If a person felt lonely
- If a person felt scared

2. How does a person know the difference between drug use and drug abuse?
Sample answers:
- If he feels the need to drink every day, it might be abuse.
- If she can't deal with everyday life without the drug, it might be abuse.
- If he feels like he has a problem, then he might have one.

3. What are some responsible ways to use alcohol and drugs?
Sample answers:
- If people use alcohol in moderation—with meals at social gatherings
- If people use anti-depressants prescribed by a doctor who fully understands the patient's lifestyle
- When people use alcohol for occasional celebrations

Talk about Your Family Rules

This is an opportunity to review your family rules. Ask your child the following question.

What are our family rules about using alcohol and other drugs?

Sample answers:
- Adults may use alcohol in moderation.
- We never drink and drive.

- No one in this family breaks the law regarding alcohol or drug use.

After the Talk

Some parents are surprised by how much kids are aware of drug abuse. Many schools have drug prevention programs that include discussions about alcohol and nicotine. Most children are open to discussing the use and abuse of drugs in a dialogue. Many parents have found having heart-to-heart talks more effective than yelling, "Use drugs and I'll kill you" or "Just say no." Your goal is to help your child understand that she can make choices about how she deals with peer pressure to experiment with drugs, and that you understand that it is far from a simple issue for young people to deal with.

A Moment to Reflect

Take a moment to reflect on the talk you just had with your child. How do you feel about it?

- What surprised you about your child's view of alcohol and drug use?
- Do you think she has the self-esteem to deal with life's pressures without needing to self-medicate? Does she seem susceptible to peer pressure? Think about whether your child has the ability to deal with everyday stresses that go with childhood and adolescence.
- How much of the time were you listening to your child?

Warning Signs

The talks may reveal potential problems that your child is facing. Does your child seem isolated or alienated from peers? Review the following warning signs to see if your child might be using alcohol or other drugs.

- He doesn't appear to care about school or friends; at home he is listless and unfocused.
- She doesn't see anything wrong with alcohol or drug abuse.
- His grades take a dramatic turn downward.
- He thinks friends who go to rehab are weak.
- She shares some problems in the course of the talk that sound like they could be serious.

Trust your instincts on how your child is doing. When you meet your child's friends, do they appear alert, sober, and attentive?

Finding Help

This talk may reveal a number of serious issues. Your child may have hinted at having problems. Or he may have made up some serious "problems" for the characters in the stories. While presented as fantasy, the situations may indeed be based on real situations in your child's life. If needed, support and help for your child are available. Your child's school will have resources and your family and friends may have helpful insights.

Success Stories

You have made it through an important talk. Talking about drug use and its relationship to sexual activity may have held a lot of surprises. One mom in Boise, Idaho, reported that her sixteen-year-old son revealed he had, indeed, gotten drunk and made out with a number of girls at a party. This led to a series of talks about drinking, double standards, and respect.

The talk is not over. We want to restate that this talk about drug use is part of many talks that may need to be facilitated. It is a very complex issue for many families. The use of alcohol and other drugs has the power to destroy families and relationships. The good news is that now there is more awareness of the problem than ever before and more resources available for people to find help for themselves and their loved ones.

Sample Talks

Between Parents and Children

Before you begin your first talk, you might want to read this sample conversation, based on excerpts of actual talks between parents and children.

Discussing the Story about Mom, Dad, and Mixed Messages

Participants: A mother and her thirteen-year-old son.

"A brother and sister are home watching their dad drink beers while mom has a few glasses of wine and smokes some cigarettes."

Mom: What is the mom thinking?
Son: Nothing.
Mom: What is the dad thinking?

Son: Nothing.

Mom: What is the daughter thinking?

Son: (Long pause)

Mom: They are watching their parents drink beer and smoking.

Son: Watching them do drugs.

Mom: What is the son thinking?

Son: Same thing.

Mom: Do the kids think their parent are "doing drugs" with the beer and the wine and the cigarettes?

Son: That's not drugs. (Brother laughs in the background.)

Mom: Do the parents think they are "doing drugs"?

Son: No.

Mom: Are the parents sending a mixed message to their kids if they told them not to drink and smoke?

Son: Yes.

Mom: Have you ever been in a situation like this?

Son: No!

Lessons Learned from This Sample Talk

The mother reported that her child was being uncooperative and inconsistent in his answers in hopes of getting out of this talk. He may have been testing her. At first glance it might appear that this short talk didn't reveal much. What effect did the younger brother in the room have? The son did not think of alcohol or cigarettes as drugs, so further talks could explore the son's definition of drug use. This talk set the groundwork for future talks—both with this child and the brother.

Discussing the Story about the Party

Participants: a mother and her ten-year-old daughter.

Mom: "A girl is at a party with some friends. Everyone seems to be drinking and smoking. The girl is offered a drink by some popular kids at school whom she likes." What is the girl thinking?

Daughter: She's thinking she kind of wants to do it to be cool, but then she kind of doesn't want to do it and get in trouble with her parents.

Mom: What is the girl saying?

Daughter: She's saying, "No thanks. I don't drink or smoke."

Mom: What kinds of excuses might the girl offer?

Daughter: "If I drink, I'm going to get in trouble and I'll be grounded for a long time." Or, "I have to go someplace. I'll be back in a moment."

Mom: What are the kinds of consequences the daughter might face if she starts drinking, something that's against her family's rules?

Daughter: She might get grounded or might even get arrested for drinking too much.

Mom: If the daughter is caught, will it break her mom's trust?

Daughter: Yes.

Lessons Learned from This Sample Talk

This mom learned a very valuable lesson: her child might not feel strong enough to say, "I don't want to smoke or drink." The child needs the strong feelings, values, and support of her parents to back her up. She is aware of the consequences and uses those as a way of avoiding pressure. Mom might use the information she has gained in this talk and figure out ways to help her daughter feel empowered to refuse alcohol and drugs when they are offered. Mom should feel good that the daughter has the right values and just needs the skills to back them up. Future talks can explore the topic of self-esteem and ways to improve refusal skills.

Discussing the Story about the Party

Participants: a mother and her fourteen-year-old daughter.

Mom: A girl is at a party with some friends. Everyone seems to be drinking and smoking. The girl is offered a drink by some popular kids at school whom she likes. What is the girl thinking?

Daughter: She's scared that she's going to get caught by the cops.

Mom: What about what her parents may say or do?

Daughter: Her parents would be upset.

Mom: Be upset at her?

Daughter: Be mad.

Mom: What is the girl saying?

Daughter: She could make a big excuse not to drink.

Mom: What kinds of excuses could she make up?

Daughter: She could say, "I don't feel good," or something like that.

Mom: What about you? What happens to you if you have a sip of wine?

Daughter: I throw up.

Mom: And what else? (Pause.) Don't you get an allergic reaction? A rash?

Daughter: Yeah.

Mom: Get all red on your face?

Daughter: Yeah.

Mom: What are the kinds of consequences the daughter might face if she starts drinking, something that's against her family's rules?

Daughter: She could get into trouble with her parents or she could, like, do something she shouldn't because she's drunk.

Mom: What kinds of consequences, punishment?

Daughter: Like be grounded for a long time and not go to any more parties.

Mom: If she were caught, would it break the trust between the mother and the daughter?

Daughter: Yeah.

Mom: How would the daughter feel about that?

Daughter: She'd probably be upset and wish she had never done it.

Mom: Have you ever been in a situation like this?

Daughter: No.

Lessons Learned from This Sample Talk

Mom gets a better picture of the peer culture's values about drinking and gets to remind her daughter that there are consequences to drinking: physical and emotional. Her daughter understands that drinking at her age is against the law and against her parents' wishes. She has also shown her mom that she knows alcohol helps people do things that are not in their best interest, and that they would regret. In fact, this talk has given the parent an excellent opportunity to remind her daughter that drinking could be life-threatening for some people, including her own daughter.

Discussing the Story about Two Friends and Many Beers

Participants: a mother and her fifteen-year-old daughter.

Mom: A high school senior and a high school freshman have been going out almost for a year. They have not been sexual. One night at a party they both get drunk and end up in a dark bedroom having sex. Hours later they wonder what they have done. What is the senior thinking?

Daughter: Well, if the high school senior is a guy, then he's probably feeling guilty, because it was something that wasn't supposed to happen and because they were both under the influence of alcohol. The girl and the guy are both regretting that their first time had to be like that, 'cause your first time is suppose to be special. Instead it was only because they were drunk.

Mom: The next question is, "What is the freshman thinking?"

Daughter: Pretty much the same thing. If the freshman is a girl, she's probably wondering if she could get pregnant and how all this is going to affect their relationship. And there's STDs to be worried about and it's really a serious situation.

Mom: Why is this a good experience for both of these people?

Daughter: The only good thing to come out of this is a lesson to not do it again. It shows what drinking can do to you. You're not yourself when you're under the influence of alcohol, but this was definitely not a good thing to have happened because it could really ruin a good relationship that they have.

Mom: How could this situation have been prevented?

Daughter: First of all, they are underage, so they shouldn't have been messing around with alcohol in the first place. It's illegal. That is also going to affect their relationship.

Mom: What do people usually do in a situation like this? I assume this means they have already gotten drunk, had sex, and are now wondering what they have done.

Daughter: If they are on good terms with their parents, have good relationships with their families, then they might be able to tell them what happened—that there was an accident. Their parents would definitely be upset that it happened, but they might be willing to understand. But if their parents are not as open-minded and they think they would get in trouble, they might first want to go for private counseling or planned parenthood, or something like that, and find out what is going on.

Mom: Have you ever been in a situation like this?

Daughter: No.

Lessons Learned from This Sample Talk

Mom learned that her daughter thinks "the first time should be special." This might make the mom want to further clarify family values—whether that means waiting until a lifetime commitment or learning how to carry condoms effectively. If mom is listening carefully, she will notice that her daughter never mentioned abstinence. She also never mentioned condoms, so she might want to have a discussion about using them. On the other hand, her daughter has described this as a "serious situation"—because of pregnancy and sexually transmitted diseases (STDs)—and has shown that she knows one or two appropriate resources to seek help if needed. The daughter has also told her mom that it would be good to seek help and advice from parents, if they are on "good terms" and "open-minded" and not going to get "in trouble." Mom might want to see how her daughter sees *their* relationship and if she could come to her if a similar situation occurred.

10

What We Believe

Talking about Your Family's Values

I grew up with very stern parents and God looking over me. And guilt was a big part of my childhood and teenage years, which, to be honest, kept me out of a lot of trouble with boys.
—Helen, mother of two, Seattle, Washington

My parents were role models for me. My brothers and sisters and I knew what was expected of us and how we were supposed to behave.
—Josh, father of one, Boise, Idaho

Our family life was a mess. Dad was gone early on. Mom drank. I basically parented myself. In middle school I took myself to church to find some direction and felt like I tumbled into a life philosophy to get me through life. —Joy, mother of two, Chicago, Illinois

You are now ready for your tenth talk! Even if you have used only a few of the talks in this book, you have addressed some of the most significant issues in your child's life. You have taken the time to listen and you have learned. Likewise, your child has heard how you feel, what you believe in, and how you would like him to act. Your relationship is more informed and even, we hope, more intimate.

Don't worry if there are stark differences between your values and your child's. The construction of family values is a brick-by-brick, conversation-by-conversation process. Every little talk matters. Hopefully, you and your child have come a fair distance, but we want you two to go one more mile. We invite you to use this last talk to look at the larger picture and build the guiding principles of your household. We want to make sure your child really sees how you look at the world and what your family values are all about.

Preparing for the Talk

In this talk we want to help you feel sure that your child has a good grasp on what is important to you—and why. To do this, we will revisit some of the important themes of this book so you both will know that you have been listened to and heard correctly.

In this talk you will let your child know that

- he can depend on you to talk about your values.
- you have expectations about his sexual behavior.
- there are family rules—and consequences if she breaks them.

What You Can Expect from This Talk

After the talk your child will

- be able to state your rules about conduct reinforcing good character.
- know that while different families have different beliefs, your beliefs are the ones that set the standard for right and wrong in your family.

- understand how your beliefs relate to your family rules about sexuality.

The Importance of Your Beliefs and Values

There are many people who will advise your child throughout her life. Teachers, coaches, religious leaders, family members, peers, and trusted friends all will have an impact on how your child approaches relationships. We have seen, however, throughout this book, that the peer culture is critically important; and books like *Reviving Ophelia* by Mary Pipher have vividly demonstrated how deeply the larger culture affects a young person's self-esteem. Your great challenge is to provide a counterweight to outside values that aren't in synch with your own. What you believe has to be stated in a heartfelt way. The good news is that you can have an impact on your child's beliefs and values in ways that even TV, the Internet, and his friends and neighbors can't.

Influence of the Media

It may be hard to find TV programs, videos, and films that express your parental values. Shows that put a loving family at the center of the action are few and far between. Maybe that was why *The Cosby Show* was so popular in the eighties and nineties. Actor Bill Cosby created a world where parents treated each other with affection, respect, and loyalty. Situations were solved ethically, albeit comically. But families looking for a similar show today would have trouble finding one.

We think you need to keep asking what your child is learning from the media. What are his favorite TV shows and personalities and why does he like them? Ask him to describe these people and to spell out their ethics. We can't tailor the media to our values, but we can talk about the values it portrays and make sure our child understands what models of behavior are on display.

I have pretty much given up on TV. Prime-time shows are so violent, sexual, or stupid. I mostly resort to videos that I handpick and watch with my kids.

—Carmen, mother of three, Denver, Colorado

Building a Strong System of Beliefs

Our beliefs and character make each of us unique. When you think about it, a person's values are his guideposts all through life. Every day requires choices. Every choice gives us the chance to be ethical or unethical. Every situation tests our beliefs.

Some decisions, like phoning someone back in a timely manner, are so small, we forget that they are part of what makes up our character. Other decisions, such as whether or not we tell the truth to a friend about why we didn't show up at his party, are more clear to us. What we may not think about, or choose not to think about, is that a lot of the time our child is with us on these occasions, listening and watching.

While this book is about how we teach our child what kind of person to be, it inevitably is also a soul-searching book for ourselves. What models do we give our children? How healthy are the relationships she sees in the household? How do we explain our own emotional outbursts or relationship failures? Our children study us, and we owe them an explanation if our values and actions don't match up.

Different Families: Different Values

Our culture presents many different values about sexuality. You have your own values and rules. So do your child's friends and teachers, as well as talk show hosts and nightly news reporters. The following scenarios illustrate how a person's beliefs are tested as she receives different messages about relationships and sexuality. The scenarios are somewhat complex and designed to prepare you for questions from your children. Even though these topics might seem very adult, they raise issues that have been brought up by elementary, middle, and high school children across the country. Feel free to choose the topics that seem most appropriate for your child.

A mother is talking to her daughter about the daughter's new boyfriend when the daughter asks, "So, mom, how old were you when you first had sex?"

Some parents would see this as an inappropriate question and quickly reply, "That is none of your business!" Other parents might truthfully answer the question, thinking that their example would persuade their child to wait until marriage or engagement. Of course, some parents might not have had sexual intercourse at an age they would like their child to have it. Regretting or feeling guilty about their own experience, they might choose to fictionalize their own biographies in hopes that it would be a better model for their child.

■

A mother and son are watching the news when they hear a report about AIDS and how the virus that causes the disease is still being passed through unprotected sex and the sharing of needles. The son asks the mom, "Why would people still get infected if everyone's known about this disease for decades?"

Some parents see this as a good way to show how emotions can be so strong that people engage in self-destructive acts. This might be a good time to show how drugs or alcohol could ruin a person's ability to make a good decision. It also might illustrate the necessity of condoms in uncommitted relationships where people cannot be sure of their partner's health history or monogamy. Others would chalk up the behavior to bad character or stupidity and say that people who have sex outside of a monogamous relationship are always at risk. Quite a few parents might feel that this is not an easy topic to discuss with a young child.

■

Your third-grade daughter comes up to you and says, "Why has Aunt Sue been married three times and still doesn't have any kids?"

Some parents are happy to comment on Aunt Sue's behavior and use it as a "teachable moment" to stress how difficult divorce is, and why marriage and committed relationships are worth working at. Other parents would say that Aunt Sue has a right to live her life the way she wants. It might be possible that Aunt Sue has a very happy life, despite her numerous relationships.

■

A mother and father hear their sixth-grade son and his friends calling each other names. They are saying, "You are gay." "No, you are gay!" They all laugh.

Some heterosexual parents feel that homosexuality is a very controversial topic and would never discuss it with their child. Others feel that children already are dealing with the concept after hearing the term "gay" on the school playground, and that a discussion about sexuality and sexual orientation is necessary. Some parents will use this moment to teach tolerance, others to teach their family values.

■

At the breakfast table, a son looks at his dad's newspaper and spots an article headline stating "Prostitutes and johns arrested." The son chews his toast and then asks his dad and mom, "What's a john?"

Some parents would be horribly embarrassed by this question, but others would find it amusing, explaining that the term "john" refers to the client of a prostitute. Some parents would use this as a chance to talk about prostitution and why people would "sell" their bodies and why others would "buy" them. Other parents might feel comfortable condemning prostitution as immoral and talk about the associated criminal activity and sexual disease that they believe surrounds the practice. Some parents would want to hear their child's point of view on prostitutes and their clients, others would find a conversation on this topic too difficult to have with their child.

The issues noted above can be very sensitive and complex. No one has prepared you to deal with such explicit topics with your child. All of these issues have aspects that you may not have thought through yourself, and you may not be able to address them the first time your child brings such topics up. When you ask your child his opinion on these questions, he may not have a good answer because he is embarrassed or because he just can't deal with talking about it with you. In fact, it may take him years—or a lifetime—to clarify his values. It's important that you work to clarify your own, because as your children start building the foundation of their own beliefs, they'll be looking to you for guidance.

Last-Minute Checkups before the Talk

Before you start the talk, think about your own upbringing and how issues of character, morals, and family beliefs were presented to you.

- Did your parents give you specific guidelines about how to treat males and females? Were there differences based on gender?
- Did they have strong beliefs about right and wrong, and communicate those beliefs to you?
- Did they pass on a set of family beliefs—religious or not—to help guide you in making ethical decisions?

How are you communicating your family beliefs to your child?

- Do you communicate your family beliefs on sexuality as well as you communicate your other beliefs?
- Do you talk to your child about the difference between right and wrong?
- Are you raising your child with a set of family beliefs—religious or not—to help him make ethical decisions?
- Do you think your behaviors make it clear how your child is to treat people? Do you differentiate between how to treat men and women? If so, in what ways?

This is a good time to think about your childhood experiences of learning about morals, beliefs, and character. Do you have any stories that you could share with your child? For example:

- A story about an adult who talked about morals and ethics with you
- A time when an adult explained the difference between right and wrong
- A story about how you developed your values and beliefs
- A story about how you specifically developed your values about sexuality
- A story about learning how to understand how to interact with people in ethical ways

What Are Your Family Rules?

In the previous nine chapters we have offered examples of family rules that were shared with us by parents from around the country. By now you have clarified your values and communicated some standards of conduct to your child. It is time to look back on all the thinking you have done and perhaps even write down what you think are the core elements of your beliefs, values, and morals. It is time to summarize what you want to pass on from that core list and the kind of character you would like your child to have.

In the stories in this upcoming talk, a parent and child have a meaningful conversation about family beliefs and values. The stories illustrate a parent asking a child a question that relates to sex and character and give you an opportunity to see how your child is perceiving your values.

As you think about the moral issues in these stories, consider what kinds of family rules need to be in place to offer your child practical guidelines. For example, do you have family rules about when your child will start dating and how you will keep track of your child's whereabouts and safety? Do you know if your child is knowledgeable about human sexuality and whether he understands how alcohol, drugs, and the media could be influencing his feelings? Are there clear guidelines about what are important ways to act and clear consequences for violations? Have you thought about whether or not your rules are reasonable, and whether you have created a climate in your household in which you and your child always will be free to discuss them? Do you feel comfortable about having the moral authority to enforce the rules if you need to? And, if you need help of any kind, do you know where you can go to find it?

Clearly, introducing family rules to a compliant six-year-old is going to be a lot easier than to a hormonally charged adolescent. But as many parents have found, you can change your parenting style at any time, whether that means having regular family talks or developing new family rules. You can develop new techniques when old ones prove ineffective. Some parents will negotiate a shared set of rules and then post guidelines on their child's wall. (It really helps to write things down so that everyone will have written proof of what they agreed to do.) Others will have informal family meetings when a problem arises. It also helps to bring in a supportive larger community: church groups or youth groups can help back up a family's values and create another place a child can go when things heat up within the family. If you can, place your child in an environment with other young people from families who share your values and rules about curfew, dating, and other important issues.

Setting rules with my middle school son has been very interesting. We have talked about looking at the family rules as guidelines. My son said that he hated the word "rules." I understand where he is coming from. When I was growing up rules were barked at me by my dad and mom. I remember thinking that when I became the mom of a teenager I would never be that way.

—Barb, mother of three, Boise, Idaho

I really had thought that my daughters knew the rules of the house. But then I realized that I had only spent a lot of time thinking about their behaviors and hoping that all would work out. Maybe I thought my girls would be telepathic. It has been good to sit down with my kids and actually articulate my values and find out how their values differ from mine.

—Kaye, mother of two, Portland, Oregon

The Talk

Introduce the Talk

Congratulations on making it to talk number ten. After nine chapters and talks, you have had the opportunity to hear how your child responds to a variety of situations and problems, and how he makes moral choices. This talk will give you a chance to hear what sex and character mean to your child and to talk about how your viewpoints may differ.

Find a time for an uninterrupted ten minutes. Ask your child, "What does the phrase 'family values' mean to you?"

Be prepared to hear "I don't know" or "Something about religion?" Family values might sound like a sophisticated phrase to an elementary school child. You could offer, "What does 'values' mean?" Your child may offer some examples. If so, proceed with the next section.

If he doesn't offer any examples of the term "values," you can suggest something like this:

"Values are what makes a person feel and act the way he does. When a person values something it means he likes or respects it. If you value honesty, then you want to be honest and be around honest people. Your values are like a guidebook for making decisions. They help you tell right from wrong. The phrase 'family values' is used by different people to mean different things. We live in a society with many religions and philosophies, which means there are many kinds of 'family values.' The challenge of living in a diverse society with differing beliefs is to hold onto one's values while simultaneously respecting the values of others."

Review These Words

Please review the terms in this section. Discussing all of them with your child is optional. You know what's appropriate for your child's age and maturity level. More than likely, even the youngest children have heard these words on TV.

beliefs: acceptance that certain things are true and real.
character: personality, moral strength.
diversity: often used to describe groups that include people of different races, ethnicities, religions, sexual orientations or genders, and speaking different languages.
ethics: moral standards, system of morals.

morals: how we define what is right or wrong.

principles: a person's basic truths or rules of conduct.

tolerance: respecting the rights of other people you may not like or agree with to live as they choose. Often this term is applied to behaving in a civilized manner toward people of a different race, religion, or sexual orientation from your own.

Why Is Talking about Family Values Important?

For some children, talking about family values seems as relevant as talking about what kind of water purification system they have in Denmark. Your child may ask, "Why do we have to talk about this stuff?"

Some responses might be:

- Your values are what you hold to be true. And I want to know if we share the same ones.
- People's values help them sort through problems. I want to know how you are doing.
- Talking about values helps families set standards for behavior.
- Talking about values helps children and parents clarify right and wrong.

Last-Minute Checkups before the Talk

Before you talk with your child, try to remember what your parents taught you about family values when you were young.

- Did a parent ever talk to you about their values related to sex and sexual relationships?

- What did they tell you to look for in relationships?
- Did they role-model their spoken values about sexual relationships?

As a parent, what are you teaching your child about your family's values?

- Do you encourage her to talk about values with regard to relationships and sexuality?
- How do you let your child know that you welcome conversations about relationships and sexuality?
- Do you talk to your child about the importance of finding friends who share your family values?
- How do you model your family's values?

Do you have any stories that you can share with your child about having values and beliefs to guide one through life? Can you share how your beliefs helped you through difficult situations or how you confronted someone who was mistreating you because you had strong beliefs? For example:

- The time a person tried to pressure you to have sex and you stood firm in your values not to
- The time you felt betrayed in a relationship and how you had the moral strength to deal with the problem

Sharing your stories lets your child know how you feel about having strong values and beliefs, and what they meant to you when you were growing up.

What Are Your Family Rules?

In the nine previous chapters we have outlined sample family rules to provide guidelines for parents and their children. As you think about your values and beliefs, you might wish to review some of the rules illustrated in the book. You'll also want to think about clear consequences for breaking them.

The Stories

In the next part of the talk, you'll be reading short stories to your child and discussing them together. You don't have to read all of the stories. Pick the ones that raise questions that are appropriate for your child. Feel free to embellish them, adding details that you think might make them more believable to your child.

The following stories present the same situation: a parent and child talking. They illustrate

- a mother talking with a daughter.
- a mother talking with a son.
- a father talking with a daughter.
- a father talking with a son.

These stories are a little different from the stories in the previous nine chapters in that the parents in the illustrated scenarios ask specific questions of their children. You may wish to review the sample talks at the end of the chapter to see what areas were explored by other parents and children. Some of the children's responses may surprise you.

The Story about a Mom and Daughter Talking about Sex

This talk gives you an opportunity to address your values about sexual activity and when it is appropriate.

"A mother asks her daughter, 'When does a person know when they are ready to have a sexual relationship?'"

Ask these questions of your child:

- What is the daughter thinking?
- What does the daughter say?
- What is the mom thinking?
- What does the mom say?

Now that your child has completed this scenario, ask the following questions:

- Does the mom have any special concerns?
- Does the daughter have any special concerns?
- Does the daughter understand why this topic would be important to talk about?
- How often does this type of talk really happen?
- Have you ever seen or been in a situation like this? If so, what did you talk about? How did you feel after the talk?

The Story about a Mom and Son
Talking about Relationships

This talk gives you an opportunity to address your values about being sexual and about the responsibility that comes with being sexually active.

"A mother is asking her son, 'What does a person need to know about another person before they become sexual?'"

Ask these questions of your child:

- What is the son thinking?
- What does the son say?
- What is the mom thinking?
- What does the mom say?

Now that your child has completed this scenario, ask the following questions:

- Does the mom have any special concerns?
- Does the son have any special concerns?
- Does the son understand why this question would be important to talk about?
- How often does this type of talk really happen?
- Have you ever seen or been in a situation like this? If so, what did you talk about?

The Story about a Dad and Daughter Talking about Parenting

This talk gives you an opportunity to address your values about when people are ready to be parents.

"A dad asks his daughter, 'When is a person ready to become a parent?'"

Ask these questions of your child:

- What is the daughter thinking?
- What does the daughter say?
- What is the dad thinking?
- What does the dad say?

Now that your child has completed this scenario, ask the following questions:

- Does the dad have any special concerns?
- Does the daughter have any special concerns?
- Does the daughter understand why this question would be important to talk about?
- How often does this type of talk really happen?
- Have you ever seen or been in a situation like this? If so, what did you talk about?

The Story about a Dad and Son Talking about Character

This talk gives you an opportunity to address your values about character and the traits you admire in a person.

"A dad is asking his son, 'What are the character traits needed to have a healthy relationship?'"

Ask these questions of your child:

- What is the son thinking?
- What does the son say?
- What is the dad thinking?
- What does the dad say?

Now that your child has completed this scenario, ask the following questions:

- Does the dad have any special concerns?
- Does the son have any special concerns?
- Does the son understand why this question would be important to talk about?
- How often does this type of talk really happen?
- Have you ever seen or been in a situation like this? If so, what did you talk about?

Clarify Your Family's Values

Discuss the following question with your child as a way of sharing your values. We have included a number of potential responses from children to help you formulate your own responses.

Ask your child: "What happens when a child is raised without any guidance on how to behave, how to expect respect, or how to treat others with respect?"

Child response #1: I don't know.

Parent: It depends. For some children, having no direction from a caring parent can be very harmful. The child never learns right from wrong. Their self-esteem is damaged and they may think badly of themselves. They may not know that they deserve respect and need to respect others. In other families, a child may learn to parent himself. This is very difficult and usually requires the support of teachers, social workers, therapists, or other trusted adults. But a child can create a strong compassionate character against the odds.

Child response #2: He has sick relationships.

Parent: That can happen. Without a loving parent to raise a child, a person can become emotionally disturbed. It's a struggle to parent yourself—though some people do it and develop into healthy adults who have healthy relationships. But people who are abusive tend to have grown up in abusive situations.

The Bare Minimum: A Quick Quiz for Kids

Ask your child the following questions to assess her knowledge of her own values.

1. What are some values that show a person is capable of having a healthy relationship?
   Sample answers:
   - The person treats other people with respect.
   - The person is always honest.

2. How does someone learn values?
   Sample answers:
   - By watching their parents
   - By watching other people, like teachers or other adults
   - From their religion

Talk about Your Family Rules

As you know, *Ten Talks* is filled with sample family rules in every chapter. Take some time to think about what family rules you need to invent, introduce, reintroduce, change, omit, add, or emphasize. You also may want to review the consequences of breaking the rules and go over these consequences with your child.

After the Talk

A Moment to Reflect

Take a moment to reflect on the talk you just had with your child. How do you feel about it?

- What surprised you about your child's values? Are you comfortable with her sense of right and wrong?
- How do you think your child felt about the talk?

367

- How much of the time were you listening to your child?
- What follow-up talk would you like to have?

Warning Signs

The talks also may reveal potential problems that your child is facing. In some families there may be what is called a crisis of character. Some children show little empathy for others, which might prove troubling. There may be cause for concern if you hear from the school, or from other parents or child-care providers, that your child:

- Feels entitled to do anything he wants, even at the expense of others
- Is extraordinarily passive and submissive to others
- Is extraordinarily aggressive to others and controlling
- Is obsessed with beliefs that show disrespect for certain groups of people

Always use your instincts as a parent when it comes to looking for warning signs. In any of these situations, you need to find out what is happening by talking with your child. If after your discussion you feel that your child needs more help than you alone can offer, visit the school counselor or look further into one of the many resources available in your community.

Finding Help

If needed, support and help for your child is available. Most teachers, school counselors, principals, and religious leaders can refer parents to caring professionals with expertise in working with young people. More and more school, community, and religious groups are offering workshops for parents to help them talk with their children about sexuality.

Success Stories

You have made it through *Ten Talks*. Great work! You now have more insights into how your child views sex and character. You have opened up communication about sexuality—which means you can now talk about pretty much anything. If we have sparked your interest in studies about child development or parent-child communication, we encourage you to visit your local book store or library where you will find a wealth of information on these topics.

Around the country, we are hearing that the *Ten Talks* approach can serve as a catalyst for productive family conversations, helping parents and their children build stronger relationships and open up the lines of communication. As a parent, you have the most important job on earth. The work you are doing with your child affects everyone. Always remember that you are supported by other parents—we're all in this together. *Ten Talks* salutes your hard work and wishes you the best for your ongoing talks with your child. Know that your work helps strengthen not only your family but the entire community as well.

Keep in Touch

We want to hear how you are doing with your talks. Future editions of *Ten Talks* will share how families all over the country are doing with their dialogues. We will also report on community events, parent workshops, and support from local and state governments for "parent-friendly" programs. We all have a lot to share and to learn from one another. We would like to end this book with a wish that you and your family enjoy good health—and great conversations! We salute the important work you are doing in the always challenging and important work of parenting.

We would enjoy hearing how your talks are going. Let us know about your successes, challenges, and creative approaches by visiting www.tentalks.com

Sample Talks

Between Parents and Children

If you are wondering how a talk based on this chapter might really sound, take a look at the following excerpts from real family talks.

Discussing the Story about a Mom and Daughter Talking about Sex

Participants: a mother and her fourteen-year-old daughter.

Mom: In this story a mother asks her daughter, "When does a person know when they are ready to have a sexual relationship?" What does the daughter say?

Daughter: She says, "When she's older?"

Mom: How do you know, though?

Daughter: What do you mean?

Mom: What makes a person think she is ready?

Daughter: When you love a person you're ready for it, right?

Mom: What is the daughter (in the story) thinking? (Pause.) What are you thinking right now?

Daughter: That you're weird.

Mom: Why am I weird asking you that?

Daughter: Because aren't I kind of young?

Mom: Kind of young? Hmm. What is the mom (in the story) thinking?

Daughter: She's hoping her daughter won't have sex at the wrong time.

Mom: Why?

Daughter: 'Cause she's not ready for the consequences.

Mom: What does the mom say?

Daughter: The mom is saying "What until marriage."

Mom: Does the mom have any special concerns?

Daughter: Yeah.

Mom: Why?

Daughter: 'Cause if the daughter gets pregnant or something.

Mom: What about if the girl has a boyfriend? Is the mother worried about that?

Daughter: She shouldn't be.

Mom: She shouldn't be?

Daughter: No.

Mom: Why?

Daughter: 'Cause. If the girl says no, then nothing will happen with the boyfriend.

Mom: The boy is a nice boy and would respect the girl's wishes?

Daughter: Yeah.

Mom: Okay. Does the daughter have any special concerns?

Daughter: No.

Mom: Not at all? (Pause.) Okay. Does the daughter understand why this would be important to talk about?

Daughter: Yeah.

Lessons Learned from This Sample Talk

Mom has learned that her daughter feels "too young" for sexual intercourse. She feels in control and worthy of being trusted. This talk has taught Mom where her daughter stands developmentally and emotionally. The daughter tells her mom that this talk is premature. Mom has learned that even though her daughter tells her that it is "weird" to be talking about this topic. An important piece of information Mom has picked up is that her daughter believes intercourse is appropriate when "you're in love." Mom might really want to have a discussion about that. She may want to dispute that idea—or indicate how hard it is to know what love is, when it is real, when it is everlasting, and other questions her daughter needs answers to.

Discussing the Story about a Mom and Daughter Talking about Sex

Participants: a father and his nine-year-old son.

(*Note:* This dad is the primary caretaker of his two children. He changed the genders of the characters in the story from "a mom and daughter" to "a father and son" to fit his situation.)

Dad: In the story the father asks his son, "When does a person know when he is ready to have a sexual relationship?" What does the son say?

Son: The guys have to know if they have some kind of disease.

Dad: What is the dad thinking? Is he thinking about how to have safe sex? What does the father say, "Don't have sex until you are older and more mature and can understand better the whole idea about being sexual?"

(The son does not respond.)

Dad: Does the dad have any special concerns?

(The son does not respond.)

Dad: The dad is concerned and wants his son to be safe . . . and not have sexual relationships before his son is much older. He doesn't want his son being involved with somebody until they both know they are ready to handle those types of activities.

(The son does not respond.)

Dad: Do you have any special concerns, son, before you become sexual?

Son: Well, that the person is not dirty and is nice to you and won't try to rape you and that's really it.

Dad: Do you understand why this would be important to talk about?

Son: That's because you could get cancer from it and die from it.

Dad: A sexually transmitted disease? It's worse now than it was before. How often does this type of talk between a father and son really happen?

Son: We don't talk about it a lot because I'm young, but when I'm older, a teenager, you should talk about it a lot.

Lesson Learned from This Sample Talk

This talk represents a nine-year-old's perception of sex as a purely physical and perhaps dangerous act. He has told his dad that they should talk about it later, because right now the subject doesn't interest him too much. Still, his dad might note that his son doesn't mention, or perhaps understand, the emotional reasons for having—or not having—sex. Dad might want to talk about the emotional as well as physical consequences of having a sexual relationship, and about the issue of responsibility as well.

Discussing the Story about a Dad and Son
Talking about Character

Participants: a father and his fourth-grade son.

Dad: A dad is asking his son, "What are the character traits needed to have a healthy relationship?" What do you say about that?

Son: Be caring. Don't rape whoever it is. Respect them. Have trust in them. Be fair to them.

Dad: What do you think about when you think of a healthy relationship?

Son: I don't usually think about it. This is the first time I've heard about it, actually, so I'm saying whatever pops into my mind.

Dad: That's good. You're doing a good job. Do you have any special concerns, son?

Son: Um?

Dad: About character traits?

Son: I can't really think of anything.

Dad: All right.

Lessons Learned from This Sample Talk

A great first talk! Dad learns that his son has a good idea about what creates ethical conduct between people. The son knows his dad is interested in his relationships and wants him to do the right thing. This little talk opens up the possibility to have more intimate—and comfortable—communication with him in the future.

Discussing the Story about a Dad and Son Talking about Character

Participants: a father and his eleven-year-old son.

Dad: A dad is asking his son, "What are character traits?" Do you know what that means?

Son: Yes.

Dad: What does the son say when the father asks him what character traits are needed to have a healthy relationship?

Son: The son says, "You need to be caring, fair, honest, and responsible."

Dad: Also a good listener, don't you think?

Son: I'm not sure that's a character trait. Oh, yeah, I guess it could be.

Dad: What do you think the son is thinking when his dad asks him about character?

Son: He thinks about the pillars of character.

Dad: That you learned about in school?

Son: Yeah.

Dad: The Character Counts program?

Son: Yes.

Dad: What do you think the dad is thinking?

Son: The dad thinks, "I wonder if he's learned about character in school?"

Dad: That's good. What did the dad say?

Son: "Good."

Dad: Good job.

Lessons Learned from This Sample Talk

Dad reinforces his son's lessons about character in school. His son learns that these lessons are something his dad feels are important. Dad is reassured, knowing that his son has retained such core concepts about character. Future talks can keep Dad up-to-date on other school coursework on character.

Discussing the Story about a Dad and Daughter Talking about Parenting

Participants: a mother and her eleven-year-old son. Note: The mother changed the gender of the parent and child in this story.

Mom: This is a story about a mom and son talking about when a person is ready to be a parent. The mom asks the son, "How does having a baby change a person's life?"

Son: They need to take a lot more responsibility in their life.

Mom: How might this new dad support himself and his baby?

Son: He might start a new job and raise or get a lot of money.

Mom: How much does it cost to raise a child?

Son: A lot. In the PE locker room there's a sign and I think it's $100,000 through the age of eighteen.

Mom: Wow. It's a good thing you noticed that.

Son: I read the sign every time I see it. (Both Mom and son laugh.)

Mom: How would a man go to college and raise a baby at the same time?

Son: He wouldn't go to college every single day. He'd take weekly classes so it wouldn't do that much damage.

Mom: Do you think it would be important to go to college, if you could, any way you could swing it?

Son: Yes. Even if it costs a lot of money.

Mom: What are the benefits of having a baby early in life?

Son: You have a better chance of being a grandparent and (Pause) that's it.

Mom: What are the benefits of having a baby later in life?

Son: You're more experienced? Yeah. (He laughs.)

Mom: Why might a man choose not to be a parent?

Son: 'Cause he wants to be buff and cool. (He laughs.)

Mom: Any other reasons?

Son: Nope.

Lessons Learned from This Sample Talk

Mom learns that her son understands what an enormous responsibility it would be to have a child while still a teen. She also learns what kinds of educational messages her child is exposed to (the poster in the locker room) and that her son is reading them. The son learns that he and his mom can be comfortable and relaxed talking about this potentially embarrassing topic. Future talks can help Mom and her son discuss everything he is learning about parenting, sexuality, and character at school.

Discussing the Story about Becoming a Parent

Participants: a mother and her ten-year-old daughter.

Mom: How does having a baby change a person's life?

Daughter: A mom has to raise it and will be busy around the house, 'cause the baby cries and you have to give it its bottle and stuff and it's a hard responsibility.

Mom: How might this new mother support herself and her baby? Support means having enough money to live.

Daughter: She'll have to get a baby-sitter, 'cause she'll have to work late, and then she'll get more money and then she'll have enough money to support her child.

Mom: What does it cost to raise a child in a month? (Long pause.) You probably don't know the answer to that question.

Daughter: Probably a lot of money.

Mom: How would a woman go to college and raise a baby at the same time?

Daughter: If her husband could stay with the baby for a little bit while she is at college, and then she comes back and takes care of it. She could give the baby to a grandparent and she could watch it while she goes back to college, and then after that she could stay with the baby and not go to college.

Mom: Is it good to have a baby early or later in life?

Daughter: The good thing about having a baby when you're older is you learn more about raising a baby and you know how to raise it. And you have enough money to raise it. When you have it in early life you don't know much about having a baby and you may not have enough money to support it.

Mom: Why might a woman choose not to be a parent? Would there be some reason why a woman might not want to be a parent?

Daughter: Because it's a really big responsibility to raise a baby and also it's very hectic.

Lessons Learned from This Sample Talk

This conversation shows that even a ten-year-old understands that raising a baby is hard work. Actually, by having the conversation, the daughter is getting a chance to really think deeply about what it might be like to raise a baby, so, in a sense, she is teaching herself about how difficult it would be to get the education she needs if she were to become a mother early in life. Future talks can help the mom and daughter further examine feelings about being a parent, pursuing educational goals, and having the healthiest and most enriching life possible.